'John Menadue brings a unique pers[decades in Australian politics, governme and aviation. This compelling and often . fresh, fascinating and first-hand insights into the character and motives of figures as diverse as Gough Whitlam, John Kerr, Malcolm Fraser and Rupert Murdoch. It will become the indispensable guide to a fuller understanding of the events surrounding 11 November 1975. Best of all, John Menadue's story testifies that honour and decency are no bar to success and achievement, even in the tough world of Australian public life.'

Graham Freudenberg

'Life at the top of Australian politics, diplomacy and business as John Menadue's ideals are tested by experience. This is an enthralling story—concise, rigorous and wise, with no excuses and no cover-ups. Menadue's honesty, not least about himself, makes this a unique work of Australian discovery.'

Edmund Campion

'This is a life lived from the country Methodist manse to the inner circles of power in Canberra. Challenging new assessments of Gough Whitlam, Malcolm Fraser and Rupert Murdoch, among others, are matched by moral candour about himself, rare in an insider's account.'

Brian Johns

'In this memoir by a substantial modern Australian, we learn a great deal about the development of similar qualities in Australia as well as the evolution of a man who became a real achiever. His story exemplifies our nation's predominant ethic, an emphasis on working behind the scenes wielding benign but effective influence and quietly dreaming big dreams.'

Geraldine Doogue

For my parents
Laurie and Elma Menadue

THINGS YOU LEARN ALONG THE WAY

JOHN MENADUE

Ruth Benton,

Best wishes –

John Menadue

March 2000

DAVID LOVELL PUBLISHING
MELBOURNE AUSTRALIA

Acknowledgements

Thanks to Glynnis Nancarrow and Nancy Campisi, who typed the many drafts. Eric Walsh and Michael Kelly SJ gave much encouragement and helpful reminders. Cathy Coles, Ray Cassin and Neil Thomas tutored me in writing a book and pointed to the areas that needed change. Beth Pitman, my sister, has a much better memory of childhood than me. She is the family memory bank. Susie Menadue gave enormous encouragement and support. My children, Susan, Rosalie, Peter and Elizabeth, were frank and encouraging as ever. David Lovell, my publisher, was quietly professional and helpful, with no fuss or drama.

First published in 1999 by
David Lovell Publishing
PO Box 822
Ringwood Victoria 3134
Australia
Tel +61 3 9879 1433
Fax +61 3 9879 1348

Cover photograph courtesy John Menadue
Design by David Lovell
Typeset in 11.5/14 Bembo
Printed in Australia by Openbook Publishers

National Library of Australia
Cataloguing-in-Publication data

Menadue, J. L. (John Laurence), 1935– .
Things you learn along the way.

Includes index.
ISBN 1 86355 073 9.

1. Menadue, J. L. (John Laurence), 1935– . 2. Australia. Dept of Prime Minister and Cabinet - Officials and employees – Biography. 3. Australia. Dept of Immigration and Ethnic Affairs – Officials and employees - Biography.
4. Ambassadors - Australia - Biography. 5. Chief executive officers - Australia - Biography. 7. Australia - Politics and government - 1965– . I. Title.

994.06092

Contents

Preface

I didn't intend to write my autobiography, although I was tempted at times to write something personal for my four children and seven grandchildren. But I did complete an oral history at the request of the National Library. A lot of time and energy was invested in that project but the result, I felt, needed more work. I decided to try to put it into better shape.

Every person's life is precious, even sacred. Why tell about mine? Perhaps I have had wider experience in my life than most people. I felt I had a story to tell—and we all like telling our story if someone will listen.

I was born into a Methodist manse and carried the influence of those first 15 years right through my life. Despite this background I joined the Catholic Church. I worked for Rupert Murdoch and saw how seductive power is. As Head of the Department of Prime Minister and Cabinet in Canberra, I was working for Gough Whitlam on the morning of 11 November 1975 and in the afternoon for Malcolm Fraser after John Kerr dismissed the Whitlam Government. The anger of what happened on that day is still with me. Working with Malcolm Fraser, I knew I was an outsider. It was liberating, however, to realise that while being an outsider was not comfortable it was manageable.

I was Australian Ambassador in Japan in the late 1970s and from that vantage point learnt most about Australia and myself. As Head of the Department of Immigration and Ethnic Affairs, I had the most satisfying job of my life, being part of nation building and doing my best to end White Australia. As CEO of Qantas I saw the opportunities in Asia and experienced the difficulties of dealing with a board and a government with agendas that weren't the same as mine—and the pressure to conform.

In telling my story I decided not to separate my public from my private life. They happened together, although for long periods my private journey came a distant second to career. As the years unfolded I think I came to integrate them better.

In the Methodist manse I learnt about the work ethic and discipline. I was determined, some would say driven.

Without habit and custom we would be exhausted having to make conscious decisions about every detail of daily life, so we live a lot of our life on 'autopilot'. Our cultural context strongly influences our attitudes and behaviour. But there were experiences in my life that were catalysts that forced me to change, to turn off the auto-pilot, although I often wasn't able to articulate or understand the changes for years, perhaps decades later.

Most of those changes were of the emotions, not of the intellect. Because of that they were more deep-seated and powerful, but also more painful. Change, whether for individuals, institutions or nations, is not easy and inevitably comes with some loss of what we previously valued or relied upon.

As a country boy from South Australia, I grew up in White Australia. Malayan students at university college unknowingly reflected White Australia back to me. It was an unpleasant experience. They changed my life and triggered my 45-year commitment to promoting Australia's relations with Asia. Aldous Huxley described this change process: 'Experience is not what happens to a man. It is what a man does with what happens to him.'

A sceptical university professor unwittingly helped me draw a link between Christian values and social justice.

Gough Whitlam awakened a new world of ideas and opportunities for me. I am ever in his debt.

My first wife's death in 1984 humbled me. I didn't have the spiritual and psychological resources to handle the circumstances in which I found myself. It helped me to understand my vulnerability. I learned the hard way that success and status weren't really important in the end. They were props that made it easier for me to shut out my inner voice. We learn best in hard times.

In the Catholic Church I encountered the same problem as in so many other institutions: the alienation of people from leaders who, despite the rhetoric, do not feel they are accountable. Power is inevitably abused.

Preface

All institutions, like people, are in need of radical daily reform. Without dissenters, institutions die. In that respect I became more radical as I grew older.

Through all the changes in my life I think I have been resilient. I have moved on to the next venture and opportunity with little looking back and few regrets. I probably learned that resilience from my days in the manse, when I was always on the move.

At the age of 64, I believe that the one thing above all else that I have learned is that we are all made incomplete. We need relationships and community to be complete.

My story is about a journey and the things I learned along the way. I am pleased with what I have done, even with the failures and mistakes. I hope you find my story encouraging.

John Menadue
July 1999

Son of the Methodist manse

'The Child is father of the Man' (William Wordsworth)

I am the son of a Methodist minister. That probably says more about me than anything else I can say about myself. So much of my life and how experiences affected me is predicated on my first 15 years in a Methodist manse.

Self-improvement and a strong work ethic were a part of daily life. We had to be 'up and doing'. Idle hands made mischief. My sister and I were told that if we believed in something, the energy and enthusiasm to achieve goals at study or sport would come. Hard work and determination would produce better results than flashy brilliance. We had a duty to try to make the world a little bit better.

My family were temperate, not given to wild flights of fancy or excess. Alcohol and gambling were taboo. Methodists were earnest. Time and effort should not be wasted on the superfluous.

I have never escaped the imprint of this upbringing. A close friend of mine often told me that I confused earnestness and competence. I think he was right.

I was born to Laurie and Elma Menadue in Cowell, South Australia, in February 1935. My sister, Beth, was two years older. I lived in Cowell until I was two. My mother was a matter-of-fact and no-nonsense woman, but she clung to an old wives' tale that I was lucky in birth and life. She enjoyed telling me that I was born in the caul, part of the sac covering my head at birth, which superstition tells brings good luck and always protects against drowning. My mother often told me of my caul, perhaps not surprisingly as her own mother had died at her birth. Maybe she was right about good luck. Born at the end of the Depression with low birthrates, it was easy for my generation to obtain scholarships and jobs. I was too young for the Second World War and too old for Vietnam. I have had very supportive families and have enjoyed good health.

Cowell, in the district of Franklin Harbour, is a small country town of a few hundred people, mainly farmers and fishermen, on Spencer Gulf in South Australia. When I was born, times were tough in Cowell. Rainfall was always unreliable, but 1935 was particularly bad. Landowners were warned about allowing sand to drift over the roads. Wheat and wool prices were poor in those post-Depression years. The local council said that the unemployed should work for rations—an early version of work for the dole. Blocks reverted to the Crown for non-payment of rates. Cowell, in February 1935, had a mice plague.

Ministers like my father left parishes or 'circuits', as we called them, with large amounts of stipend unpaid. In Cowell, the Methodist minister's car allowance remained unchanged for over 20 years and the marriage fee unchanged for 50 years. Laurie was often paid in kind: meat and eggs.

I went back to Cowell, with Beth, for the first time 60 years later. I was not surprised that I tasted and smelled the salty air from Spencer Gulf. In my mind's eye nothing had changed; it was still a sleepy town which came to life only on shopping and sale days and Saturdays for sport. The main street, with a few shops, a post office and a pub, led to a jetty in a quiet and protected harbour which in earlier days had been used to load grain in bags. The large blue sky merged into the vast grey sea with a fuzzy line in between tracing the curvature of the earth.

The town's folk museum was designed to give some sense of history and belonging. There was no sign that Aborigines had ever been there when the first land was leased to a Scotsman in 1853. The *Back to Franklin Harbour Souvenir* of 1938, however, records that after the fatal spearing of a shepherd, 'four natives were taken to Adelaide, tried and condemned to be hung in the Franklin Harbour District. This was done in the presence of a band of natives so that as early as 1855 the Aborigines were shown the ways of the white man's justice'.

Cars were a large part of our life in the manse. We had to have a car, usually a patched-up old Pontiac or Chrysler with a canvas top, so that Laurie could travel to his preaching appointments and sick calls. He enjoyed cars but for Elma they meant garage debts following us from town to town. When we went for holidays in midsummer, with the rear baggage rack and the passenger side running board weighed down with luggage, the car invariably boiled in the Hummocks, the hills outside Port Wakefield at the top of St Vincent's Gulf. In the early morning, after travelling all night, we were tired and irritable, with Laurie cursing old and unreliable cars. Elma tried to calm him down with mushy tomato sandwiches and tea from the thermos.

The Methodist Church was at the centre of our lives. An evangelical movement, Methodism grew out of the established Church of England in the mid-18th century. Methodists were dissenters and 'methodical' in their devotions. They found that the Church of England had lost spiritual vitality. Their reform movement finally broke away and pursued its own course with emphasis on the New Testament, a very personal spiritual experience and social concern. The enthusiastic and confident singing of Charles Wesley hymns, set to Welsh tunes, and evangelical preaching are my warm and nostalgic recollections of Methodism. At church, bosomy organists pedalled furiously to get maximum volume out of the organ and led the singing at the top of their voices. Methodism was born in song.

My paternal great-great-grandparents, Hugh and Jane Menadue, came to South Australia from Cornwall in 1847 in the SS *Northumberland* and settled at Port Willunga, south of Adelaide. From 1834 land had been sold to finance the migration of free settlers. Hugh and Jane had 17 children. They followed a stream of Cornish copper miners who had come to Moonta, Kapunda and Burra in South Australia. The area was known as 'Little Cornwall'. Laurie's family came as farmers. Menadue is a Cornish name meaning 'dark hills'. Perhaps 'dark hills' reasonably describes the Menadues, as we have often been seen as a bit distant and certainly not given to flashiness.

In 1910 my grandfather, John Henry Menadue, secured a cheap and large block of land at Wynarka, in the Mallee. The official history of the region published in 1986 records that Laurie together with his father, John, and older brother, Clarrie,

> came from Salisbury with a horse team and wagon. Some of the
> way from Tailem Bend to beyond Chapman's Bore they had to
> cut their way following survey pegs and tracks to their scrub
> block. Water and supplies, including feed for horses, were carted

19 miles from Tailem Bend. The horses were hobbled at night and turned into the scrub with a bell so that they could be found in the morning until a fence was built and some clearing was done. In March 1911 a small home of iron walls and dirt floor covered with tar was built. In 1915 the house was burnt down.

Wynarka was an unfortunate experience for those early Menadues. Most farmers lost their land and few survived the Depression. They made farming mistakes, flattening the scrub and causing erosion. Fertilisers were expensive or unavailable. Seasons and prices were poor. If the Menadues came to Australia seeking streets lined with gold, they were disappointed in the Mallee.

My father, Laurie, seldom referred to hardships. He was quite laconic. Although intelligent and an avid reader, he went only to fourth grade of primary school and then only for three days a week. He had to travel by horse and buggy into town, and horses couldn't make the 16-mile round trip every day. He could freely recite Henry Lawson and C. J. Dennis. He told Cornish stories about the 'cousin Jacks and cousin Jennys' of Moonta. He read a lot about the heroes of Empire, Walter Scott, Livingstone and Wilberforce. He had books by Studdert Kennedy, an English army chaplain in the First World War, and Woodbine Willie.

It was a very lonely life for a young boy like Laurie, not interested in farming. Sitting on the plough with nothing much to do except watch the horses gave him time to think about life and compose droll, inconsequential stories about a mythical 'my father'. Thinking of Laurie 40 years later I am sure that he had a much richer inner life than I thought at the time—a hidden life of memory and imagination.

Laurie was very active in the local Methodist Church. There wasn't much other social activity at Wynarka. The church was the only public building in Wynarka for twenty years. He became a local preacher at the age of 16. In 1924, at the age of 21, he went to the Methodist theological training college at Brighton, in Adelaide. He found the studies hard and had to take a year of sick leave. I was never told why and didn't ask. Later I surmised that it was depression.

In his studies he was supported by Elma Florence Menear, whom he later married after a seven-year courtship. It worked well for both of them without being a terribly romantic arrangement. She was a trained teacher of deaf students at Brighton, within a half a mile of the Methodist training college. They met at the Brighton Methodist church.

Laurie's faith was very much part and parcel of him and the choices that he made. He told me that the real divide was not between people, but between good and evil in people's hearts. We each had a dark and light side. Service was at the core of his life. He was very scriptural in his preaching. 'The Scripture text today is …' and then he'd expound for precisely 20 minutes on the text. His favourite was 'For God so loved the world that he gave his only begotten Son, that whosoever believes in Him shall not die but have life everlasting' (John 3:16). Preaching didn't come easily to him; he spent all day Saturday preparing the Sunday sermon, which he preached three or four times. On Thursday nights over tea and in time for choir practice that evening we would make our suggestions for the Sunday hymns. My favourite was number 110 in the Methodist Hymn Book 'Jesus, Lover of my Soul', with the words by Charles Wesley to the tune 'Hollingside'. Fifty years later, whenever I take time on my own to play a CD of old Wesleyan hymns, feelings and emotions take me back to the warmth of those childhood days. Those feelings are as much part of me as my hands and feet.

Laurie didn't have particularly developed political views. He had come from a conservative farming family. The only time that I can recall politics being seriously discussed was in 1947 when bank nationalisation was on the agenda. To Laurie, Catholics seemed more likely to vote Labor, which, for him, was a strike against Labor. In his early life, I am certain that he voted conservative. In later years he voted Labor—perhaps on account of my influence.

In my mind's eye, Laurie was well groomed and bespectacled. Outside the house he always wore a three-piece suit and hat; never sports clothes. He had a lot of hernia operations and popped indigestion pills with aplomb. To me he exaggerated his health problem. I think he was bored a lot of the time. He was stocky and moderately overweight from eating and lack of exercise. As an ex-farmer and with a large manse yard his only exercise was gardening. His principal at theological college told me that he had a 'formidable tennis serve', but I never saw him play tennis.

Quite loud at times, he enjoyed risqué stories that made my mother blush. He loved standing with his back to the open fire and telling us he was warming the 'hole' of his body. He loved stories about the foibles of priests and nuns. Didn't all non-Catholics tell those stories? He always seemed old to me although there was only 32 years difference. There was no 'tom foolery' or wrestling on the floor; no coaching on how to kick a ball or hold a tennis racquet.

Because of his flexible work hours, he had time to look after Beth and me—to pick us up from school if necessary and come and watch us play sport, which I found embarrassing. I was the only boy who would have a father barracking for him on a week day. He was a very partisan supporter and didn't know the rules well. But he was so loyal to us. With understandable irritation, Elma and Beth mimicked Laurie for so often extolling the exploits of 'my son John'.

He got into arguments with fundamentalists who thought he should be preaching more 'fire and brimstone'. He saw them as very narrow-minded and mean people. He knew that life was a lot more complicated than they thought. They hurt him a lot. His temper flared with them, but always passed quickly. He was a member of the Masonic Lodge, but not very active.

Elma Florence Menear, my mother, was born in Kapunda in 1906. Menear, a Cornish name, means 'long stone'. She was the rock in our family, solid and dependable. Elma's father, Seth Menear, migrated to South Australia on his own in the 1880s. He had been a tin miner in Cornwall and came to Kapunda, north of Adelaide, when the copper mines opened.

My maternal grandmother, Elizabeth Ann, Seth's wife, died six weeks after Elma's birth and Elma was reared by her sisters and particularly her eldest sister, Blanche, who later had four children of her own. Elma was financially supported from time to time by Seth who worked as a fettler on the railways when the copper mines finally closed in 1923. He would be away for months at a time. Blanche's husband also worked on the railways.

Living in Adelaide, Elma had more educational opportunities than Laurie. She was a very good student at Adelaide Girls' High School, although she didn't go to university. Few women did. Instead, she went as a governess to country properties before teacher training, and then as a professional teacher at Townsend House for deaf children at Brighton.

Her sister Gert, a teacher, was a big influence on my mother, Beth and me. We hadn't heard of feminism, but she was a feminist well ahead of her time. She was different. She didn't conform. She went to the races on her own, smoked, 'had a drink or two' and saved money to go overseas to attend Pan Pacific women's conferences in the 1930s. She never married. She had many arguments with Laurie about St Paul. In Gert's view, Paul was a woman hater and stamped his prejudices all over the early church. I felt embarrassed that Gert seemed to have the better of the arguments. The established order was being attacked and Laurie didn't seem to have an adequate answer. He tried to laugh Gert off as eccentric.

Gert told Beth and me about her experiences as a teacher at towns along the Port Augusta-Kalgoorlie railway line. Elma often lived with her. The townspeople along the line were supplied each fortnight by the 'tea and sugar train'. She told us exciting stories of big railway strikes when all residents in those isolated towns had to pack up and leave with their dogs, cats and chooks when a strike was pending. With the strike over, they would go back to places like Tarcoola or Cook, with their awful railway houses, which in 110-degree heat and dust were stifling. Gert ran a free night school for train crews at Cook. It was a tough life for her. She looked anything but a frontier woman; thin, almost spidery, meticulously well-groomed, old-fashioned and prim in her dress, bespectacled and always precise, almost pedantic, in her speech.

She took a great interest in our education. She was appalled when Beth and I were sent to private Methodist colleges. I played sport, didn't study and got bad results in my first year. That confirmed to her everything she had ever thought about private church schools.

My mother, Elma, was like Gert in appearance and manner but maternal, not an 'old maid' like Gert. Elma was very dark haired and handsome as a young woman. Laurie speculated that she must have some Spanish blood from the sailors of the Spanish Armada who were shipwrecked on the Cornish coast. With a father away, and brought up by older sisters, Elma was conscious of the need to be strong. It was a real burden she carried.

In every family difficulty Elma was the strength. A strong and firm handshake was essential. 'Don't extend your hand like a wet fish', she would tell me. Laurie used to affectionately call her 'ramrod'. Whenever Elma spoke to me there was no raised voice or tantrums. I never saw her cry. She always seemed cool and in control. So much was bottled up. She was a good manager. She didn't waste a thing. 'Look after the pennies and the pounds will look after themselves.' Even in latter years, she washed and reused plastic. She was often sick with kidney trouble and had persistent asthma. In retrospect, I think she felt quite lonely with the responsibility she carried. Sickness was a respite. It was her way of asking for help.

She was more radical than my father, but not political like Gert. She was single-minded and so determined. I admired that. She was a wonderful carer. The sick and the lame unerringly found Elma.

With Laurie an itinerant preacher, we were always on the move from town to town and school to school. We were wandering Methodists; newcomers working hard at being accepted. Lasting friendships were hard to maintain. We learned to accept it—on to the next town, the next school, the next church.

After Cowell, we were transferred to Bute and then Ardrossan on Yorke Peninsula, both farming towns but more prosperous than Cowell, with better topsoil and more reliable rainfall. Ardrossan, like Cowell, also had a small fishing fleet. I remember that because at Ardrossan, as a student working on vacation ten years later, a fishing boat was sunk and I recall accusing fingers being pointed at a battling fisherman with many children. He had complained about the wealthy hobby fishing families. They had been issued additional licences that threatened his livelihood. The good people of the town and the Methodist church people sided with the wealthy hobby fishing families against the struggling fisherman on the social fringe of town. No charges were laid. While I am vague about the facts, I recall very clearly my feeling then and almost 50 years later that there was something unfair about it all.

From Ardrossan, in 1941 Laurie was appointed a chaplain in the RAAF. We had no minister's manse for the three years that he was away. Elma, Beth and I lived in ten houses during that time, floating between the houses of church people and relatives. We were strangers, tolerated but not accepted. The adults were more two-faced with Elma, but they didn't conceal their attitudes from eight- and six-year-olds like Beth and me. We had good antennae and knew we were not welcome. We were niggled at continually; not turning off the lights, not cleaning up the kitchen, using too much hot water in the bath. I remember an aunty gave me an awful hiding with a thick stick for upsetting her two daughters. It was my first experience of the abuse of power. I never forgot what it was like to feel helpless and powerless. It always seemed to be women in these houses that were pushing me around. At that age, I was probably looking for the company of men and boys.

What we missed was the sense of home where we could be ourselves without pressure or pretence. I knew when Elma was upset, though she never let on to outsiders. Under strain, her body went taut like fencing wire. I learnt from her to hold it in. Years later, I wondered why Elma accepted it all so stoically. It must have been because she had been passed around between sisters after her mother died. She didn't expect or hope that the Methodist Church would treat her any differently.

But in those dark and dingy houses we did have one place of warmth and safety: Elma's bed. Cosy in her bed, we discussed the affairs of the day and Elma read to us from her Bible and devotional book, *The Upper Room*. I still recall the warmth and intimacy of those occasions. And it wasn't all devotions. The ears of our creepy and unfriendly landlords would have been burning if they knew what we were saying about them. When things became too unpleasant, Elma pulled up stakes and we moved on. By the time I was 22, I had lived in 17 houses and attended 12 schools.

The first week in all those schools was painful. Even today, I feel alone in a schoolyard. I can still smell the bitumen playground in a February heatwave when we started at the new schools. On the first morning my mother would escort us. The headmaster would try to cheer us up, but didn't help much. If you feel alone on the inside, outsiders can't really help. Beth would be with me. She would be lonely too, although she was a better talker than me. But sisters are not much use in the schoolyard. You can't stand talking to your sister all day. At lunchtime I would quickly eat my mother's soggy white sandwiches with tomato sprinkled with sugar, then I would sit close to a group of boys and wait until they started playing with a tennis or cricket ball. Then I would join them uninvited. I knew that I was good at sport and, given half a chance, I would be admitted to the group. Sport was my way out of loneliness in the schoolyard. In all those anxious experiences, my mother seemed to show more confidence in me than I had in myself.

It was a great relief when, in late 1942, we went to Murray Bridge. It was clear by then that Laurie's appointment in the RAAF was not short term and, with our garage debts paid off and with the help of his chaplain's salary, we could afford to rent a house of our own. It seemed, at the time, to be very large and comfortable. Returning 30 years later, it was really quite small. I had changed, not the house, like the cranes in

Basho's poem, 'Patiently fishing in the lake, the crane's long legs have shortened since the rains'.

Murray Bridge was chosen because Laurie's family lived in the area. It was close to Wynarka. We boarded a high school teacher to help our budget. I was 'the man about the house' and close to my mother, doing the gardening, chopping the wood and tending the fowls. I was broken-hearted when at night a large tomcat jumped through the rusty wire netting enclosing my homing pigeons. Next morning I had to get an axe and cut the heads off the mangled survivors.

The war years now seem long ago, with ration coupons, trenches in the schoolyard and identification discs around our necks with our blood group. We collected paper, tyres, scrap metal and toothpaste tubes to raise money for the School Patriotic Fund. Stamps for War Savings Bonds were sold at the schools. I learned to make camouflage nets and knit army socks with four needles. Elma had to turn the heel. Windows were blacked out and streetlights dimmed, even in country towns in South Australia. In the Brighton Primary schoolyard we speculated that a wealthy German living on the Brighton esplanade was signalling at night to a German submarine in St Vincent's Gulf.

My mother did aeroplane spotting in Diamond Park, Murray Bridge. Beth and I joined her after school for tea and scones and to check whether any Japanese planes had intruded into Murray Bridge airspace. We packed the Saturday film matinees to see patriotic films like *The First of the Few*, starring Leslie Howard, about Spitfire pilots. When we were less patriotic, our favourites were *Mrs Miniver*, about an English housewife surviving the war, and *Blossoms in the Dust*, about a Welsh mining village with Greer Garson and Walter Pidgeon. To foot stamping and cheering, the main feature was followed by the serial, starring Roy Rogers and his horse, Trigger, or the Lone Ranger and his Indian friend, Tonto.

When Laurie returned home on leave, we were very proud of him in his officer's uniform; we had plenty of chocolate and chewing gum to show off at school. The war was a financial saver. Laurie now got a reliable RAAF salary and Elma managed it well. There were later benefits of war service: a part pension, a chaplaincy at Daws Road Repatriation Hospital in Adelaide and a war service home loan on retirement. The part pension was due to Laurie's digestion problems as a result of war service. My mother said the real problem was Laurie's mother's poor cooking.

Those three years in the air force were the greatest years of my father's life. He often spoke of them: the pleasure of male companionship after female-dominated local churches, travel to new places like Townsville, new work and status, and without the grind of the circuit and the financial problems and parochialism that went with it.

In 1944, after Laurie finished as chaplain, we went to Renmark on the Upper Murray, a fruit-growing area. We spent three happy years there. We went from Renmark to Naracoorte, where people had bigger cars and less tolerance for newcomers.

In the seven manses where I lived Laurie always had a separate study—something of a no-go area for the rest of the family. The small bathroom usually had a galvanised-iron bath with chip heater and washbasin. There were no showers and we bathed twice a week. Boils and skin infections were common. We feared polio.

The kitchen had a Metters wood stove, with a cast-iron fountain on top for constant hot water. The Naracoorte kitchen had a Silent Knight kerosene refrigerator. Until that happy time, we relied in summer on a Coolgardie safe with hessian sides, dripping with water, to keep fruit and vegetables cool—with the ice chest reserved for butter, milk and meat. It was my job each morning in summer to carry home blocks of ice from the iceworks in a hessian bag across the handlebars of my bike. Flies in the house were killed by a Mortein pump spray or came to grief on a sticky strip hung from the light.

Elma was a plain cook; Methodists had little interest in *haute cuisine*. Cornish pasties were my favourite. You could tell they were cooked when you could smell them through the whole house. The smell was a better guide than a timer. Elma would tell us about the real Cornish pasties for copper miners with meat, potato, swede and turnips at one end and apricot or apple at the other end. Two courses in one.

Every Saturday lunch we had mutton and vegetables, roasted in dripping. We were not allowed to leave any food on the plate. Beth and I were told, 'Eat up—Indian children are starving.' I still feel guilty if I leave food on my plate. The mutton was recycled as cold meat on Sunday. Before I went to school on Monday, I minced the mutton ready for shepherd's pie on Monday night. Rabbit stew with white sauce and parsley and corned beef with beetroot and plum sauce were certainties during the week. With mulberry trees in the fowlyard, eggs were purple in the season. Sweets were often rhubarb and quinces in winter and fresh or stewed stone fruit in summer. Not surprisingly, my tastes in food are plain rather than fancy. Elma didn't seem to enjoy cooking. I wasn't enthused either but I was good at food preparation and cleaning up the dishes. We never ate out, except for church teas and suppers. 'Bring a plate.'

Elma was good with cakes, puddings and trifles, with brandy or 'the doings' added. Brandy for drinking was not acceptable but in cooking it was fine. 'Invalid brandy' was kept at the back of the top shelf in the kitchen dresser. Stale cake and bread always finished in puddings or trifles. Tomato sauce was made in bulk in February. But the big cooking event of the year was in late summer, when we preserved white clingstone peaches by boiling them in Vacola jars in a large galvanised sterilising pot.

Eating together in the kitchen was the centrepiece of family life. Grace was always said before meals, either 'For all his mercies, God's holy name be praised, Amen', or 'Bless this food which now we take, to do us good for Jesus' sake, Amen'. Serviettes were in a personal holder. The table was well set, usually on a damask tablecloth. Knives, forks and spoons were always precisely set and had to be politely used. Permission was essential to leave the table. Years later at lunch at Yarralumla, I recall Queen Elizabeth pulled out her face powder and puff at the lunch table and proceeded to dust her face in front of me and other guests. My mother would never have done that.

The washhouse was outside, with a copper, cement troughs, one for plain rinse water and one for Reckitts blue, a wringer, scrubbing board and a mangle with wooden rollers for pressing dried sheets. The clothes line was strung between the shed and a strong tree with two or three forked poles to keep the clothes off the ground. Monday, the minister's day off, was always washing day with Laurie kicking off by lighting the fire under the copper. He was a very impatient washing hand, dropping sheets on the dirt floor, streaking them with too much blue or putting the woollens in the hot water. Elma would have preferred him to play golf but that was a silly hope. Only the top people in town played golf.

Long-drop toilets away from the house were common, with their cut newspaper and lime bucket. A new pit was dug before each summer. Usually it was quite a walk and, at Ardrossan, we were swooped by magpies in the season. Laurie got out his rifle and shot them. The toilet was often near the woodheap and under a pepper tree or a dollacus creeper, with a blue-mauve flower growing over it. Back lanes for toilet bucket removal were more common in the newer country towns. We enjoyed the fun of the night-soil truck running out of control at Naracoorte, down the hill from the Presbyterian church and into the Lutheran minister's house at the bottom of the hill. We always thought that Presbyterians believed they were better than the rest of us—even their night-soil. Years later, when Gough Whitlam spoke about the 'effluent society' and the need to sewer the outer suburbs in the big cities, I knew exactly what he meant.

As I grew older, I usually drove Laurie to his Sunday preaching appointments. I didn't have a driver's licence, so Laurie would drive out to the edge of town and I would drive from there. He could then do the final preparations on his sermon. But he was never relaxed with me driving. If I wasn't driving out of town, Sunday was very predictable: Christian Endeavour at 9.30 am, church at 11.00 am, Sunday School at 2.30 pm, church again at 7.00 pm and prayer meeting and hymn singing at 8.30. All that leaves an imprint.

Youth groups during the week were segregated. Rays and Comrades were for the girls. The Order of Knights, based on King Arthur and the Knights of the Round Table, was for the boys. I was taught the religious, moral and social codes of chivalry: honour, courage, defence of the weak and protection of women. There were heavy doses of regalia and ceremony, perhaps to make up for the lack of it in the Methodist Church. Dancing was forbidden. Sport and shopping on Sunday were also out. In country towns like Renmark the 'Roman Catholic' children went to convent schools and we had little to do with them. Their church appeared exclusive and dominated by priests. Roman Catholics were evasive over combined services on Anzac Day. They seemed to keep raising the bar against other Christians by developing doctrines like papal infallibility. I never considered what they thought of us.

Beth and I were both members of the Band of Hope, with its pledge of abstinence from 'demon drink'. We learned that alcohol was 'good for the engine but not the engineer', that the lion was strong because he drank only water. I letterboxed houses with leaflets to encourage 'no' votes in the local option polls, whereby local residents could determine whether they wanted an extra liquor licence in their area. We had a high success rate with the 'no' campaigns. We knew we were called 'wowsers' but we believed we had a good cause. Alcohol and gambling were causing the enslavement and impoverishment of working people everywhere. I didn't drink alcohol until I was 27. Margaret Whitlam brought me undone in Paris. But more about that later.

For the Sunday School anniversaries a special platform was erected in the church. We practised for weeks. We sang at the top of our voices 'Jesus loves the little children, all the children of the world. Red and yellow, black and white, all are precious in his sight.' With Methodist gusto we sang 'The Church's one foundation is Jesus Christ our Lord'. This seemed to me a way of saying that our church was built on Christ and not Peter like the Catholics'. They were great family days. It was a chance to get 'the dads' to church. Not surprisingly as the minister's children, Beth and I won attendance prizes. I didn't win prizes for behaviour or diligence.

Sunday School picnics were a great opportunity to show off sporting skills to the girls. We ran flat races, then the novelty races: egg and spoon, sack and three-legged. I didn't like being beaten and won a lot of prizes. We ate curried egg sandwiches, Cornish pasties, lamingtons and sweet cakes and drank raspberry cordial.

Like policemen's children, ministers' children were expected to be well behaved. There was great pressure to be a 'good boy', respectful and dutiful. Beth and I were told of the misdemeanours of others. The implication was 'Don't let the Methodist side down'. We had a highly developed puritan view of right and wrong, with an exaggerated sense of guilt–whether it was about alcohol, gambling or sex. God would love us if we were good and probably not otherwise. I was hard on myself and hard on others. A good Methodist boy had to live by a strict moral code. There was to be no playing around with girls. Illegitimacy was a common subject of discussion at home or in the schoolyard. The stigma of illegitimacy was terrifying—a fate almost worse than death. What amazed me was that, despite the stigma, people kept doing those things outside marriage. What was the attraction? It takes a while to work that out of one's system. It probably explains why, in later life, I found my Irish friends so attractive, and harboured a vicarious longing for their lifestyle. How could you enjoy life, feeling guilty?

We didn't discuss many emotional or psychological issues within the family. There were no therapy sessions in our house. We knew the rules very clearly. Within those boundaries, Beth and I were expected to work things out for ourselves. We knew what had to be done and were urged to get cracking. We learnt that we were responsible for success or failure. There was no point in blaming parents or the 'system'.

The Methodist Church knew it was getting a package when it appointed a minister. Elma was busier than Laurie. On top of running the house and family, she was expected to be President of the Ladies' Guild, whose main function was to raise money in fetes and jumble sales for the minister's stipend. She was President of the Women's Auxiliary of Overseas Missions and President of the Women's Christian Temperance Union with its motto: 'Prohibition, world peace and world piety'.

She ran a guest house for church visitors as well. The only paid accommodation in town was at the local hotel. We would never think of putting our guests in a public house. Beth or I usually had to vacate our bedrooms for the visitors at weekends. The President of the Methodist Conference paid official visits, along with the Director of the Young People's Department and representatives of the British and Foreign Bible Society. There were deputations from home and overseas missions. The missionaries from India seemed to be copies of Gandhi, sun-tanned, gaunt and with wire-rimmed spectacles.

I recall a visit by David Unaipon, who stayed at our house. He features on our $50 note. As a scientist, inventor and musician, he was called the Leonardo da Vinci of the Aboriginal people. In his *History of Australia*, Manning Clark described David Unaipon as 'sustained by the image of Christ in his heart ... he wanted the white man to cease patronising the black fellows as "little children" who had a chance in the kingdom of Heaven, but drew blanks and never prizes in the white man's world'. I am sure he drew blanks in the Methodist manse in Renmark in 1946.

At Sunday School we were encouraged to note the good Methodist families in Adelaide who fostered or adopted Aboriginal children—the stolen children as we later called them. How Christian we thought they were. Race never seemed an issue in the manse. I can't recall it ever being discussed in any serious way, although Laurie would often refer to someone of mixed parentage as 'having a touch of the tar brush' or someone being 'a real white man'. I didn't get much sense of malice from that. Didn't everyone talk that way?

There always seemed to be people at the front door or on the telephone; someone was sick and needed to be visited; someone needed food. Laurie supplied meal vouchers from his own pocket to the needy to take to a friendly cafe owner. He would never give money as it could be spent on liquor. Laurie and Elma were always at the beck and call of the church, the church community and the general public. It was not surprising that Beth became a teacher and I became a public servant.

From 12 years old, I had vacation jobs, doing deliveries for a grocery store or cutting stone fruit in the season. Annual holidays were with family and friends. The best holidays were at Port Elliott, where the Methodist Church had holiday houses for ministers and their families. Except for Sundays it was at the beach all day in fine weather. In bad weather we went 'window shopping'—looking but not touching or buying.

When I look at the photos of Beth and me, I am struck by how neat and tidy we looked even with a limited wardrobe. My short trousers were ironed and creased, the tie carefully knotted and the coat buttoned up. Socks were held up with elastic bands, my shoes were cleaned and my hair was slicked down with Brylcreem. Elma did present us well. She was not a good sewer, but she knitted our jumpers and socks. Parishioners we knew well would discreetly help with some hand-me-downs. Beth got a new dress each summer, and Aunty Blanche sewed pants for me. Ironing was done with the Mrs Potts iron. The plates were heated on the top of the stove and then a curved handle clamped on top. I was taught to iron my trousers and shirts when we bought an electric iron. Laurie was always rummaging through second-hand shops and disposal stores. At Naracoorte he bought army green legging boots for me, cut them down and dyed them black. The girls at school laughed.

Banned on church property, dancing at Boy Scout and school socials was like forbidden fruit. It was a great opportunity to meet girls as they never came to our house, although a couple of times they masqueraded as Beth's friends. I loved the King's Waltz, the Pride of Erin and the Tango. At the dances the girls sat around the walls, with the boys milling about the door, discussing their prowess and who were the good sorts and the good dancers. I was too awkward and embarrassed to sit next to girls and hold a conversation for more than ten seconds. When we were invited to 'Take your partners for the military two-step', I would sweep across the floor quickly and, as nonchalantly as possible, claim my partner.

At Renmark I think I had my first girlfriend. She wrote in my autograph book, 'The friends thou hast and their adoption tried, grapple them to thy soul with hoops of steel'! I liked her but I was too shy and nervous to know how to respond to lines from Hamlet.

Swimming was also a chance to show off to the girls. Diving to get attention, I broke off two front teeth when I hit the bottom of the pool. I made a real mess of my face. After dental repairs, I did the same again, diving into an irrigation channel to impress the girl who had written the lines from Shakespeare. I don't know whether she was impressed by my daring or thought I was a slow learner.

Only sissies wore hats and real boys didn't wear shirts in the water or out of the pool. We were outdoors all the time. The sunburn was predictable. First there was the pain which was partially relieved by a vinegar sponge. After a few days of itchiness the peeling started. Each morning I had to shake out the peeled skin from my bed sheets. I would be careful for a month or two and then repeat the folly.

As with family and church, discipline at school was always strict. At Bute, my class teacher was away and the headmaster took to me with a cane. I was five years old. I refused to go to school until my class teacher returned. Whether my rebellion was due to fear or stubbornness I don't know. Probably a bit of both. Within the family, the Bute school story improved with the telling over the years.

Every Monday we saluted the flag and, with hand over heart, pledged allegiance to King George VI. After the headmaster's daily parade in the bitumen yard we marched into class to the accompaniment of the school band. I played the triangle. My borrowings from the town library were cricket books, *Biggles, Tom Brown's Schooldays* and books about exploration and colonial adventure like *Scott in Antarctica*.

I liked being a leader in the schoolyard. Beth usually won academic prizes and I won all-rounder, leadership or sports prizes. I worked hard to sell myself. I remember only one fight, at Murray Bridge. It was over who was the top group in the schoolyard. I was the organiser of a group and was surprised when I had to be the enforcer as well. I was scared, but got in a lucky punch. My opponent ran away, to my great surprise and enormous relief.

At Renmark High School I sneaked a look in my class teacher's file. I learned that my IQ was average. My results reflected that. But in 1949, for the external Intermediate Certificate at Naracoorte, I worked hard for about six months and got good results. My subjects included woodwork. I learned that if I was determined I could succeed.

I was mad about cricket, Australian Rules football, tennis and athletics. In country towns there was plenty of open space and sports facilities. Sport was always my way, as a boy, of belonging—of the outsider becoming an insider. Cricket took pride of place. Without fail in those early years I was the captain, opened the batting and kept wicket if I wasn't bowling. The family was delighted, as I was, by the headline in the sports pages of the *Renmark Pioneer*: '12-year-old boy scores 44 not out'. I played for the school during the week and the town team on Saturday.

I bought my first cricket bat in Renmark by catching rabbits in traps and with ferrets and selling the carcases to the iceworks, and the skins that had been stretched and dried on wire. However, I was so delighted with my new cricket bat that I oiled it too much to prevent splitting. It became too heavy. Practising an off drive with it, I broke the bedroom lampshade of Laurie's minister friend in Adelaide, where we stayed for our holidays. He was very understanding.

At Naracoorte I was the high school tennis champion as a second year student. I was very competitive, keen to prove that I was as good as or better than the graziers' or bank managers' sons. I couldn't understand why others didn't hit to an opponent's weakness, usually the backhand. I led a team of school cricketers and footballers to Adelaide for state competitions. I loved sport and couldn't play enough. Studies were a fill-in between sports.

In 1949, my Intermediate Certificate year, Laurie made inquiries about jobs for me in Naracoorte. I was 14 so it was time for a job. He was always planning my future, anxious for me to succeed. He spoke to a bank manager about a job as a trainee teller in the ES&A Bank. He spoke to the postmaster about me becoming a trainee linesman. We talked about it over the meal table but I didn't really feel involved. Laurie was going to make decisions for me anyhow.

He then talked to some leading Methodist laymen in the town and a new world opened up. Many of the Methodist families in Naracoorte were old boys of Prince Alfred College in Adelaide. Laurie quizzed them about scholarships. I didn't see a formal application, although I provided newspaper clippings of my sporting activities and school reports. I assume the Methodist network went to work on the telephone and did the rest. Within a couple of months I had a sports scholarship at 'Prince's'. As a son of the manse, I also got reduced fees for boarding and an Old Boys' scholarship as well. Beth went to Methodist Ladies' College, but as a day girl. Boys invariably got the better deal.

Study hard, get a job, get married, buy a house and have children

'Times change and we change with them' (Anon)

Prince Alfred College opened a new world for me. I loved my three years there. I became close friends with boys who expected to go to university. I decided to follow them. To my knowledge, no one in my family had ever been to university.

I commenced as a boarder at Prince's in January 1950. I was almost 15. I spent most of my waking hours in 1950 playing sport or thinking of girls.

After years on the move from country school to country school, Princes was stabilising and exciting. It was also well endowed. There were no asphalt schoolyards for sport but well-manicured green ovals and lawn tennis courts. Assembly was not outdoors in all weathers, but in the large assembly hall with wall-to-wall honour boards of old boys. I never felt homesick. Neither did I have a sense that Laurie or Elma were trying to hang on to me, to stop me doing new things or going to new places. They were proud of me and, on later reflection, were living out their own unrealised ambitions through me.

Methodist in inspiration and with a motto appealing to students to do brave things and endure (*FAC FORTIA ET PATERE*), Prince's was modelled on English Public Schools. I had read a lot of ripping yarns about young heroes at schools: boys who single-handedly solved a school mystery, topped the form and ran the length of the field to score the winning try against all the odds. They were good young lads; white, Protestant and socially adept. I admired them. And I was joining them. Like the boys in the books, the boys at Prince's came from families with middle-class and socially conservative backgrounds: farming, the professions and manufacturing. Their parents exercised power naturally and easily as a birthright. It was a chance for me to observe at close quarters the manners of the well-born. At the time there was little analysis in my head. I was just exploring new things, too busy for any reflection. The teachers were wonderful 'Mr Chips' types; classes were small. The chaplain, a famous ex-footballer, told us more about football than faith.

At the first under 15 cricket practice after joining Prince's, Frank Hambly, who was captain and was to become a lifelong friend, sidled up to me and confidentially whispered, 'Consider yourself selected in the under 15s'. I thought, 'I should certainly hope so'. After making a century in quick time with the under 15s I was included in the first XI cricket team in my first year. St Peter's, the Anglican school which was even more socially conservative than Prince's, was the traditional rival. Methodists and Lutherans produced the state's wealth and the Anglicans owned a disproportionate share of its property. In the intercollegiate match against St Peter's at Adelaide Oval I made a duck. For one and a half days my risible score was displayed on the Adelaide Oval scoreboard, with my name misspelt. I did much better in my second and third years scoring 48, 52, 17 and 73.

In my second and third years I won colours for representing the college in three sports: cricket, football and athletics.

It was a great life but academically my first year at Prince's was a flop. I passed only one subject in my Leaving Certificate and had to repeat. My parents must have been disappointed but they didn't show it. I learnt a lot from that year, mainly the need to be focused and disciplined. Perhaps too much sport, mucking around and not enough study was a reaction against 14 years at the manse and its rules. It opened a new world for me and was an inevitable transition; away from a country manse to a city boarding school and meeting boys and some girls with very different educational and social backgrounds and expectations.

My second year was quite different. My parents had been transferred to Port Adelaide in 1951. I became a dayboy. I changed many subjects, dropping the so called 'hard' academic subjects in favour of economics, geography and history. I applied myself to study and got good external Leaving Certificate results. I continued to play sport but on a lesser scale than before. I was rebuked a couple of times by masters on the grounds that, as a sports scholarship holder, I should be playing more sport and studying less. Perhaps sports scholarship holders weren't expected to have serious career prospects.

The final year at Prince's, 1952, was very light academically. I was a prefect so could dish out a caning or two. I did Leaving Honours in name only as I was preparing myself for Adelaide University. For university entry I had to have a foreign language. Twenty-five years later I applauded that policy as the way to promote foreign language study but in 1952 it was a pain. I hated Latin but finally passed. I played a lot of sport again.

Prince's was my first real public encounter with sectarianism. The grudge football matches were against the Catholic schools, particularly Rostrevor; Anglo-Saxon Methodists against Irish Catholics. I shared a common view then about Catholics and their exclusiveness. What galled us most was the treatment of non-Catholics in mixed marriages. In my family and amongst other Protestants this was a regular conversation topic. They wouldn't even let us put flowers on the altar for such a marriage. What was the point of discussing church union with Catholics when their view was simply that we should join them: the one true church. That put an edge on our football rivalry.

In my last year at Prince Alfred College, Laurie again was actively looking for jobs for me. Using his Methodist network, I got a job offer from Wiltshire, Denton and Turner, a leading Adelaide firm of Methodist accountants. But it was Frank and Peter Hambly who, unknowingly, took me on a different path. Their father was a well-known scholar and a leading Methodist preacher. Frank and Peter's expectation was that they would go to university, like their father before them. I decided that I would do the same. It was as simple as that. So I applied for a Commonwealth Scholarship to study accountancy at university and was successful. In my age group, scholarships were easy to obtain. I subsequently changed from accountancy to economics and off I went to Adelaide University.

After I left Prince's I never felt any desire to go back and never joined the Old Boys' association. Yet all my children went to Methodist or similar private colleges.

In my last year at Prince's I met Cynthia Trowbridge. We were both 17 years old. We married five years later. She was from the same Methodist background; her father was a farmer and a Methodist circuit steward from Lameroo, 130 miles north-east of Adelaide. We met at a school dance at Methodist Ladies' College, where she was a boarder. I had gone on sufferance because one of the girls at the college had difficulty in finding a partner. I was prevailed upon by her parents from Naracoorte who had helped me get the sports scholarship. I was rewarded by meeting Cynthia, who was squired on the night by a grazier's son from Naracoorte. She wore blue taffeta. I was awkward but she was so easy to be with and talk to. It was love at first sight. Always outgoing, she was a brunette with brown eyes, had arching eyebrows and a smile that rarely left her.

After she finished college she went back to Lameroo and taught the piano to country students. But after six months she found that living in a country town was not for her; neither was marrying a farmer's son. She came back to Adelaide and lived in a women's hostel, obtained a librarian's diploma and became a professional librarian.

Our friendship continued throughout my university days, a friendship that was very conventional and predictable for the son and daughter of two Methodist families in the 1950s. Sex came after marriage, not before. There was little calculation or planning about accumulating assets and then thinking about marriage and children. The personal path was clear for both of us: finish study, get a job, get married, buy a house and have children. We did just that. Forty years later I would not have wanted it any different.

The Commonwealth Scholarship paid tuition fees and a living allowance at Adelaide University for four years, from 1953. I knew that if I worked hard and focused I could get good results. Accordingly, I largely gave up sport, which now I regret. I changed my focus from sport to study. I was worried that if I didn't keep my head down and study hard I might lose my scholarship. I was a Methodist self-improver.

Although my major was in economics, it was political science that had the most influence on me, particularly as taught by Professor W. G. K. Duncan, an old leftie. At secondary school I had been used to lecturers presenting facts and views to me. I would write the notes down and, if I was smart, reproduce them at examination time. It was more like indoc-trination than teaching. But, in Duncan, I had a lecturer who asked repeated questions. I found it very frustrating for the whole first term. What was this fellow all about? He wouldn't tell me what to accept or believe.

It took me a whole term to get over my frustration and irritation with him. It was the most brilliant and challenging teaching I have ever experienced. He respected my freedom and right to choose. There is a kernel of truth to be found but you have to work to get inside the shell and find out what it is. And once you find it, the truth is your own. I didn't realise it at the time but this exploring, challenging and finding is where life's energy comes from.

I found the debates in Oliver Cromwell's army novel and exciting. The plain soldier and his views were as valued as the officers'. The influences of R. H. Tawney's *Equality* and *Religion and the Rise of Capitalism* and Laski's *Grammar of Politics* are still with me. I read about the radical Archbishop William Temple, Charles Kingsley, the Anglican priest, and the Christian socialists in England. Unknowingly, Duncan helped me draw out the link between faith and social justice. I could see in later years that my commitment to social justice was anchored in my early days in the manse. It profoundly affected my life and career choices.

A decade later I was thrilled by the American civil rights movement which grew out of the Protestant churches of the South with their prophetic preaching and vibrant singing. I felt part of the same tradition.

From the beginning the Methodist Church, wherever it went, was active in social justice. A lot of early Unionist and Labor Members of Parliament in England, such as Arthur Henderson and Keir Hardie, came from Methodist chapels. The religious aspect of English socialism gave it an ethical bent that distinguished it from European socialism, which was more Marxist and anti-clerical. 'Labor owes more to Methodism than Marxism' as Arthur Calwell often said.

Methodist action for social justice had two strands. The first was public agitation by its members in solidarity with others. The second was private: hard work, self-improvement and sobriety to improve one's lot. In time, a political division opened up. Many laymen were so successful in self-improvement that, in getting ahead themselves, they turned their back on others. They privatised their faith. Limited public welfare was fine but structural change to redress structural evil and injustice in society was unnecessary. 'I have made it, why can't others?' Methodist clergy such as Alan Walker, a hero of mine, Donald Soper in England and some of the laity remained more radical and in keeping with the roots of Methodist social activism as I came to see it. My father had often admiringly spoken of an earlier Cornish Methodist local preacher, John Verran, who in 1910 was the first Labor Premier of South Australia with a clear majority. He was described as 'folksy, flamboyant and nearly illiterate'. In South Australia in my time, Norman Makin was fairly typical of the Methodist and Labor links; a minister in the Curtin Government and a Methodist lay preacher.

South Australia had quite a radical tradition. The first Labor candidates in Australia were elected in South Australia in 1891. Women's suffrage followed three years later.

Professor Duncan helped me draw a social and political conclusion from my Methodist and biblical background, in a way that my parents had not. The beautiful poetry of the Bible came alive to me as a political challenge. It was thrilling to feel and know what those stories meant to me in a quite new way; texts that I had read for years and could readily recite.

'Let justice roll down like waters and righteousness like a mighty river' (Amos 5:24).

'Is not this the part that pleases me; To break unjust fetters; To undo the thongs of the yoke; To let the opposed go free; Is it not sharing your food with the hungry; And sheltering the homeless poor?' (Isaiah 58:6).

'There is neither Jew nor Greek, slave nor free, male or female … all are one …' (Galatians 3:28).

Duncan's politics lectures were transforming. My heart was engaged and I knew that for me the other side of the coin of faith was social justice. We were all equal souls. Years later I came to understand equal souls also includes the unborn and the terminally ill. Human life is a seamless web. It is always sacred.

I found the values underpinning socialism—equality, cooperation and solidarity—very appealing, but I was never attracted to Marxist economic theories and communism was morally unacceptable, or, as I awkwardly and piously described it at the time, 'communists hate the rich, more than they love the poor'. Capitalism was proving a more efficient system than any other. We had to live with it as best we could. But, like communism, it was morally flawed, based at best on self-interest and at worst on greed.

The economics department at Adelaide University, headed by Professor Peter Karmel, was also very influential. Together with Eric Russell, Russell Matthews, Geoffrey Harcourt and Keith Hancock, they made up, what I like to think, was the best economics department in the country. It was strongly Keynesian. They were people who had been shaped by the Depression. They were more than interpreters of history and events. They had a passion for reform. Capitalism could be saved from itself; it was only a means to an end. The end was people and their happiness. Economic orthodoxy changed later when it moved to supply side and 'rational' economics. It then took on the hallmarks of fundamentalism, with different objectives and values.

I was pleased with my Bachelor of Economics results but was disappointed with my honours result, a 2A. But, on reflection, I didn't really have cause for complaint. My thesis was on the Australian banking system. Cynthia typed it for me.

Just as I had followed Frank Hambly to Adelaide University, I also followed him to Lincoln College where his father was the principal. The college had been named after John Wesley's college at Oxford. In addition to my Commonwealth Scholarship I got a discount at Lincoln as a son of the manse and earned extra money from vacation jobs. My parents paid the balance.

In my first year at Lincoln College I roomed with three Malayan students, Joy Seevaratnam and S. K. Cheung, both medical students, and Ray Thong, an architectural student. In subsequent years I shared a room with Ray Thong only. The unofficial leader of the Malayan students at Lincoln was Sam Abraham. He became the first Asian to be president of the National Union of Australian University Students.

I came from country towns in South Australia where I had not thought about White Australia. It was a given and not discussed. My attitudes had been reinforced over the years by family, school and church. I could only remember one Chinese student at Brighton Primary School and in country towns I had lived in there was not even a Chinese restaurant. Those three Malayan students I roomed with and Sam Abraham changed my life. They helped me confront my ignorance and prejudice on race. I learnt something from them about Malaya, its history and cuisine but, more importantly, I learnt something about Australia and myself. For me they held a mirror up to White Australia and I didn't like what I saw.

Until Lincoln I had a stereotyped view about Asians as poor, unskilled workers or hustlers working street stalls in Bombay and Singapore. A threat! But in Australia in 1953 there was a group of articulate and educated young Asian students. Their presence was reassuring. Not surprisingly the push to abolish White Australia came out of the universities and, particularly, Melbourne University. I recall the pamphlet *Control or Colour Bar*, published a few years later, which argued the moral case against White Australia but recognised that there had to be some restrictions on numbers or it would frighten the Australian community.

Lincoln College changed so many things for me. That experience, and other 'foreign' experiences, whether in Australia or Japan, taught me about Australia and myself. We are not often changed by the intellect but by experiences of the heart and emotions. As a result their influence is long lasting. It is also painful to admit error and then change. No wonder the Israelites murmured against Moses. They preferred the predictable life of slaves in Egypt rather than change and be free and uncertain in the wilderness.

My student days were very ordered. I rode a bike during the week to lectures at the university. Private study, tutorials and socialising, over Asian cooking or bread toasted on the radiator, took place at the college. On Friday nights Cynthia and I went to the theatre, films or ballet. I would ride my bike to her hostel to take her out and ride back to college at the end of the evening. We often queued for many hours for tickets to the Bolshoi Ballet. I didn't like it much, but Cynthia loved the ballet. We didn't dine out very often.

On Saturday afternoons in winter I played football and Cynthia came to watch when she wasn't playing with her social tennis group. In summer we both played for a church tennis club in competitions but, with no practice, I found it frustrating that I didn't play better. I always wanted to win. Occasionally we would join Laurie and Elma for a drive in the Adelaide Hills with a thermos of tea and date scones. In retrospect it was boring but I can't recall thinking so at the time. I was being dutiful.

Sunday was the most predictable of all as it had always been for me in the manse for 15 years before I went to boarding school. Cynthia and I would meet in the city, catch a bus to Alberton and later Goodwood and spend the whole afternoon at the manse, filling in time having a large afternoon tea, often toasted bacon fingers or Cornish pasties. I sensed that Cynthia found it all boring and why wouldn't she? I am surprised how we stuck at it. I didn't see my parents much during the week and this was the least I could do. Obligations. Obligations.

In each university vacation I worked for two or three months for pocket money—often together with Frank and Peter Hambly—stripping fruit trees in Adelaide during a fruit fly outbreak, picking grapes at Renmark (only for dried fruit, never for wine), sampling barley at Ardrossan to identify green grain, and National Service Training at Woodside in 1954.

I enjoyed Woodside, meeting a wider range of young men, even though I felt the whole exercise was a great waste of public money in response to a trumped-up threat from China. Army corporals, veterans of Korea, must have found cheeky university students a real pain. For me it was a chance to break a few rules. My peers and I never aspired to a rank. Only the bosses' stooges, medical students and young Liberals got stripes. I remember at Woodside the suicide of a young man in the hut next to mine on the first night. He was an only son, studying philosophy, who had applied for but been refused conscientious objection. I had never thought about such strong-felt opposition to war. At the time I had a mixture of sorrow and admiration for this sensitive young man.

Apart from study and time with Cynthia at weekends, the only activity that interested me was the university ALP Club. I joined in 1953 and became president in 1955, the year of the Hobart Conference and the Labor Party Split. The right-wing anti-communist Catholic movement led by B. A. Santamaria was expelled from the ALP and set up what was to become the DLP throughout Australia. It transferred traditional Catholic Labor votes to the Liberals for 17 years, demoralised the ALP and on at least two occasions kept Federal Labor out of power until 1972.

Robert Menzies was in power in Canberra and Tom Playford in Adelaide. Playford held office because of a heavy electoral loading of rural votes, despite a solid and growing ALP vote in Adelaide. It looked as if the Menzies and Playford reigns would never end.

South Australia had had only free settlers and fewer Irish than other states. In the ALP this was reflected in a less Irish and Catholic influence. The ALP in South Australia was exceptionally well led by such people as Clyde Cameron, Jim Toohey, Reg Bishop, Jim Cavanagh and, later, Mick Young. Because of the pragmatism of this ALP leadership and also the Catholic hierarchy in South Australia, the Split of 1955 and its aftermath was not as bitter and destructive as elsewhere. The DLP ran candidates but they never really made much impact in South Australia. It just wasn't fertile ground for them.

There were debates at the university on the Petrov Royal Commission and the controversy following the Split. We had the editor of the *News*, Rohan Rivett, come to Lincoln College and speak about the Split. Somehow it seemed remote. But perhaps my views were coloured by the sectarian background from which I had come, sceptical and suspicious of Catholics and the role of the Catholic Church within the Labor Party.

The principal issue which concerned us in the ALP Club was the abolition of White Australia, even though it was long-entrenched ALP policy. To pursue our campaign we held meetings on campus and wrote letters to the *Adelaide Advertiser*. It was certainly not a boisterous campaign, in contrast to the anti-Vietnam campaign a decade later. But to students of my generation with a left-wing inclination White Australia was the important issue. With many Asian students on campus our attitudes and prejudices were challenged. We couldn't avoid the issue.

The main outside political contact was with Don Dunstan, an aspiring young Labor politician and lawyer from Norwood. We greatly admired him, particularly his stand on White Australia. He had been at the University of Adelaide before us and represented the new Labor Party. He was articulate, young and professional and gave us hope when it was in very short supply.

If people like Menzies clung to the strings of British Empire, young people like me clung to the strings of British socialism. I subscribed to the *New Statesman* and the *Tribune* in England and avidly followed what the British Labour Party was doing.

For those like me leaving university at the end of 1956, there was seldom concern about a job. It was simply a matter of picking and choosing. It was a lucky period for most Australians. There was economic growth and widening prosperity. For Prime Minister Menzies the British Empire still held sway and the countries of our region were becoming more prosperous but no threat strategically or economically. There was large-scale white immigration. Aborigines looked like disappearing as a people and a problem. Foreign investment was pouring in. God seemed to be in his heaven and all was going well in our closed white world. The one cloud on the horizon was communism, with conservative governments everywhere thriving on anti-communist rhetoric. The 'red menace' was exploited to the limit.

In my last year at university I wrote to Harold Souter, Secretary of the ACTU, about a position as research officer in Melbourne. I didn't get an acknowledgment. My first job was as a junior research officer in the Commonwealth Bureau of Census and Statistics in Adelaide. My father played no part in finding this job. I was moving into an area outside his knowledge and experience but I still lived at home with my parents and paid five pounds a week board out of the 25 pounds I earned.

I found the work in the Bureau of Census and Statistics dreadful, working on coding retail census forms. It was the pits. Coming out of university I had delusions about myself and my value. But here I was sweating out my first nine months writing codes across the top of two A4 pages on the type of enterprise, the industry classification, the number of employees and the turnover. My coding enabled the operator to punch in the details for compilation purposes. I learnt with a vengeance that work was not always going to be exciting and satisfying.

I joined the Goodwood branch of the ALP. I also became the Secretary of the Fabian Society of South Australia. Affiliated to the Fabian Society of Great Britain, its aims were 'the establishment of a society in which equality of opportunity will be assured and the economic power and privileges of individuals and class is abolished through the collective ownership and democratic control of the economic resources of the community. It seeks to secure these ends by the methods of political democracy'. Among its active members were Clyde Cameron, Jim Toohey, Don Dunstan, Norman Makin and Ken Inglis. The early membership of the Fabians in South Australia was almost interchangeable with those who controlled the State Executive of the ALP as well as the Trades and Labour Council.

Among the membership was a woman who Clyde Cameron believed, probably correctly, was an ASIO spy. I was surprised to think that anyone would think we were worth spying on. It was very open and quite uncontroversial, so much so that Rupert Murdoch was one of the early speakers at meetings held in the library of the Zoology Department at the University of Adelaide.

In my first year of work, I started playing football again with Alberton Methodists in the United Churches Association. It was hard going, not being really fit and playing against retired and canny ex-league football stars on the rough, hard Adelaide parklands. I had frequent concussion. It was a relief at the end of the season to play for the Port Adelaide Senior Colts, along with players such as Peter Obst, Rex Johns and Geoff Motley who went on to become league stars. But the most exciting player was an Aborigine, Wilf Huddleston. He was amazing and appeared capable of bouncing back on to his feet whenever he was knocked over. He was never hurried and always had the football on a string. He was a sporting genius. Later Charlie Perkins told me that racism broke Huddleston's heart and he gave football away.

In September 1955, before I had finished studies, Cynthia Trowbridge and I decided to get married. We were both 20 and had been courting for three years. She was the only serious girlfriend I ever had. As was the custom, I asked permission of her father, Max. He was hard of hearing in his left ear so I had to position myself on his right. He readily agreed to me becoming his son-in-law. We weren't married for another two years.

Cynthia was very supportive over our five-year courtship. She was very much the giver. She must have often felt like an afterthought, squeezed in between study, job, politics and occasional football games. We always went together to church. Socially we met each weekend during term and more often during vacation. I regularly went to Lameroo to stay with her parents on their farm. They were very welcoming. Debutante balls were still very important for young women 'coming out', so in black tie and dancing pumps I partnered Cynthia to the Methodist Ladies' College Old Girls' Debutante Ball at the Palais on North Terrace. Balls at the Palais were always big occasions, with large crowds, big bands and excellent suppers.

The year 1957 was a difficult one for me; it was then I suffered my first real setback. Lifestyle changes made me anxious about the future. I hated my job and was apprehensive each day I went to work. I had a wonderful and supportive relationship with Cynthia but marriage and the changes it would bring were worrying. I would have my own family rather than be part of Laurie and Elma's. For the first time in my life I felt uncertain. In retrospect I know I went through a period of depression. I felt as if I was in prison and didn't know my way out. I can now understand that experience because of two later bouts of more severe depression.

I felt very vulnerable and alone. I didn't talk to anyone about it, not even Cynthia. It is remarkable how she put up with me and my melancholy. Twenty years later she told the children about it. In retrospect I can see that she had a pretty good understanding of what was happening. I didn't know enough about depression to articulate it to anyone. Even if I had been able to understand, I don't think I would have mentioned it. That would have shown weakness. I didn't get medical treatment. Time was the healer, not medication or counselling. How can you address a problem if you can't name it. I thought I was just having a downer for a month, two months, three months … It lasted about nine months. I was becalmed and frightened. I was yet to learn that setbacks are part of being human. We are born to both life and trouble.

Cynthia and I married in October 1957, in the Hare Street Methodist Church in Laurie's circuit. Frank Hambly was my best man. My Lincoln College room-mates attended. It was to be a wonderful partnership of two young, unformed people growing and changing together. We honeymooned at Victor Harbor, 50 kilometres from Adelaide, where both of us had holidayed as children. We borrowed Laurie's car for the week.

When we returned we moved into a house that Laurie had built with the help of a War Service home loan. He was so excited about owning his first and only home at the age of 60. His pleasure was palpable.

It was financially convenient for us but socially restrictive. He never really left us alone, always visiting to check on the house.

My mood improved but I still looked for ways to get out of that awful job in Adelaide. I hated going to work and took quite a few sickies. I thought to myself for a period that Cynthia's father might employ me on the farm at Lameroo. Perhaps physical rather than mental work would be better.

A respite, if not a solution, was at hand. There had been a round of promotions in Adelaide at the Bureau of Census and Statistics which, not surprisingly, I had missed out on after only nine months in the job. My supervisors could hardly have been impressed with the quality of my work. They suggested, however, that it might be worth applying for something in Canberra, where there were many more opportunities. So I applied and got a promotion to a research officer in Canberra.

The trip to Canberra was not an auspicious start for a new life and a new career for Cynthia and me. We bought a second-hand Holden FX on hire purchase with the help of one of Laurie's Methodist network in the second-hand car business. Unfortunately it boiled in the Adelaide Hills with 800 kilometres to go. A generous taxi driver saw us marooned, stopped, adjusted the loose fan belt in 30 seconds and we were back on our way to the biggest adventure of our lives. We were like the Scotsman described by Samuel Johnson who saw the noblest prospect being the high road that leads to London; in our case it was Canberra.

Years later I could see that I needed that physical separation from my background to find my own direction. I would also see how enriched and influenced I had been by that background.

When we arrived in March 1958, Canberra had a population of just over 50,000. It was like a large country town, except for the public buildings: Parliament House, the War Memorial, East and West Blocks and Civic Centre. It was sleepy and quiet. The parks and fields were brown and dry. Yet I got a real buzz in seeing, for the first time, these buildings that I had read so much about.

In later years, as I lived away from Canberra, the more I regarded Canberra as a great mistake, a remote and privileged city. I recall Japanese officials visiting Australia to look at the Canberra experiment and to advise their government on the location of government departments outside Tokyo. I advised them, 'Don't—ever!'

But for Cynthia and me in 1958 it was new and exciting, doing things together without the constraints of South Australia and family. We first stayed at the Hotel Acton; it had a view over the basin which was later to become Lake Burley Griffin. There were a large number of such hotels and hostels which provided accommodation for newly arrived public servants. Life was very ordered in a government boarding house. We had to get used to noisy children in high chairs who shared the table with us and who seemed to enjoy throwing half-digested food or worse, across the table.

After a few weeks we rented a house in Deakin. It was much more to our liking. It provided more privacy, a garden and guests. Together with old friends Frank Hambly and Ray Thong, visits from in-laws soon followed. We visited the sites and went on picnics with the Canberra flies. We upset our Deakin neighbours by keeping fowls against the back fence. How could you have a home without red Orpingtons?

With help of a loan from Cynthia's parents we put a deposit on a new 'spec' house in Narrabundah which we extended as the family grew. We established a garden, planted a lawn and got our free issue of trees from the Department of the Interior. As was the fashion in those days we laid cork tiles in the living rooms and lounge and seagrass matting in the rest. Cynthia made all the curtains. On Sunday picnics we collected firewood by the roadside. Married life was very happy. We were active in the Methodist Church at Forrest and I played football, briefly, with the Manuka Football Club. We commenced our twice annual car treks to South Australia for holidays. I transferred my membership to the Labor Party in Canberra and together with Cynthia attended meetings of the Canberra South branch at the old Burns Club on National Circuit.

Cynthia worked in the Bureau of Census and Statistics library before our first child, Susan, was born in January 1959. We were parents at 23, but in those days wasn't everyone?

My first 18 months in Canberra were spent working in the Bureau of Census and Statistics; first on new capital raisings, then on the inflow of foreign investment into Australia. I found the work was much more enjoyable than coding retail census forms in South Australia. In late 1959, I secured a position with Treasury in the Financial and Economic Policy Branch. My promotion to Treasury was assisted by Harold Heinrich with whom I had studied economics in Adelaide. He persuaded me to apply and obviously had a few words with his Treasury seniors. But I didn't really have time to settle into Treasury. I was only there for four months. A big opportunity was just around the corner: working for Gough Whitlam.

The seven lean years

With Gough Whitlam

*'And the seven years of famine set in as Joseph
had predicted' (Genesis 41:54)*

W orking with Gough
Whitlam was the most exciting work experience of my life. His energy
and zest for ideas were boundless. He became a firm friend and still is.
He penned on my farewell card, 'To my companion through the seven
lean years, March 1960–October 1967'.

It was hard going in opposition. But those years were laying the
ground for success in 1972, just as Menzies had done after the formation
of the Liberal Party in 1944. It took Menzies five years to become prime
minister the second time. It took Whitlam 12 years. Modern political
parties now seem to think that policies can be developed in a few months
and presented to the electorate in a four-week election campaign.

Voters are very perceptive. They can recognise very quickly when
the policy cupboard is bare: as they did with Kim Beazley in 1998. This
is no great problem for conservative parties, but more is expected of
reformist parties.

My South Australian connections served me well in getting the job
with Whitlam. My most active continuing political contact from South
Australia was Clyde Cameron. In Adelaide he had been kind enough to
speak a couple of times at my Goodwood Labor sub-branch. I also kept
in touch with Don Dunstan, who was active on the Federal Executive
of the ALP.

When Whitlam was elected Deputy Leader of the Federal

Parliamentary Labor Party in March 1960, I got a phone call from Cameron to say that Whitlam was looking for a private secretary. Was I interested? I thought it a silly question. Of course I was interested. Shortly afterwards Whitlam rang and said that he would like to see me. I went over to old Parliament House as fast as my legs could carry me to see him in his small Deputy Leader's office just off King's Hall. The office faced onto a large courtyard of poplar trees, lawn and white masonry. But the light from the courtyard seemed to be absorbed by the heavy, conservative office furniture and the dark green of the carpets and upholstered cushions, the distinctive colour of the House of Representatives. Whitlam struck me as very alert, bright-eyed, angular, well groomed and dressed, friendly but not at ease socially. He never was. He was very precise. We had not met before but I had read a lot about the 'new rising star' in federal politics.

He outlined what he wanted: mainly help on research and speeches. It was very clear that he was not going through any elaborate process of advertising or head hunting. How to run a small office was not discussed. I didn't know and neither did he. He was playing it very much by ear on the basis of a personal recommendation from Cameron. It suited me. Apart from my South Australian connections and my economics degree I had something else going for me. I wasn't then a Catholic. The Split was very much alive and Cameron didn't want Whitlam to put a Catholic on his staff. Cameron was very frank and explicit to me on the matter. As a South Australian Methodist I was quite receptive to his view.

Cameron was also in touch with Dr John Burton, former Head of the Department of Foreign Affairs, who then ran a Canberra bookshop. Burton spoke to the Reverend George Wheen, the Methodist minister in Canberra at our church. Wheen rang and urged me to take the position if it was offered. It was important not to let Catholics get these sorts of positions, he said.

One reason why Whitlam had won as Deputy against Eddie Ward, the aggressive but ageing member for East Sydney, was that Whitlam was not a Catholic. The three other 'leaders', Arthur Calwell and the Leader and Deputy Leader in the Senate, Senators Nick McKenna and Senator Pat Kennelly were all Catholics. If Eddie Ward had been elected Deputy Leader it would have been four Catholics. Some thought that too many. Ward was very bitter about sectarianism being used against him. Whitlam may not agree that not being a Catholic helped his election as Deputy Leader, but I have no doubt it certainly helped me.

So Whitlam, without much due process, offered the job to me. Cynthia, who had witnessed my frustration with uninteresting jobs, was very encouraging. 'Grab it', she said. I gladly took it. Without really knowing it I had fallen on my feet. I was 25, careful rather than brash, but very ambitious and with a vague sense of public service.

I became in effect Whitlam's chief of staff. There were only three other staff: an electoral secretary who was based in Sydney serviced Whitlam's western suburbs electorate of Werriwa, which included Liverpool and Cabramatta; one staff member in Canberra was a receptionist and typist; and the other staff member worked with me. With a heavy workload we had to muck in and do things together. The office was too small and work pressures too great to indulge ourselves in office politics.

Our staff establishment, administration support and general infrastructures were determined by the Government in association with the Public Service Board. We had little discretion, except the power of appointment. Because of our limited resources we had to rely increasingly on people of goodwill to contribute their time and ideas gratis. They did so very willingly. Times have changed. In 1999 the Deputy Leader of the Opposition has a staff of eight.

The Canberra office in Parliament House was poky. I had a bank of green filing cabinets next to me; I ran the filing system. I was the only staff member near a window. Looking out that window I saw the poplars bud and shed their leaves over seven years.

Whitlam was always open to ideas. He scanned the newspapers and tore out stories. We followed up interesting ideas by getting copies of speeches. He carried envelopes in his suit pocket on which he would jot down ideas which seemed to occur to him every hour of the day. 'Comrade, have you got a minute?' and I would be called in. He would then run through his notes about what he wanted done. These envelopes were his agenda and it kept growing. It became my work program. There was little discussion of philosophy and ideology. There was even less discussion on how the office should be run and priorities determined. We essentially responded to the 'in tray' and the daily demands of the job.

I was also speech writer and responsible for media liaison. I was better at media liaison than speech writing. Many politicians lived by the newspapers, which set their agenda for the day. Whitlam was much less so, but we needed to watch and manage as best we could the political debate, particularly as it affected him. As a result I established good media contacts: Eric Walsh on the *Daily Mirror,* Brian Johns on the *Australian* and Ian Fitchett on the Melbourne *Age* and the *Sydney Morning Herald.* Fitchett enjoyed the coffee, laced with whisky, that we served on his daily call in the office. Alan Reid, the political correspondent for the Sydney *Daily Telegraph,* was always hostile and we treated him very cautiously. I did give him a few news titbits. To teach me a lesson, Fitchett gave Whitlam a couple of paybacks in his columns to warn me not to play with his opponent. The ABC had a reliable news coverage supplied by good shorthand writers but its political commentary was in its infancy. Daily public affairs programs were in the future. I wandered through the Press Gallery on the roof of Parliament House three or four times a day to pick up news and gossip. Whitlam never directed or queried any of my briefing of the press and I did a lot of it. The term 'spin doctor' hadn't been invented. Our media strategy was to project Whitlam and his ideas in as favourable a light as possible. But it was all very ad hoc. To pretend it was more thought-out than that would be untrue. I was always anxious about the private briefings or documents I gave to the press. What would I say if I was confronted about a leak to the press? Would I confirm or deny it? Fortunately I was never confronted. Perhaps everyone was doing it.

I had to supervise Whitlam's visits around Australia, arranging meetings and preparing speeches. To my embarrassment and the annoyance of inviting groups, I was instructed to delay acceptance of invitations as long as possible to give the widest choice of venues and audiences. The object always was to speak to the largest number of people who could influence change in the ALP and in the electorate. I was told 'You be the bastard' if we had to delay a response. I had to inform ALP and union secretaries and parliamentary colleagues on his program. He was busy with other things, often to the detriment of close contacts with them. The excuse of business suited him as he was uneasy with people and close to only a few. He often reminded me that I should present a good excuse why he could not be in contact with them. I know that his colleagues did not enjoy getting telephone calls from me. I covered as best I could.

Lacking a political power base, Whitlam's strength was knowledge and the articulation of ideas. He was eclectic in calling knowledge to his aid—Hansard, the classics, Acts of Parliament, the Bible, even the dictionary. Knowledge and words were the way to beat his opponents. Like Vaclav Havel, he understood 'the power of words to change history'. He made his mark best as a speaker at parliamentary lunches or dinners for visiting presidents and prime ministers. Opinion leaders in the country were there and saw him perform. Well prepared, he spoke as well as Menzies and much better than Calwell. Later Holt, Gorton and McMahon, with their lacklustre and embarrassing performances, trailed badly behind his erudition and humour. As a boy he had been surrounded by books and words; they were his world. On being asked to give an example of his view of equality he described where he had come from and what he wanted for others, 'I want every kid to have a desk with a lamp and his own room to study'.

I was conscious and occasionally embarrassed about the privileged position which staff have in working for a senior Member of Parliament. In my own career and the overview I got on issues, events and people, the benefits were enormous. There is an opportunity to influence public outcomes. I often thought it sobering that I had more influence as a member of Whitlam's staff than I would have had as a backbench MP. I observed a lot of them. Some worked excessively; some were idle. Most were very careful with money. Some milked the system like the senator who employed his 70-year-old retarded sister or the senator who, for years, slept in his office at Parliament and strolled down each morning for a free breakfast at the Hotel Kurrajong. He became blasé about this practice and complained about the quality of the food. Members of Parliament in my view are not well paid so they make up for it in travel allowances and superannuation benefits.

In seven years I got to know the old Parliament House like the back of my hand, the chamber, the library, the 'papers office', King's Hall and the Press Gallery. But not the Non-Members Bar. Eric Walsh got me down there a few times but I didn't feel comfortable. Parliament House was like a boarding house for adults, unreal and isolated and removed from family. Marriages often suffered. I usually went home for dinner at night for an hour but took a sandwich from home for lunch at my desk. I didn't enjoy socialising in the staff dining room. I saw enough of people rubbing shoulders with them over a 14-hour day.

I spent as much time in the Parliamentary Library as in my office. It was a great research resource, particularly in Opposition. The information backup of the Parliamentary Library and its research service were critical in the preparation of Whitlam for leadership of the ALP and becoming prime minister. Library staff were thrilled and became Whitlam devotees. He was an exceptional advocate and advertisement for well-funded public libraries. I had never known how valuable a library could be.

In addition to the library, no MP, before or since, used questions like Whitlam. In failing to do so, they deny themselves a great source of information. Scores of questions, well thought-out, went on the notice paper at the beginning of each parliamentary session. Answers enabled us to draw on the resources of the Government. They were an enormous help in building an information bank on a wide range of public issues; and none more than health and particularly the poor performance of private health funds. As the focus of the questions sharpened year after year, they disclosed the poor coverage of patients and range of medical services provided, the high cost of administration and the high level of reserves of the health funds. Whitlam was highlighting 30 years ago the gaps and inefficiencies of private health insurance. It was done in parliamentary questions.

Ministers privately complained that he was tying up public service resources with his barrage of questions. The Speaker of the House of Representatives, Sir John McLeay, however, took me aside to comment how inventive and diligent Whitlam was in framing questions on notice. To the casual observer it looked excessively detailed but on close examination his interrogation of ministers on the notice paper followed a very clear pattern and was designed to extract enormous amounts of information to help him in the preparation of speeches and the development of policy. In 1999, friendly members of parliament still ask questions on his behalf.

That interest dates back to the 1960s, when he asked scores of questions about who had signed and ratified a whole raft of international treaties and conventions. Australia did not have a good record. By 1964, for example, as the answers to questions on notice showed, Australia had ratified only 17 out of 31 General Assembly conventions, seven out of 52 ILO conventions and none of the nine UNESCO conventions. The

Commonwealth Government had power to make international treaties but Whitlam was looking forward to the day when the Commonwealth's treaty-making power would carry with it the power of the Commonwealth to override state laws that were inconsistent with the treaties the Commonwealth Government had entered into.

In his 1961 Curtin Memorial Lecture, Whitlam said, 'the Commonwealth could greatly enlarge its economic and social authority by exercising its constitutional right to make laws with respect to external affairs'. In the 1960s, beavering away in the Parliamentary Library and in the preparation of questions, I could not have envisaged the High Court decision 20 years later in the Franklin Dam case which set out, for the first time, an expanded view of the Commonwealth's treaty-making powers. In a telegram to the Labor Minister for the Environment, Barry Cohen, Whitlam commented 'after the dam, the flood'. With globalisation, the 'information super highway' and the power of multinational companies, national governments will have to negotiate more treaties with other countries to protect their national interests. It is essential as financial and economic power migrates from the national to the international arena.

Detail never slipped Whitlam's notice. He was particular, sometimes pedantic. Wherever we travelled a pile of Hansards went with us. Hansard staff were too slow in publishing the bound and indexed volumes. His questions and speeches were listed in handwriting on the left-hand side of the front cover. Any interesting speeches or questions by other MPs were listed on the right side. The left-hand listing was always much longer. He didn't need a Gideon Bible at motel overnight stops around Australia. Hansard would do. Correspondence was checked carefully. He occasionally detected mistakes in the *Oxford Dictionary* and invariably bested its editor in correspondence. Sloppiness in anyone's work was unacceptable. Instructions were invariably in his handwriting to prevent misunderstanding. We were admonished to 'write it down' to avoid mistakes.

The work load was enormous but excitement overcame fatigue. It was like working in a powerhouse. He took little exercise, ate heartily and was seldom sick. The energy just kept flowing.

When the House was sitting I would be away from home from eight o'clock in the morning until midnight. I would be home on Sundays but very often travelling on Fridays, Saturdays and Mondays. Even on

Sundays I would do a run through the Press Gallery with a press statement and to give some spin on what Whitlam was saying or doing. Our smudged blue carbon copies of press statements became well known. They were not very professional. If we were lucky we got a line or two in the Monday newspapers. Well thought-out policy ideas were invariably ignored but if he was in a political or personal dispute we could be sure of extensive coverage. The media haven't changed much.

Whitlam did, however, have a major breakthrough with the ABC. Liberal ministers, reluctant to debate him, refused to appear on television or set unreasonable conditions. In this way a pliant ABC allowed ministers to veto any proposed interview or debate. Whitlam persuaded the ABC that interviews should go ahead, even if abridged and amended, if one side of politics refused to appear. Liberal ministers quickly came to heel. It was reasonable for one political side to refuse to participate but it was unreasonable for either side to have a veto. Thirty years later, in the 1996 and 1998 elections, the Liberal Party recovered lost ground in refusing to participate in the Great Debates on the ABC. Channel 9 with its folksier, softer approach won the day.

In Canberra, Whitlam refused to stay at the Hotel Kurrajong, where most ALP and Country Party members stayed. He was a loner who preferred the privacy and modern amenities of a motel. In visits around Australia we avoided hotels, particularly the 'Irish Catholic' pubs. He saw the Split as having at least one advantage: it allowed him to avoid those awful Labor pubs with the smell of stale beer and tobacco smoke and where the publican was invariably the president of the ALP branch and chairman of the St Vincent de Paul Society. We encountered it a lot in Western Victoria in towns like Warrnambool and Hamilton. I agreed with him.

I worked for Gough Whitlam before the latter-day myth makers got to work and made him larger than life—the public icon, the national, even international treasure. One of my first recollections of him is the tall man stooping in the House of Representatives to be less conspicuous. One of his travelling companions on the train each morning from Cronulla to the city in the 1950s described him to me as 'quiet as a church mouse'. I found him awkward with ALP members and ill at ease with small talk. I had to try to carry the conversation. Through his bravado he made it harder for people to get near the private person. And, as a public person, he was right to do so. He was too dignified to cry on television, but he was shy, painfully so at times. That is my enduring and endearing recollection of Whitlam.

But he was ready-made for the myth makers, tall, sharp and funny, irreverent, given to self-mockery and with an unlikely education in the classics and European history for a Labor Party leader. When Margaret Whitlam caught a cold in Paris he commented, 'Comrade, the European winter brought Margaret to her knees, just like one of Napoleon's horses'!

We all project a public persona to protect our private self. For politicians it is even more important. Gough Whitlam was no exception. His confidence on the public platform was often at variance with the diffident private person. Through necessity and decades of practice, the public persona came to dominate or replace the shy, private persona. It is sometimes hard to distinguish between the two.

He was inspiring to work with, iconoclastic and with big-picture ideas tumbling out all the time. He was always growing and developing. But he was irritating on so much detail and oblivious to the reactions of others. During one of his disputes with the Federal Executive of the ALP he recited at lunch, to Tony Crosland of the British Labour Party, in detail poured on detail, conference resolutions, executive decisions and dates. Crosland almost fell asleep in his soup. At times he was his own worst enemy, lacking discretion and not always wise. He was too smart by half for many in the party. In that three-person Canberra office we irreverently and privately referred to him as GGLP–God's Gift to the Labor Party.

Unlike some of his successors he was unimpressed by money and people who flaunted it. He has always lived modestly, whether at Cabramatta in the heart of his electorate in western Sydney or at Darling Point in retirement. He did not tug the forelock to captains of industry with their money and power and was never overawed or cowed by the big end of town. He was tempted but didn't succumb. He was secure in his own values. He often told me, 'Comrade, I will not be beholden to anyone, inside or outside the ALP'.

Yet he was overly impressed by people with university degrees and judicial robes. He needed a people's and party person to complement his intellectual skills. Mick Young, rather than John Menadue, might have been a better choice for him as a private secretary. But Mick Young would never have got the job in 1960. Someone with a university degree was necessary. It was only down the track that he appreciated the skills which Mick Young brought to politics. Until that happy day he made his way forward with his intellectual clout and enormous energy. He survived his mistakes because even his critics believed that he might be a winner.

With some of the staff, Whitlam was tough. Tears were not uncommon. He drove himself hard and sometimes expected too much of others. Years later I often thought that I should have supported the younger members of staff more than I did. To me and my family he was always generous. He light-heartedly quipped that Cynthia always seemed to be having another baby when election time came around. Every VIP who came to the office was meticulously introduced to all the staff. There was 'old world' courtesy. He never forgot a birthday.

The tongue that could entertain could also lacerate. A Senate colleague was described as having a 'conflict of disloyalty'. He retorted to a New Zealand academic in Canberra who irritated him that 'the best New Zealand academics make it to Oxford and Cambridge and the second raters make it only to Canberra'. A Liberal Member of Parliament, a former Presbyterian minister and oil exploration executive was referred to as 'his oiliness'. He said a certain minister owed his promotion not to how he stood in Cabinet, but how he crawled outside it. He didn't always win the exchanges. Richie Gunn, a Labour member of parliament from South Australia, said that Whitlam regarded him as one of the party's intellectuals. When Whitlam challenged this assessment, Gunn retorted that Whitlam had called him a 'know-all'.

He was intolerant to some of his less well educated colleagues like veteran Eddie Ward, an ex-boxer. Ward felt slighted by a Whitlam riposte and threw a punch at him. In our poky Canberra office I heard raised voices and the scuffle in the corridor. The door slammed quickly as Whitlam escaped inside. He told me what happened as he viewed his minor lip damage in the office mirror. Years later Ward said he knew he was losing his punch when he threw one at Whitlam and missed.

Whitlam usually preferred to throw his barbs from a distance in a letter or speech and then withdraw. There was no hand-to-hand combat. He avoided close confrontation if at all possible. I never saw him in an intense head-to-head argument, the sort of argument that Clyde Cameron and Mick Young were so adept at. I recognised in Whitlam what was also true of me.

In the early 1960s, Jack Lang's *Century* called him 'Winsome Whitlam'. He wasn't from a patrician background although his parents were reasonably well off. He never pretended to be something he wasn't: a battler with a working-class accent. He was hardworking and sober. He said that no matter how much he drank, no one would believe that he was drunk—and no matter how little a certain political opponent drank, no one would believe he was sober.

When I joined him in 1960, I was very conscious that he was accused of being an opportunist, that he chose the ALP rather than the Liberal Party because it had better prospects. In 39 years, I never saw any sign of that. When he was close to expulsion from the ALP over the State Aid dispute in March 1966, he was approached by John Murray, the Liberal Member for Herbert in North Queensland, about joining the Liberal Party. To this day, I can recall Whitlam's outrage at the approach. It was not affected. The accusation of opportunist was class snobbery: an educated and literary person should be a Liberal. Little did they understand that he was developing a radical program that was further from the Liberal Party than anything in more than two decades. He was always dignified, a quality which the Australian public greatly admired, particularly after the embarrassment of 'Silly Billy' McMahon as prime minister. McMahon had been asked in 1971 by *Time Magazine* about his vision for the future. He requested from his press secretary the 'file on the future', and on being told there was no such file McMahon replied that he had nothing on the future.

Fred Whitlam, Gough's father and Commonwealth Crown Solicitor, was a very principled and proper person who was imbued with a sense of public service and an enduring commitment to social, religious and racial equality. Like his son, Fred Whitlam was trusting. Gough Whitlam followed in his father's footsteps, although not as a churchman, describing himself to David Frost as a 'Christian fellow traveller'. Fred Whitlam would have been better pleased with Freda Whitlam, Gough's sister, who became the Moderator of the Uniting Church in Australia. Gough was very loyal to Freda when, as Principal of Sydney's PLC, she had difficulties with her governing council.

He believed passionately in public discussion and education. To the BBC in 1973 he said, 'the public meeting is part of the continuous education process that politicians have to engage in'. The barrister was always trying to persuade. Working with him was like being part of an unending seminar or tutorial.

I am perhaps running ahead of myself. In Opposition in the 1960s so much was yet to unfold. Opposition is a hard and thankless life. It destroys more Opposition leaders than it makes prime ministers. Whitlam described the problems he faced in his 1957 Chifley Lecture. 'The way of the reformer is hard in Australia. Our Parliaments work within a constitutional framework which enshrines Liberal policy but bans Labor policy. Labor has to persuade the electorate to take two steps before it can implement its reform, first to elect a Labor Government, then to alter the Constitution.'

Under the Menzies hegemony and the Split, Labor seemed doomed to indefinite Opposition. It was a period of deep pessimism and disappointment for Labor supporters. What was remarkable was that, in the political wasteland on the left at the time, Whitlam didn't wilt. He had the vision and the stamina to see it through.

Margaret Whitlam was an enormous help in stabilising and sustaining him: calm, sensible, her feet always firmly planted on the ground. Even when irritated by her good advice he could say, 'She is a good wife to me'. 'Bugger the Whitlams', she sometimes exclaimed to cut through the uncritical adulation he often received, and enjoyed. He was also sustained by two other factors. One was that he hadn't been in government and didn't know what he was missing. He hadn't been seduced by the power and the trappings of office. He wasn't waiting around expecting deliverance from opposition as if government would fall into his hands as the political pendulum swung. He didn't ever believe that. He believed that it required contemporary ideas, a modern party machinery and hard work.

The other factor that sustained his spirit and for which he was so often criticised was the refreshment he got from overseas travel. When he read in the newspaper that the UN had admitted Yemen and Upper Volta, he protested, 'They are creating new states faster than I can visit them'. Travel in the 'lean years' was a great relief from the parochial grind. It was an opportunity to pick up ideas, meet interesting people and get a new perspective on the tasks at hand in Australia. Travel revived his sagging spirits in a quite remarkable way. The institutional ALP seemed so often to be in its death throes. Whitlam had to get away or he would have been sapped of all energy and probably destroyed.

Despite his classical education and his encyclopedic knowledge of European and particularly Roman and Greek civilisations, Gough Whitlam did not visit Europe until 1962, when he was 46 years old. I was 27. United Kingdom entry into the European Common Market was in prospect and Prime Minister Menzies had agreed to the four Opposition heads—Arthur Calwell, Gough Whitlam, Nick McKenna and Pat Kennelly—visiting Europe. We were to meet Nick McKenna in Europe, who planned to visit the major Christian shrines, starting at Lourdes. Gough Whitlam had other things in mind: the galleries and ruins of Europe that he had so lovingly read about since his school days. He agreed with Samuel Johnson that the grand object of travelling is to see the shores of the Mediterranean. Standing in the Roman Forum he told me, 'Comrade, this is the most important place on earth, much more so than Jerusalem'. I wasn't entirely convinced. I carried home a small, white memento stone from Golgotha and not Rome.

He was the self-appointed tour guide for Margaret and me on all our visits. She was a wonderful companion, warm and easy to be with, a 'tower of strength' as I called her. His detailed knowledge, even on the location of art in particular salons in galleries, was breathtaking. Local gallery guides stood back in awe with this large man striding from room to room and gallery to gallery describing picture after picture. He hardly stopped to draw breath. It was an exciting new world for me but after six or seven hours my mind was numbed and my legs were aching. 'Dame Margaret', as she later became, knew when it was time to call a halt. 'Gough', she would say, 'John and I have had enough for today. Leave something for tomorrow.' He would grind his teeth, mutter to himself and obey. He was very much at home in Europe, visiting the places he had read and dreamed about and being entertained by diplomats and meeting the leaders of Europe. It gave him new perceptions and reference points. He loved it and so did I. It was a world away from the South Australian country towns of my childhood.

Ambassadors entertained us extravagantly in ways that I had never experienced. I had read about the way some people lived but this elegant living was new to me. In Paris, Margaret and the Ambassador's French-speaking Belgian wife persuaded me to try some French wine. Margaret said, 'You cannot be in France and not drink French wine with French food'. It didn't lead to my ruin. The old habits of moderation, however, remained strong. Back in Canberra we made do with Blue Nun, Liebfraumilch and Mateus Rosé.

On his European sabbaticals Whitlam always had an eye for his electorate at home with large numbers of constituents from European countries. On return he would speak at their clubs. Malta was on our itinerary for that reason. I can't think of any other reason for the visit. We met the irascible Dom Mintoff, the Prime Minister of Malta, who was in continual dispute with his own Labor Party and the Catholic Church. After meeting him Whitlam described him as prickly and difficult: 'the Lee Kuan Yew of the Mediterranean'.

In Venice I had to take a photo of Whitlam standing on the Rialto with a Lazzarini shop sign over his shoulder. Lazzarini was the former Member for Werriwa. Margaret and I swanned down the Grand Canal in a gondola.

On early visits I carried his hat and maintained his log of airflights, a legacy from his days as an RAAF navigator. But he found me unreliable on both counts. He caught me making up aircraft serial numbers that I had forgotten to record. At least Tim Fischer carries his own hat.

We met a kaleidoscope of people, from Pope Paul VI to President Lyndon Johnson. Paul was ascetic and retiring. Johnson was direct and overpowering. The White House seemed designed to intimidate friend and foe alike. Whitlam grabbed Johnson's interest by recognising a portrait of Andrew Jackson, a southerner who had been President of the Union before the Civil War. Johnson introduced Whitlam and me to Billy Graham, who even in the morning seemed made up for television or a photo opportunity. In Los Angeles I met the Black Panthers, whom I had read so much about and admired for their radicalism. They were no 'Uncle Toms', pleading for a place in the sun; they confronted white racism head-on and didn't pull their punches. I made a line for their newsstand to buy their weekly newspaper. An act of solidarity I thought, as I handed my 50 cents to the tall, imposing black man. Once I took the paper I was greeted with, 'Fifty cents won't save you, whitey'. So much for brotherhood.

In 1963 and again in 1967, I was enthralled by Israel's struggle to maintain democracy and its institutions and practices under unrelenting outside pressure. It was thrilling to see Israel's modesty after its 1967 victory. We met Prime Minister Eshkol and Foreign Minister Eban. On return to Canberra I inquired from the Israeli Ambassador whether our children might be able to live and work on a kibbutz with its communalism and socialist inspiration. He was delighted and said he would pursue it with me when the children were ready. In 1971 I visited Israel again. Israeli modesty had turned to arrogance. Solidarity with others had become contempt for the Palestinians they had displaced. The only opinion that seemed to count was their own. The King of Jordan, who had lost territory on the West Bank to the Israelis, was now derided as the 'Mayor of Amman'. I forgot about the Israeli kibbutz for the children and from that time became increasingly sympathetic to the Palestinians. It seems to me that only more blood and tears lie ahead.

Visits to Israel with Whitlam were not all politics. It was a chance to visit the biblical places, the Mount of Olives, Bethlehem and Golgotha. I was appalled at the grubby competition of the Christian groups for positions in the Church of the Holy Sepulchre. Perhaps the Catholic Church is lucky that the focus of Christian life is in Rome rather than Jerusalem.

Gough loved Europe and the Middle East. Our visits to Asia, however, were harder work but more important. We received the normal hard sell in Vietnam in 1966, in support of the United States and the Australian government line. The US Commander, General Westmoreland, was clear he could win the war. He just needed more soldiers. The risk was that the US Government might 'go soft'. Whitlam commented afterwards that Westmoreland sounded like the British general Douglas Haig, who squandered so much life in the battlefields of France in the First World War.

Until I went to Vietnam in 1966 I was inclined to the view that, morality aside, US military power would prevail there. I changed my mind when I visited Hoa Long, a small village within three kilometres of the Australian Task Force at Nui Dat. Every day Australian soldiers went through the village to win the hearts and minds of the villagers with educational, medical and food supplies and a few lollies for the children. But at night, when the Australians withdrew, the Vietcong came down from the hills and back into Hoa Long to visit their families. If Australian soldiers couldn't secure a village that was almost at their task force front gate then the cause was lost—as it proved to be.

At the Australian Embassy residence for dinner in Saigon, I sat next to Colonel Nguyen Ngoc Loan, the head of South Vietnamese Security. He had a 'bad head', as my father would have said. I can still recall my strong feelings of that night, an uneasy and brooding sense of evil at the table. It was spooky. I felt sick later when I saw the infamous photo of General Loan, during the Tet offensive in February 1968, holding his pistol to the head of a Vietcong suspect and killing him in cold blood. I was not surprised. Loan had done what I had sensed, two years before, he was capable of. Australia had strange dinner guests at the Embassy in South Vietnam.

After the war zone of Saigon, with its decadence and corruption, we flew to Phnom Penh. It was quiet and peaceful. The contrast with Saigon is still vivid in my mind. But the CIA had the Government of Cambodia overthrown because it wouldn't and couldn't toe the US line. Henry Kissinger unleashed a secret bombing war on Cambodia and precipitated Pol Pot and the killing fields. To this day I can still see and feel the quiet and peaceful Phnom Penh and wonder if Henry Kissinger feels any remorse. The powerful seldom get called to account for their deeds.

In Manila we met Ferdinand and Imelda Marcos, both good singers and speakers. Visiting them at the Presidential Palace was like entering a Hollywood Wild West film set. The palace grounds were teaming with hangers-on queuing up for favours and cronies wanting concessions. The anteroom outside the President's office carried a sign above a rack, 'Hang your guns up here'. Gough commented, 'It's a different world here, comrade. The Filipinos can't work out whether they want to live in the Vatican or Hollywood'.

In India I visited Old Delhi to see the poverty of India that my Sunday School teachers had told me about. Gough Whitlam visited the Taj Mahal. Aside from poverty, two things struck me about India. The first was how firmly the British parliamentary and legal systems were rooted and how fervently they were admired. They loved things English. Politicians and bureaucrats we met spoke like Peter Sellers. The other thing that struck me was how India had copied some of the worst features of British bureaucracy, particularly its pedantry and pettiness. I experienced it whether meeting senior ministers and officials or confronting the tyrannical immigration officials at the airport.

We visited Papua New Guinea several times. During each visit

Whitlam put independence on the public agenda. He was not impressed with the argument that independence would bring disorder and slow development. People were entitled to independence and with anticolonial winds blowing everywhere in the world it was better to grant independence sooner rather than later. The message was not well received, particularly among the white planters in the highlands. The undercurrent, and sometimes the accusation, was that by talking independence Whitlam was promoting violence and possible bloodshed. We found Australian government officials well-meaning but paternalistic. We were often taken on inspections of private homes by district commissioners when the owners were away or at work. There was no sense of invasion of their privacy. Whitlam described such government officials as 'third-rate Australians doing a fourth-rate job'. Toilets were for 'Marys' and 'boys'; indigenous people were 'non expatriates'!

Whitlam was always impressed by President Sukarno's political achievements in Indonesia, beating the Dutch in an anticolonial war and welding a nation out of such a vast and disparate archipelago. He spoke many times of it being a turning point in history and of the important role which the Chifley Government played in helping the birth of this new nation. He never had any doubt that the last vestiges of colonialism, the Dutch in West New Guinea and the Portuguese in East Timor, were aberrations and that the United States would not pay attention to Australia's concern about Indonesian actions. The *Realpolitik* of such a large and diverse nation, the largest Muslim population in the world, living on our doorstep could not be avoided. For good or ill it would determine Australia's future.

In 1966 after the failed coup we found the Jakarta streets in chaos, burnt-out trucks and cars obstructing the roads and shops boarded up. Above the ruins, however, were the Sukarno monuments towering over the people. He had given them monuments of himself and the revolution but had forgotten to feed them—stones instead of bread.

We had a memorable meeting in August 1966 with Sukarno and, by accident, with Lieutenant General Soeharto. Sukarno was still in Merdeka Palace being slowly squeezed out. We were invited to have breakfast with him on the back patio of the palace, together with a large number of artists.

I had always had an image of Sukarno in his uniform, cap and medals, the great orator, the charismatic leader. But at 7.30 in the morning, with no hat to hide his bald head, without his uniform and medals and wearing what seemed like a grey shearer's singlet, he was paunchy and anything but charismatic. He was, however, very impressed by the young Indonesian women army officers who were serving on the table. He was popping handfuls of pills, to what advantage I don't know. His humour was very schoolboyish and smutty. It was an uncomfortable occasion. We were both a little prudish—after all Whitlam had a Presbyterian father and I had Methodist parents.

Towards the end of breakfast, Soeharto arrived, dressed in his army fatigues, with his driver in an open jeep. He sat at the back of the patio, away from the breakfast, for almost an hour. He held very substantial military power. A large number of people had been killed. Not for a moment, however, did Soeharto presume to interfere or press himself on the President. He showed great political skill, respecting authority and power but, at the same time, he was moving slowly and carefully to oust Sukarno. Step by step, Sukarno was stripped of power and moved out of Merdeka Palace.

But while we were experiencing a refreshing new world in our overseas odysseys, problems at home made for a hard slog. In the end what carried the day for Whitlam in the ALP was his standing in the electorate, an ever-present help in time of trouble. Without that standing among voters he would not have survived. He was clearly more popular than the party leader Arthur Calwell.

Queensland was the pilot state for Whitlam to publicise his policies and to hone his skills in the electorate. Up and down the state in 1960 and 1961, he recited figures to prove that Queensland was getting a raw deal from the Menzies Government, whether it was on roads, education or health, or whatever unfavourable comparison he could make. Queenslanders, even the most conservative, responded to the anti-southern and particularly the anti-Canberra message. It was very tribal, as if Whitlam was barracking for Queensland in a State of Origin football match. He laid it on with a trowel. The story fell on very fertile ground in Queensland. Here was a great state, the 'sleeping giant' ready to develop but being restrained by unfair treatment from Canberra. Later, Bjelke-Petersen developed this story into an art form, blaming all his mistakes and problems on Canberra.

We crisscrossed Queensland by road as well as by air.Whitlam always sat in the front seat to tune the radio for ABC news.The longest safari was in 1960 up the coast to Cairns and down the centre via Charters Towers, Winton, Longreach and Toowoomba. Unfortunately, the sun visor kept slipping down on the passenger side. For three days he kept pushing it back up, time and time again. In desperation he tore the visor from its mounting and flung it out the window into the spinifex as we sped between Longreach and Winton. With a smile the driver stopped to recover it.

The Menzies/Holt 'horror budget' of 1961 provided a great opportunity for the ALP. Foreign policy and the Cold War, which had dominated most elections, were pushed aside and Arthur Calwell, a good man, had replaced the un-electable Doctor Evatt. I didn't think for a moment that Labor would win in 1961. I was used to voting for losers. Gough Whitlam was more optimistic but he was also surprised by the result.

With its classified advertising revenue down following the 'horror budget', the *Sydney Morning Herald* strongly supported Arthur Calwell and the Labor Party, which won five seats in New South Wales. But the landslide was in Queensland, where Labor won eight seats, largely due to Whitlam's tireless and skilful campaign.The election produced a new Member for Oxley, Bill Hayden, a young policeman who campaigned in support of dairy farmers against choice by consumers to buy margarine.

Labor almost made it into government but was thwarted by the celebrated victory of Jim Killen and the Liberal Party in the Queensland seat of Moreton. But no seats came to Labor in Victoria, the state where the Labor Split was most deep-seated and virulent. Clearly something had to be done in Victoria for Labor to win federally.

The 1961 result proved a false dawn, promoting a mistaken view that if the Labor Party could just hang on, the pendulum would swing and Labor would fall into government. It papered over the ALP's problems: the Split, decrepit party machinery and out-of-date policy. In a similar way, Keating's 1993 victory obscured the party's underlying problems; people were being hurt by rapid economic change and the party seemed oblivious and contemptuous of cries for help.

The 1961 result boosted Arthur Calwell's standing not least in the eyes of the *Sydney Morning Herald*. Bereft of ideas and under increasing pressure within the ALP he became heavily dependent on its owners, editorial writers and journalists for ideas and speeches, right through into 1963. They also helped with some of Whitlam's speeches. Max Newton, the editor of the *Financial Review*, spent a day in our family dining room in Narrabundah preparing Whitlam's budget speech in 1962.

Prime Minister Menzies skilfully persuaded the Australian public that he had learnt from his 1961 mistakes. Importantly, he set about to exploit the ALP's problems. That wasn't hard. As a result, the ALP lost ten seats in 1963. The economy had improved and there had been a major public relations debacle for the Labor Party: its '36 faceless men', in March 1963. In 1962 Menzies had announced that the US would be building a 'wireless station' at north-western Cape in northern Western Australia. In fact its main purpose was to communicate with its worldwide nuclear-armed submarine fleet. It was a foreign base outside the control of Australia and a potential target in the event of a nuclear war. Not being members of the party's ruling body, Arthur Calwell and Gough Whitlam sat outside the Federal Conference at the Kingston Hotel in Canberra waiting until a decision was made about ALP policy on the base. The conference had six delegates from each of the states. Calwell and Whitlam had participated extensively in the development of the policy to ensure joint control of the base but were photographed waiting under a streetlight outside the conference while ALP officials and trade union representatives made decisions inside. It was of course a publicity disaster. The ALP Conference was seen to be telling Labor leaders how to vote in Parliament. It was pushed along by Alan Reid in Frank Packer's *Daily Telegraph,* which never let up on the ALP.

Another important factor in the 1963 defeat was that Menzies proposed science grants for schools, including Catholic schools. This was the first public step at the federal level to resolving the State Aid issue which had dogged Australian political life for over a century. Menzies's support for science grants was a sleeper. It was a politically astute ploy from the conservative establishment which Menzies personified, and which was overwhelmingly anti-Catholic. Significant Catholic support swung to Menzies because of this policy in 1963.

In 1962 and 1963 Indonesian pressure on Dutch New Guinea intensified and Calwell took a hostile position towards Indonesia, largely at the urging of the *Sydney Morning Herald*. Consistent with his stridency over Indonesia and as something of a diversion over the faceless men debacle, Graham Freudenberg, Calwell's press secretary, and I encouraged Calwell to support an upgrade of the RAAF Canberra bomber, which we knew was being pressed by the RAAF, without success, on the Menzies Government. The choice was between either the American F-111 or the British TSR2. We drafted a paragraph, for his consideration, saying that Australia's defence forces should have equipment 'having sufficient range and strike power to deter aggression'. It was code for the RAAF having a new bomber capable of striking Jakarta. We then spoke to Charlie Oliver, the President of the ALP in NSW and a state secretary of the Australian Workers' Union. He was also chairman of the Federal Executive's Foreign Affairs Committee. Oliver persuaded his committee to include the paragraph Freudenberg and I had drafted. It was passed without dissent at the full ALP Conference in Perth in August 1963 on the motion of right-winger Oliver. It was seconded by left-winger Clyde Cameron. Anti-Indonesian sentiment was popular in the ALP and in the electorate. It wasn't Freudenberg's or my finest hour.

In the hysteria over the Indonesian threat at the time and ALP pressure, Menzies announced, in October 1963, in the run-up to the November election that Australia would acquire 24 F-111 aircraft. Because of the rush to decision, delivery of the aircraft was long delayed and costs escalated dramatically.

Calwell's views about Indonesia were not shared by Whitlam, who believed that the threat to Australia was exaggerated and that the Americans would not lift a finger against an Indonesian takeover of Dutch New Guinea. That difference over policy on Indonesia laid the grounds for Calwell's survival after the 1963 election when Labor lost many seats. To beat off Whitlam's challenge after 1963, Calwell threw himself into the arms of the left, which was never his natural home. One of the conditions of the left's support was that he change his attitude towards Indonesia. That was the start of three years of infighting, ending in the 1966 election.

The turning point in relations between the two men was in Hobart in February 1964, after the Denison by-election. Whitlam told Calwell that he believed he should stand down before the 1966 election; but Whitlam also said he would not challenge. Calwell rejected any notion that he would be a caretaker leader. He said, 'Evatt had three goes at becoming Prime Minister and I am entitled to three goes'. The relationship went downhill from there.

I mention the 1961 and 1963 elections at some length because they turned out to be wasted years. Reform of the party machinery and party policy was put on hold. The hard work was not done. The 1961 and, indeed even more so, the 1963 result showed that the party had to reform itself before the people would support it. So after 1963 it was back to the drawing board for Whitlam and his supporters. Calwell's use-by date had passed. Major policy issues in the Labor Party still needed addressing. The Split remained.

For the ALP, the Australian Constitution was a major obstacle. In the banking case of 1947, the High Court had ruled against nationalisation, which was a key tenet of faith, if not of action, for the ALP. Section 92, concerning free trade between the states had been absurdly interpreted by the High Court to make nationalisation unconstitutional. In the 1961 election, at the urging of the *Sydney Morning Herald*, Calwell had pledged, 'there will be no nationalisation during the next Parliament'. Evatt had done the same in earlier elections. To Whitlam that was nonsense. If one could not live with the policy platform it should be changed. It should not be repudiated at election time. He was determined to explore ways whereby a modern Labor Party could work with, around, or if necessary, change the Constitution. How could the party platform and the Constitution be reconciled? That was the central issue.

Whitlam's ex-air force colleagues told me how persuasive and excited he was about John Curtin's unsuccessful efforts in the 1944 referendum to change the Constitution. But Whitlam's real education on the Constitution began when, as a 40-year-old, he became a member of the Parliamentary Constitutional Review Committee in 1958. The report was tabled in 1959. If I had to name one document that most influenced and informed Whitlam's public life it would be that report, not Marx's *Das Capital*, John Maynard Keynes's *General Theory of Employment, Interest and Money*, or Rousseau's *Social Contract*. In those early years, the blue-covered Constitutional Review Report went everywhere with us. Dog-eared and torn, it was his guide on how to overcome the obstacles in the Constitution.

A commitment to equality of opportunity, which only the Commonwealth Government could achieve for its citizens, rather than the philosophy of socialism was Whitlam's chief motivation. Governments had to do for the disadvantaged what the private sector could or would not do. Only the Commonwealth Government had the money. From his experience on the Constitutional Review Committee he developed a unique package of programs. He certainly took to heart the advice of Clem Attlee, the British Labour Prime Minister, to 'join a parliamentary committee and keep out of the bar'.

The committee's terms of reference included relations between the House of Representatives and the Senate, electoral reform, inclusion of Aborigines in the population count, transport, industrial relations, corporations, restrictive practices and economic powers. Its members included Alexander Downer (Snr), Senator O'Sullivan, Percy Joske, Arthur Calwell and Eddie Ward. The committee's work, which produced a high degree of agreement, was marked by real generosity across political parties. The patrician Alexander Downer and the firebrand Eddie Ward came from different sides of the track and got on well. Ward was poorly educated but very articulate, able and passionate. I recall both Whitlam and Alexander Downer (Jnr) recalling fondly the rapport which Downer (Snr) and Ward developed. Whitlam was also a lifelong admirer of Downer senior's personal decency and political liberalism. Over almost two years on that committee, Whitlam was exposed to a range of expert advice from premiers, heads of departments, justices, bankers, business and rural leaders on how the Constitution might be adapted to best advantage our emerging national economy. The report of 1959 was a mine of information and ideas. We mined it voraciously.

One thing stood out from that report for Whitlam. Under Section 96 of the Constitution the Commonwealth Parliament 'may grant financial assistance to any state on such terms and conditions as the Parliament sees fit'. We could repeat those words in our sleep, we heard them so often. If Section 92 precluded nationalisation, Section 96 of the Constitution could become the 'charter for public enterprise', as Whitlam called it. In his 1961 Curtin Lecture in Perth, which I helped draft at a motel near the airport, he described his position: 'In our obsession with Section 92, which is held up as the bulwark of private enterprise, we forget Section 96, which is the charter of public enterprise'. It was a very inventive way to break the impasse, particularly with the Federal Government's increasing financial dominance. Almost all the major programs which Whitlam inspired in health, education, housing and cities were dependent on the ability of the Federal Government to make grants under Section 96. A way through the logjam had been found for a Federal Labor government to fund its reform programs. Very few in the ALP or outside appreciated the great significance of this breakthrough in policy thinking. It was to have major implications particularly in the Whitlam Government. In the 1960s the prospect of winning seemed so remote that new policy was discounted across the board as interesting but not particularly relevant.

For the programs that we were looking to implement with Section 96 grants we sought precedents in other federal systems. What were the federal governments in the United States, Canada and West Germany doing in such areas as transport, arts, education and housing? A large part of our overseas trips was spent examining and discussing such programs with overseas federal agencies. I also spent long hours visiting their embassies or high commissions in Canberra or researching in the Parliamentary Library to find precedents in other federal systems to get around the Australian Constitution. In speech after speech Whitlam referred to what other federations were doing through federal funding of programs. We were searching everywhere for precedents in 'countries with which we choose to compare ourselves'.

Like most Australians we also had something of a cultural cringe— we were impressed by things British. In policy development we were influenced by the British Labour Party, particularly its National Health Scheme. The Wilson Labour Government had also promised Britain 'a white-hot scientific revolution', whereby science could open up new economic and social benefits for British people. We worked hard on both health and science policy, influenced by the British experience.

These ideas and programs had to be marshalled to rewrite the party platform and to provide input into speeches. So, after the false dawn of 1961 and the poor results in the 1963 election, a large amount of my time from then on was spent organising a network of advisers to Whitlam and through him to the party. Calwell was sidelined in this project.

Whitlam and I were at one on this. We knew that there was a whole new constituency of people with ideas who were attracted to the values of the ALP but lacked a means to contribute and participate. In fact they were actively discouraged by some in the party. Party insiders lacked new ideas and resented 'eggheads' intruding. The ALP had not seriously considered policy development since the defeat of Chifley in 1949.

We developed a network of people across most policy areas. Not all were party members. Most were from universities. Professor Sol Encel, a sociologist at ANU and later at the University of New South Wales, was the link person that I worked with. Whitlam and I were attracted by an article he wrote in *Nation,* a fortnightly public affairs magazine, in mid-1961, headed 'Gold Rush', about the propriety of Commonwealth Directors-General of Health resigning and taking lucrative positions with foreign pharmaceutical companies who wanted their drugs on the Commonwealth-funded list. At our request, Encel sent more information about precedents in other countries to regulate such conduct by former bureaucrats. From that contact Encel sent us other briefings on health and science matters.

At the Fabian Society Conference at Olinda outside Melbourne in January 1962, Whitlam appealed to people with ideas to assist him on speeches and policy development. Encel, who was at Olinda, returned to the ANU and spoke to Professor Ted Wheelwright, who was at the ANU on a six-month sabbatical. He was Associate Professor of Economics at the University of Sydney. Encel and Wheelwright drew up a list of about 30 people who would help. It was all in 'The Network' folder. Encel gave me the names and I made the contacts. The network included, over several years, economists Bruce McFarlane, Max Corden and Brian Brogan; health economists John Deeble, Richard Scotton and Ruth Inall; urban planners Don Gazzard and George Clarke; scientists Ken Inall, Frank Hird, Cyril Applebee and Keith Crook; educationalists David Bennett and Henry Schoenheimer; and historian Jamie Mackie. Most of the network were from Sydney, Canberra and Melbourne. We started slowly but got into stride after the 1963 election. The quality of the network was patchy. Some were great contributors such as Deeble and Scotten and Crook. Others were good critics but could just not bring themselves to help develop policy. Some talked a lot, but didn't perform. We sent budget papers to one senior economist who promised to help but he wouldn't even return my phone calls. We put him on the bottom of our network list.

I would arrange a group of advisers to meet Whitlam. At the meeting, he would outline his ideas and get their input both for speeches and policy change. When they looked at the Federal Party Platform they almost all had a fit when they saw how dated it was. This was not surprising given that resolutions to the Federal Conference came from State

Conferences in a haphazard form. Passing resolutions was more important and certainly easier than developing policies. With Whitlam as the patron, members of the network saw very quickly their policies and programs become official party policies. The old decrepit party policy formulation machinery was being outflanked.

Public education was an important part of the process. New ideas were canvassed in public speeches. The reactions were assessed and the policy revised. By the time they were finally launched, it was hoped that errors had been corrected and any gaps filled. The Liberal Party was unlikely to copy because the philosophical underpinnings were very different to anything it had in mind.

Our priorities naturally reflected Whitlam's interests. Even though he was only Deputy Leader, he was forcing change as the committee reports that we substantially wrote were invariably endorsed by the Federal Executive and Federal Conference. While Arthur Calwell informally allocated bills to executive members of the Parliamentary Labor Party for debate in the Parliament, there was no Shadow Cabinet. That made it much easier for Whitlam to move across many policy areas.

Whitlam claimed that at the 1965 Party Conference in Perth as much as 60 per cent of the platform had been rewritten. In his speech at the conclusion of the conference he observed that there were radically changed policies in health, housing, transport, immigration, broadcasting and television, labour and industry, foreign affairs, welfare, Aboriginal affairs, science and national development. He praised the contribution of the ALP's policy review committees and welcomed the ALP's affiliation with the Socialist International, the admission of the press to the conference and the involvement of intellectuals in party policy-making. 'It is the first time for fifty years a bearded man has taken part in [the party's] deliberations'.

'White Australia' was dropped from the platform. This reform was led by Don Dunstan, who had influenced me on this and social justice issues ten years earlier as a student in Adelaide.

There were big rewrites of the platform in 1967 and 1969. By 1972, Whitlam had virtually rewritten the whole of the party platform. At senior levels of the party he received little serious opposition. It was like refreshing rain falling on dry and arid earth. The party had not done anything like that in its history nor has done so since. Unlike Evatt and Calwell, Whitlam would not be repudiating the platform when he opened future election campaigns. He wouldn't need to. He had largely rewritten the party platform himself.

One of the most important advisory groups was in health, which Dr Moss Cass put together. Cass was in charge of a trade union health clinic in Victoria. He was the most far-sighted thinker on health policy I knew. He understood the need to focus on health care delivery in hospitals and not just health insurance. I did, however, have a problem in involving Cass as Whitlam and he didn't get on well. Whitlam saw Cass as part of the sectarian left in Victoria. Cass was also small in stature.

My own interest in health policy went back to endless late night discussions as a student at Adelaide University. I recall a tutor asking, 'Why should anyone be financially disadvantaged through sickness?' It is still a question I ask myself. I regret that in my public career I have not had much of an opportunity to work on health policy.

Like many others in the ALP in the 1960s, I was attracted to the National Health Service (NHS) which the British Labour Party, with Aneurin Bevan as Health Minister, had introduced in the 1940s. Margaret Thatcher retained it. It has stood the test of time much better than its many critics.

With Cass's assistance, I read the literature on different health care schemes. I was particularly taken with the *New England Journal of Medicine,* which was not only at the cutting edge of medicine but was pioneering the sociological imperatives of health care. What caught my eye were many surveys and analyses which showed that fee-driven, private medicine resulted in excessive treatment and high costs. The journal reported on the development of Health Maintenance Organisations (HMO) in the United States in response to escalating private health costs. HMOs contracted with doctors on salary to provide health services to their members. Kaiser Steel had pioneered an HMO for its staff in America. In later years 'managed care' developed in the United States, originating in the same concern that gave rise to HMOs, the need to cap or manage escalating private health costs.

In 1961 Whitlam described his path for health reform in his Curtin Lecture: 'the best way to achieve a proper National Health Service is to establish a National Hospital System'. He added, 'the proper approach is for the Commonwealth to make additional grants to the States on condition that they regionalise their hospital services and establish salaried and sessional medical and ancillary staff in hospitals. Such measures would attack costs where they are greatest, both for the individual and for the community.'

In government, Whitlam introduced a five-year program of capital assistance for public hospitals. They were Section 96 'special purpose grants'. The Fraser Government did not renew it. Nor did the Hawke or Keating governments. Health reform was to go down another path: Medibank or, as it was later named, Medicare. It was more politically popular at the time.

The genesis of Medicare was at a meeting at Cass's home in Melbourne in midwinter 1967. Many years later Whitlam asked me at what time of the year the meeting was held. I was certain it was midwinter because Cass had a log fire at his home. Whitlam quipped that it would have been the only illumination that Cass provided that night. It was unfair. That meeting in mid-1967 was both illuminating and critical in the development of Medicare.

Cass had invited Dr Rod Andrew, Dean of Medicine at Monash University, Dr John Lawson, Superintendent at the Footscray Hospital, and Dr Harry Jenkins, who later became a Member of Parliament. Key attendees, however, were two researchers from the Institute of Applied Economic and Social Research at Melbourne University, John Deeble and Dick Scotton. Deeble had previously been Deputy General Manager of the Peter MacCallum Clinic in Melbourne. Scotton had been an economist at the Commercial Banking Company in Sydney. They had done groundbreaking research on the pharmaceutical industry, hospital costs and compulsory and voluntary health insurance.

From that midwinter meeting in 1967, Deeble and Scotton developed a comprehensive health insurance scheme with a compulsory tax levy. It was clear that the Liberal Government's voluntary private health insurance scheme, supported by taxpayers' funds, was wasteful. Early the next year at a speech at the Sydney Royal Prince Alfred Hospital and almost five years before he became prime minister, Whitlam outlined an 'Alternative National Health Program', which later became so much part of Australian national life: Medicare. Once again, a compelling Whitlam speech pre-empted party policy.

In working with Whitlam I enjoyed the development of health policy more than any other, even though I think too much attention was subsequently given to the way health care was financed through Medicare and inadequate attention to how health care could be better delivered.

While we were developing domestic social programs, Australia was becoming engulfed in the Vietnam War. The greatest speech I heard in the Parliament was Calwell's opposition in May 1965 to the commitment of Australian troops to Vietnam. The moral passion was electrifying. Graham Freudenberg asked Jim Cairns and me for comments on the draft. Whitlam was deliberately not consulted. His relationship with Calwell was increasingly difficult. The division between the two was popular knowledge, for which an electoral price would be paid.

In announcing the ALP position to 'firmly and completely' oppose the sending of 800 men to fight in Vietnam, Freudenberg had drafted that the decision was made after 'earnest and prayerful' consideration. I suggested that calling on God with such a rhetorical flourish be deleted. It was my only suggested change. He agreed. Addressing ALP supporters in the country, Calwell said:

> I offer you the probability that you will be traduced, that your motives will be misrepresented, that your patriotism will be impugned, that your courage will be called into question. But I also offer you the sure and certain knowledge that we will be vindicated: that generations to come will record with gratitude that when a reckless Government wilfully endangered the security of this nation, the voice of the Australian Labor Party was heard, strong and clear, on the side of sanity and in the cause of humanity and in the interests of Australia's security.

The speech galvanised opposition to the war but was vague on withdrawal, a cause of later confusion.

Whitlam was strongly opposed to the war but more cautious on how peace and Australian withdrawal could be achieved. His caution was due to two concerns. The first was his insistence that the best way to end Australia's military commitment was to elect a Labor government and that Vietnam was only one amongst many other issues that concerned voters. He was reluctant to share platforms with other organisations at anti-Vietnam rallies. 'The Parliament is my forum.' His second ground for caution was the anti-Americanism which came to dominate so much of the anti-Vietnam debate. He pointed out that the main opposition to the war was coming from within America itself and particularly from within the Democratic Party whose own president had sunk them in the Vietnam quagmire. Menzies warned about 'the downward thrust of Communism' and the importance of the alliance with the US. The ALP was portrayed as being anti-American. Whitlam was determined to shake off that tag.

But the real confrontation on policy with the ALP organisation was over State Aid to independent schools. Whitlam described his approach as 'crash through or crash'. He did crash over State Aid and after a bad bruising, he only narrowly escaped expulsion from the party.

State Aid illustrated how Whitlam deliberately took reform over the heads of the party machine to ALP members and voters. He had good reason to believe that the ALP would require a crisis before it would change. It is true of most things in life. After 15 years in opposition, the federal ALP was defeatist. The party was conservative; its culture was averse to change. The state party bureaucracies were more concerned about their narrow state interests and ignored wider national issues. The ALP was also excessively loyal to failed leaders.

In his confrontations with the ALP, Whitlam never seemed to have any doubt or indecision. He seemed to trust himself while others, including me, had doubts. In fact, I can't recall him expressing doubts on anything. As I grew older I thought how unreal that was. Perhaps he had more than he acknowledged, even to himself.

His attitude on State Aid was very pragmatic. It was a sectarian leftover and the sooner it was addressed and got out of the way the better. Society had changed, but not the ALP; and the kids of poor Catholic parents, mainly Labor voters, were still denied opportunities. The two people in Australia who probably did most to put sectarianism behind us, at least in education, were Menzies and Whitlam, both non-Catholics. Whitlam also helped temper my scepticism about Catholics.

State Aid brought out the worst sectarianism within the Labor Party in the 1960s. A lot of Catholics had been driven out or had left the ALP despite the fact that in its whole history Catholics were the one group of people who had supported it more consistently than any other. A substantial anti-Catholic rump remained in the ALP, which flexed its muscles in February 1966, when the Federal Executive led by Joe

Chamberlain, the Federal Secretary, decided that not only must ALP members oppose any future State Aid but that it would support a legal challenge to existing benefits. Whitlam's anger knew no bounds at this stupidity. He returned to Parliament House early in the afternoon from the executive to galvanise opposition. He commenced calling parliamentary colleagues across Australia. Many were out but about an hour later they started calling back. We couldn't manage the calls without a switchboard as we were temporarily housed in the large Caucus room, so we took the calls as best we could with Whitlam darting from telephone to telephone. It was pandemonium. Under the stress, he blew up, tore a telephone headset out of its socket and threw it out of the window into the courtyard below. That relieved the tension. Ten minutes later a parliamentary attendant gingerly carried a shattered telephone handset back into the Caucus room and enquired, 'Mr Whitlam, we found a telephone in the courtyard. Is it yours?'

After the practice run on the telephone, he composed a letter to his parliamentary colleagues about the behaviour of the Federal Executive.

> The issue is not the Right or the Left, it is between those who want a broadly based socialist and radical Party and petty men who want to reduce it to their personal plaything ... this extremist group breaches the Party policy, it humiliates the Party's Parliamentarians, it ignores the Party's rank and file, it is neither representative nor responsible. It will and must be repudiated.

Not a bad opening attack.

The letter went to all Federal Labour MPs. Sending it to so many people, it was impossible to preserve confidentiality. We didn't intend to do so. So the letter went to the media knowing it was impossible for the Federal Executive to check leaks from dozens of MPs. We did that often to destabilise the party hierarchy who sought to tightly control debates and manipulate the process among three or four people. Some were Stalinists at heart with the pretence of rank and file democracy. Party members were sick of them. It was a bit like the Catholic Church's ruling that the faithful can't even discuss the ordination of women.

Whitlam added to the furore a few day later on 15 February 1966, with a television interview with Peter Westerway on Channel 7's 'Seven Days' program. Following the leaking of his letter there had been a lot of very favourable publicity for Whitlam over the weekend. At Brisbane airport and elsewhere, supporters applauded him for taking on the Federal Executive. The responses were very spontaneous. He was thrilled. The party hierarchy was appalled.

I had stayed in Sydney where I got a call from Peter Westerway: 'Would Gough Whitlam do an interview for "Seven Days"?' I told him that I would have to speak to him first. Westerway rang back when I had gone to lunch. He spoke to Norma Thompson, Whitlam's electorate secretary. She said that he could come in and set up his cameras and lights. Whitlam returned from Brisbane to the office in the Commonwealth Bank Building in Martin Place in what a journalist told me later could only be described as a 'very exhilarated mood'. He welcomed the possibility of doing something on 'Seven Days'. He assumed that I had agreed, but he was on a high and didn't need much encouragement.

I was a bit late coming back from lunch, which was rare for me. I could not get into the room, partly because the interview had started and the room was crowded with cameras, cables and people. I saw Whitlam afterwards. He was very excited with the way it had gone. He said it was the best television performance he had given in his life.

Later that afternoon Westerway sent me a transcript of the interview. My heart sank. I was alarmed by what I read, particularly the intemperate language. It was the most vehement public condemnation of the Federal Executive it was possible to imagine. He described the Federal Executive as 'incompetent and irresponsible' who 'don't seem to be able to understand policy'. He described the proposal to refer the matter to the High Court as 'preposterous'. His king hit was 'We have only just got rid of the thirty-six faceless men stigma to be faced with the twelve witless men'. There were twelve members on the Federal Executive. He attacked Calwell's leadership and proclaimed, 'I have been destined to be Leader of the Party for at least a year as soon as there is a ballot for the position'. He asserted that Labor 'led by me would beat the Coalition'. Pressed to predict the result if Calwell remained as Leader he answered, 'No comment'.

I went into damage control again. In so many disputes that Whitlam had with the party I spent a lot of time picking up the pieces. He knew what I was doing but never told me to stop. I rang Westerway and asked him to consider some revisions. He made a few minor adjustments but the story basically went to air as it was. He had a great story.

Not surprisingly, it incited the furore that I feared. One critic described the Whitlam performance as 'Bonapartesque'. It brought him to the brink of expulsion from the party.

In March, a month later, the Federal Executive charged him with disloyalty and the numbers looked seven to five against him. Calwell chortled that 'we have got the numbers to get rid of the big bastard'. Whitlam was saved by his standing in Queensland and particularly by the Dawson by-election on 26 February 1966. In that by-election Labor had an excellent candidate, Dr Rex Patterson, who made it clear that he didn't want Calwell in his campaign. It was Whitlam's campaign and it was run against the background of his attacks on the Federal Executive. The swing to the Labor Party was a dramatic 14 per cent. It was acknowledged that Whitlam was responsible for the result.

On the morning of the Federal Executive meeting in Canberra, in early March, there were hasty instructions from Jack Egerton, the President of the ALP in Queensland, to the two Queensland delegates, Jim Keeffe and Fred Whitby. Egerton threatened that he would 'cut [their] balls off' if they voted to expel Whitlam. That concentrated their minds. They switched their votes and Whitlam was saved seven votes to five, although he was reprimanded for his behaviour. It was a long day waiting with journalists on the median strip in Ainslie Avenue, Canberra, outside the Federal Executive's offices. The crisis had created the momentum for change. In July 1966, the Federal Conference of the ALP adopted State Aid for independent schools.

Success was due to Whitlam's single-mindedness, the same single-mindedness he brought to bear later on Sir John Kerr, with very different results. All through it he had confidence and style; 'grace under pressure' as Graham Freudenberg called it. Even under great stress his sense of humour wasn't ever far away. Arriving at the Federal Executive meeting and facing expulsion he greeted the journalists, 'Have you got the tumbrel ready?'

Despite the bravado he had considered that expulsion was possible. Next morning, when the heat was off, I discussed with him what he would have done if he had been expelled. He set out clearly his course of action. He would first resign from Parliament. Elected as an ALP candidate, he could not stay as a Member of Parliament if his party endorsement was withdrawn. He would not recontest as an independent. Margaret Whitlam could get the ALP endorsement for Werriwa and would be elected as the MP. When he was readmitted to the party she would stand down and he would come back as the Member for Werriwa. This would have been a long process but he had certainly thought it through. I am not sure to this day whether Margaret knew much about it. But throughout it all he did show loyalty to the party, even though it was highly tinged with contempt for some of the key people in it. In his mind acting properly and honestly was very important.

Reform was a hard slog. My view at the time was that Whitlam's confrontations with the party were badly managed. I found it frustrating. Clearly he didn't have the patience or the skills for incremental reform. Yet now I appreciate that a crisis, a confrontation, is sometimes the only way to push aside the vested interests who oppose change and cling tenaciously to their power. Prisoners of any system cannot imagine a different system. I don't think Whitlam thought of other tactics he might employ because he lacked the people and political skills necessary for more incremental reform. A crisis was the only weapon he could employ. As leader it was a tactic he also used against the Victorian executive of the ALP, with the cooperation of Clyde Cameron.

In April 1966 he challenged Calwell for the leadership but was beaten 49 votes to 24. Calwell survived because of sentimental support, even for a failed leader, and doubts about Whitlam's judgment and confrontational style.

But the reforms were under way. The real breakthroughs, however, did not come until after he became leader in 1967. Reform is a long and hard process.

I had no doubt that I was doing a job that I wanted and greatly enjoyed. I became a political addict. Imbued with the Protestant work ethic I became a workaholic. In the rush of work, success and status I seldom met myself. My identity was submerged in activity and what I believed was a worthy cause. I ignored the effect on family life. Cynthia and the children were long-suffering. After Susan in January 1959, Rosalie was born in September 1960 and Peter in April 1962. Elizabeth was born in July 1968, when I was in Sydney with Rupert Murdoch. Financially the job in Canberra was ordinary but I don't think Cynthia and I ever thought of it in those terms. It was just so exciting to be working for Gough Whitlam.

Fortunately, Cynthia's great homemaking abilities kept family life on a reasonably level keel. She nurtured the family. She was the homemaker and supporter of the children and me. She got the three children off to school. She kept friendships in repair.

I was away so much I had to give up some family chores. I used to change the engine oil on our second-hand FJ Holden. My car maintenance also extended to jacking the car up and rotating the tyres. But called away on one occasion to the phone, I forgot to tighten the wheel nuts. The wheels almost came off at the first corner. It was a sign to give up pretending I was a mechanic. An improving salary helped Cynthia force a change, without reflecting too much on my mechanical skills.

On occasions I was able to do the ordinary things that normal parents do. A night at the drive-in theatre in Canberra was a family experience, much more memorable than the film. I remember once that Peter was hidden under a blanket to avoid the admission charge. On a cold winter's night the windows were always fogged. Food and drinks were on a tray attached to a bracket on the window ledge. Sue, Rosalie and Peter went back and forth to the toilets and cafe. They argued incessantly—'Turn the sound up', 'Turn the sound down', 'I can't see'— and generally created much more drama than we had paid to see.

Despite work commitments we managed to keep our family holidays reasonably intact. They were an adventure, three children in a Holden station wagon, from Canberra to Lameroo non-stop for a boring 13 hours. It was a long haul—'I want to go to the toilet', 'I am hungry', 'Peter is biting me'. Then it was 'I spy with my little eye something beginning with "s"' and there was a lot of sky between Narrandera and Hay. When the game got too dull it was back to 'How much longer to go?', 'I feel sick', 'Who farted?', then on again, 'I spy with my little eye something beginning with "r"' and there was a lot of road between Hay and Balranald. And so on for hour after hour. Not surprisingly, Chevy Chase's film *American Vacation* is a great family favourite.

We maintained our church links and the children all went to Sunday School in the way that we had done 20 years before. But my work was more important than the family. The balance was all out of kilter. The job defined me. I was marching to the beat of Gough Whitlam's drum and not my own. It was not until afterwards that I saw the loss. I was much too driven in my work. The job and the public esteem that went with it got in the way of my gaining a sense of who I really was.

If I had had a more rounded life I would have better absorbed and interpreted my experience. At the age of 30 I was very single-minded, with a lot of energy. I was caught up in the process without much mature reflection and was unaware of the need to integrate my personal and public lives.

Moving out of the shadow
The Hume election

'John, John Menadue, he knows the problems and what to do'

I saw politics as offering the means to influence the way power was exercised. I held the view that politics was a noble vocation, even if frustrating and criticised. I was attracted to a political career and Whitlam gave me full support and encouragement to try to find a seat in Parliament.

By 1965 I had been with him five years and, despite the excitement of the battles for reform within the ALP, there was a limit to how long I wanted to be always in his large shadow. I was also growing tired of being away from home so much.

The federal seat of Hume, adjoining Canberra, seemed worth a try. It included historic towns like Yass, Harden, Gundagai, Tumut, Young and Cootamundra. Arthur Fuller had been the Labor candidate for Hume for 20 years. In the eight elections from 1946, Hume had changed hands five times. At the most recent election, in 1963, it had been won by the Country Party by only 600 votes. At the centre of the Hume electorate was the state Labor seat of Burrinjuck, whose member, Billy Sheahan, drew on the traditional Irish Catholic vote. He said he had 300 relatives to vote for him.

I decided to throw my hat into the ring. Gough Whitlam spoke to a few key party people in the area and I followed up the contacts, invariably in a hotel bar, the venue for most ALP politics. Arthur Fuller, reluctantly, decided not to run. He could have been the candidate. He had a large branch in his home town of Tumut, made up mainly of pensioners.

My parents came from Adelaide for the launch of my campaign. It was a gala Sunday rally at Bill Johnson's soldier settler farm, near Harden, in October 1965. Over 1000 turned up. It was organised by branch members; a farmer, a publican, an SP bookie, a truck driver and a railway driver. They had experiences of life very different to mine. They were marvellous at organising functions whether it was for the ALP, their local school, church or the Rugby League club. As a new boy, wet behind the ears, I admired their knock-about way of life, practical skills and ingrained sense of what was fair and what was not. Gough Whitlam and Billy Sheahan were the star attractions at the rally, speaking about the future of the Snowy Mountains Authority, a Canberra–Yass rail link, a road link between Canberra and Tumut and, of course, the big issue of the day, conscription for the Vietnam War. It was my first public speech outside a university campus. My throat was parched with nervousness after one minute. But people had not come to hear me. Gough was the hope of the side.

After the political speeches, the day got into full swing. Bill Johnson announced that the liquor booth was open and that crown & anchor and blackjack were waiting for high rollers. The Reverend Laurie Menadue blinked but didn't join in. As the hot day rolled on, political debate gave way to personal argument. It was topped off by a brawl between two supporters behind the liquor booth when one of them objected to the other chap trying to run off with his wife. I didn't know what to do but the SP bookie and the truck driver sorted it out as if they did it all the time. Laurie took it all in his stride but on the way home in the car commented, 'Son, it is a bit different, isn't it?' He was dead right.

I had over 12 months in the campaign while still on Gough's staff. Looking back, it was a new and rewarding experience, although it was hard campaigning in a large electorate that stretched from the Victorian border near Mt Kosciusko up to the edge of Bathurst in the north. Cynthia was a great help. We got parents and housekeepers to look after the children while we were away. We stayed with party members or at pubs. Almost all weekends were spent on the road, with speeches and introductions to ALP meetings and social functions. We got to know all the RSL and Rugby League clubs up and down the electorate. It was hard work. Stranded on a country road at night and climbing through a hotel window after lights out were par for the course.

We doorknocked about 6000 homes, usually on different sides of the same street so that we could keep in touch. I would knock on the door and say, 'I am John Menadue, I am the Labor candidate for Hume at the next election. I am calling to introduce myself. If you want to get in touch with me please do so'. I would give them a brochure about myself and the campaign with contact details and off I would go. Sometimes residents would want to discuss political matters but, more often, they were pleased to see the back of me. Cynthia was serving up much the same pitch. She was wonderful.

I was very conscious that I was an 'outsider' even though Canberra adjoined the Hume electorate. I promised that if I was successful I would live in the electorate. I had the artwork for my brochure prepared by friends in Sydney but I decided, against their advice, to have it printed in the electorate. The printing, by the *Tumut and Adelong Times*, was faded and the type was out of register. I rejected the proofs several times but there was no discernible improvement. I was embarrassed every time I handed it out. So much for supporting local industry!

In campaigning, Cynthia and I could never get away from the ubiquitous pub. It was the centre of social life. We never felt comfortable. We came to detest Clayton's Tonic but Eric Walsh and Brian Johns, our mentors in such worldly matters, said we couldn't avoid the pubs. I always seemed to get cornered by the bar drunk. It was nice to be described in the media and by my opponents as 'a fine type of bloke', but I knew that they were closest to the mark when Eric Walsh, writing under a pseudonym in *Nation* magazine, commented 'Like his boss, Menadue doesn't hold a glass of beer convincingly'.

My campaign in 1966 was in the middle of the Labor Split. In Hume the DLP polled about ten per cent of the vote. Many were former ALP voters and mainly Catholic. I tried to neutralise some of the antagonistic Catholic priests. Father Ed Campion from Sydney gave me a profile of the Catholic priests in the electorate and where they stood in the Split. It was an interesting insight for me about the diversity within the Catholic church. The 'Irish Mafia'—Ed Campion, Brian Johns and Eric Walsh—were a great help in the campaign with ideas, advice, press releases and television production. I got to know Mick Young, another member of the 'Irish Mafia' a few years later.

Gough Whitlam contributed generously right through the campaign. I played my association with him to the limit although his interventions were not always a great success. We visited about ten asparagus growers on the banks of the Murrumbidgee near Jugiong. Gough went through the normal pleasantries about prices, the future and any problems they were having. But the pleasantries were lost sight of when he asked, 'Why is that when you eat asparagus, your urine smells?' Good one, Gough! He got no satisfactory answer so kept asking grower after grower. The more I tried to tell him to lay off the more he seemed to enjoy asking the question.

In August 1965, he told the Australian Planning Institute, Sydney Division, that 'Cities and civilisations go hand in hand. Great civilisations have been identified with cities. By derivation, civilised men are those who live in cities, pagans are those who live in the country'. That was a good line for town planners and architects in Sydney but, in the badlands of Hume, to tell country people that they were pagans was not helpful. His comments received extensive coverage in newspapers in the electorate. The Country Party had a real meal of it for about three months.

The campaign was topped off by a jingle for use at meetings and on television and radio. Good friends Jack Neary and Bobby Limb arranged the score and music:

> 'Action starts with Menadue,
> John, John Menadue,
> He knows the problems and what to do,
> John, John Menadue,
> Hume needs a younger man today,
> John, John Menadue,
> John Menadue means business ...'

My grandchildren still call me John-John, in recall of my days as a candidate for Parliament.

The Twilighters, a folk trio, were invited by Jack Neary to Yass in November for the 'champagne launch' of the final campaign and the jingle in the Church of England hall. We advertised widely but, as the *Canberra Times* described the launch, 'The bubbly was cool but flat'. We set 200 seats in the hall; 19 people turned up: Cynthia and me, four campaign workers, six journalists and seven others. Toting their twelve-string guitars, the Twilighters sang about the need for a steady job, the troubles of the worker, the campaign jingle and 'Puff the Magic Dragon'. They adapted 'All the way with LBJ', to 'All the way with John Menadue'. A nice old lady said, 'I know LBJ, but who is John Menadue?'

We did a little better than my grazier opponent, Ian Pettitt, did with his Country Party launch. He opened his campaign with a main street meeting at 5.00 pm at Harden. The local paper reported that 'Counting the captive audience in parked cars, he drew a crowd of between 12 and 15 and, of course, the inevitable dog. At least it was a big dog. A Labrador.'

It was the wrong time to be a Labor candidate, at the height of the Split and with the very strong public feeling flowing then in favour of Australian troops in Vietnam. I received the most hostile reception to Labor policies on withdrawal from Vietnam in traditional Labor areas such as the railway workshops in Junee and in the construction camps on the Snowy Mountains at Talbingo. At both venues I got a lot of heckling. It was the old White Australia syndrome, 'Fight the yellow hordes as far as possible from Australia'. President Lyndon Johnson visited Australia just before the election to rally support for Harold Holt and his 'All the way with LBJ'.

On election day there was a swing against Labor of three per cent in Hume, the smallest in the state where there was a swing of six per cent. Nationally, the result for Labor was the worst since 1931.

It was painful at the time but if I had been successful I certainly would not have survived long. It was a marginal electorate with the demographics moving against Labor. Kindly as ever, Arthur Calwell was the only person who enquired about our family's financial state as a result of the failed election.

I said at the declaration of the poll that the Labor Party, if it continued as it was, would become a dogmatic sect. It had to become a mass party and both its policy and its appeal had to be broadened and its structure and organisation changed. One clear view I got from that 1966 campaign was how remote ALP voters and even ALP members were from real political influence. A handful of ALP members chose the candidates. ALP voters had no say in policy. Political bosses excluded the community from meaningful participation except on election day. My report to the Hume Electorate Council of the ALP in 1967 said:

> branch members must make it clear that they are tired of being

wood and water joeys expected to faithfully observe party decisions yet denied any real participation in formulating them. Members cannot be expected to carry out their functions at the local level if they are estranged from the policy making process … The branch member is too remote to feel that there is any rank and file control. We have all been at branch and electorate council meetings when members have protested about the futility of resolutions and policy statements which they know will be circumvented or ignored at the discretion of agenda committees.

At the time Whitlam and I had discussions and correspondence with Professor Stephen Murray-Smith about the American primary system and how it might be adapted in Australia to generate political activity at the grass-roots level. We discussed how the leader of the Parliamentary Labor Party might be directly elected by all members of the party in the country.

The reform of the Labor Party proceeded after 1967 and it is now a slightly broader-based organisation than it was in 1966 but there is still no direct representation of party members at Federal Conferences. Labor supporters and voters have no participation at all. The same is true of the Liberal Party. The ALP in 1999 has *Insider*, a newsletter 'exclusively for ALP supporters' club members'. As a supporter the most interactive thing that I am invited to do is participate in 'the Labor quiz'. What is the smallest electorate in Australia? Who is Kim Beazley's new deputy? I suppose a trivia quiz is a start.

So having learnt from the experience of defeat in the 1966 election, I returned to Whitlam's staff on a full-time basis to work again on party policy and party reform. I only considered standing as a Labor candidate on one other occasion. In 1973 Mick Young asked me if I was interested in the seat of Port Adelaide. I had lived in Port Adelaide in 1951–1953 and had played football for Port Adelaide. Typically, it was a very generous offer by Mick. It would have been at his expense. I declined. He became the Member for Port Adelaide after the 1974 election.

A cold day in Geelong

'1967, the party; 1968, the policy; 1969, the people'

Gough Whitlam had said that the ALP could not win the 1966 election with Arthur Calwell as leader. It is unlikely that any ALP leader could have won with the Split unresolved and the strong pro-Vietnam war sentiment in the country.

When Calwell finally made good his promise not to contest the leadership again, Calwell supported Frank Crean. But Whitlam won easily on 8 February 1967, my thirty-second birthday. He won against Frank Crean, Jim Cairns, Fred Daly and Kim Beazley senior, who was the most talented speaker of all but lacked the hunger and passion to be leader. Lance Barnard was elected Deputy Leader. Unlike Cairns, he was not regarded as a competitor to Whitlam.

Whitlam immediately created a shadow ministry, the first in Australian political history. It transformed the role of Opposition, giving key shadow ministers a status and responsibility in a defined area.

So it was back to reform of the party and policy, the cause which really only commenced seriously after 1963, but which had waxed and waned throughout the personal and party crises which Whitlam often provoked. If he had been more skilful the reform process and the winning of government may have come earlier. Close to the action at the time, I thought that he was too petulant and indiscreet. Three decades later Australia and the ALP took him to its heart in a way that I would not have thought possible in crisis after crisis in the 1960s.

As a result of the leadership changes in February 1967, there was a mood of optimism in the ALP. Whitlam was risky but he was worth the risk. He was really the only one who had the intellectual energy, stamina and the public appeal to pull it off.

Being promoted from Deputy Leader to Leader in 1967 gave Whitlam authority which he had not had before. He also had the great help of Graham Freudenberg, who joined his staff as speech writer. Our staff resources were expanded from four to six. The Leader of the Opposition now has 30 staff.

Together with Whitlam and other colleagues, we developed at the beginning of 1967 a forward program for the next three years in the lead-up to the 1969 election. The sketch I proposed was 'This year the party; next year the policy; 1969 the people'.

I revived the policy advisory network which had fallen into some decline in 1966 due to other competing priorities and my absence campaigning in Hume. With Whitlam as leader it was now easier for the network to feed directly into the party policy review committees. Policy continued to be researched and revised right across the board. It was exciting work.

On party organisational reform there were two principal objectives. The first was reform of the Federal Conference (the faceless men) and the Federal Executive (the witless men) and the second was to either sack or reform the Victorian Executive of the ALP, which was drunk with power and incompetent to boot.

Whitlam's belief in the powers of the Commonwealth Parliament and Government was reflected in his view of the party. At the 1965 Perth Conference he described how the 36 Conference delegates were composed: '15 delegates are officials of trade unions, 5 are officials of the Party, 9 are Federal parliamentarians, 4 State parliamentarians and 2 local government heads. Only 1 delegate is self-employed. The other 35 are sustained by the Labor movement'. Over 30 years later it is much the same. Party and union officials, paid employees, control the party. If there was to be a national party there had to be a national organisation chosen by rank and file members and not paid officials. Why pretend to have a national organisation which only entrenched state party and state union rights and state officials? As Whitlam said on many occasions, 'We haven't got a national Party; we've got six state Parties'. Tasmania had as many delegates as NSW. In his view there should be direct representation of party members at the Federal Conference.

His other major objection to the party machinery was the exclusion of parliamentary leaders from decision-making, particularly after the 'faceless men' debacle in 1963. He pressed hard for the inclusion of the Leader and Deputy Leader of the Federal Parliamentary Labor Party on both the Federal Conference and the Federal Executive of the party.

In May 1967, his proposals for reform of the party structure were put in cold storage by the Federal Executive, a clear signal about the struggle ahead. Change is always painful and state officials who dominated the party knew that they would lose power. Whitlam took his case over the heads of the Federal Executive to the public and the state ALP conferences. Western Australia supported him against the pleas of Joe Chamberlain, his long-time but highly principled opponent. In Western Australia, Kim Beazley junior became a strong Whitlam supporter. The New South Wales Conference also supported Whitlam. Tasmania followed a little later. South Australia, which always had a tightly organised party, was opposed and Queensland was divided. The opposition from Victoria was bitter.

Nothing could illustrate Whitlam's 'crash through or crash' attitude better than his speech to the Victorian Conference of the ALP on the evening of 9 June 1967. It was the most courageous and passionate speech I ever heard him make. He was in the lion's den, living dangerously that night. He put his proposition bluntly:

> We euphemise deep disasters as 'temporary setbacks'; the nearer Labor approaches electoral annihilation the more fervently we proclaim its indestructibility. We juggle with percentages, distributions and voting systems to show how we shall, infallibly, at the present rate of progress win office in 1998. Worse, we construct a philosophy of failure which finds in defeat a form of justification and a proof of the purity of our principles. Certainly the impotent are pure ... There is nothing more disloyal to the traditions of Labor than the new heresy that power is not important or that the attainment of political power is not fundamental to our purposes. The men who formed the Labor Party in the 1890s knew all about power. They were not ashamed to seek it and they were not embarrassed when they won it.

The Conference was in uproar.

Afterwards he commented to me, 'Comrade, I think we have ruffled a few feathers'. The line was indelibly drawn in the sand in Victoria. It was only a matter of time before the final battle would be joined in September 1970, with Clyde Cameron leading the rout of the Victorian Branch and Mick Young, the healer, doing the rebuilding.

Just after the Victorian confrontation in June and in the run-up to the Federal Conference in Adelaide on 25 July, Whitlam was given an enormous boost. Hubert Opperman had resigned as the member for Corio. Whitlam asked Bob Hawke to run again but he refused. Gordon Scholes, a well-known local councillor and Geelong Trades Hall Council President, was chosen as the candidate. He subsequently was Speaker at the dismissal in 1975. Our private office was transferred to a Geelong motel for the Corio by-election. The result was a stunning swing of over 11 per cent. The victory was only three months after a disastrous state election and it was the first capture of a seat from the Liberals in Victoria for 15 years. Whitlam had proven, yet again, to his critics that he could win. It gave him enormous leverage in the party.

That stay in Geelong in midwinter was a turning point for me. It was my winter of discontent. I had just come back with Whitlam from the United States and Europe. Most of my time in the by-election seemed to be spent twiddling my fingers on cold street corners in Geelong. I suggested to Gough that I could be more effective back in Canberra where I had my information and network. Frankly, it also would have suited me privately to be with my family. Whitlam said no. That triggered my decision to leave.

There were other important contributing factors. After seven years of exciting work and doing my own thing in Hume, it was time for a change. But Geelong in midwinter was the trigger. I must say I didn't think that Whitlam would make it as prime minister; I felt that he was brilliant but too erratic. On many occasions, I had to clean up what I saw as problems that he had created by too much aggression and careless language. These seemed flaws that would prevent him from becoming prime minister. But then again, I rationalised to myself that successful leaders are different sorts of people!

Mick Young summarised a common view: 'Whitlam subscribed to the theory that ultimately the leader could always get his way. The application of this theory had Whitlam riding on the brink of disaster for years'.

A cold day in Geelong

After the Corio by-election, Whitlam was focused on the Federal Conference in Adelaide so I decided to keep my counsel until then.

Cyril Wyndham had been appointed full-time General Secretary of the ALP in 1963. He set about building a national organisation. Up to that time the Federal Secretary had been a state official who doubled as a part-time Federal Secretary. There was no federal office. Wyndham had come to this position via the British Labour Party and Evatt's and Calwell's staff. He had also been Secretary of the Victorian ALP Branch. In his new role as Federal Secretary, Cyril Wyndham had the blessing of Joe Chamberlain, the party's 'king-maker'. I think Chamberlain accepted the inevitability of change but thought that Wyndham would be a 'friend at court' in Canberra to curb Whitlam.

In Canberra, close to Whitlam and away from Chamberlain and the Victorian Executive of the ALP, Wyndham found his feet. He proved to be the right man at the right time. Unfortunately, he left the party after his great success at the 1967 Conference.

In Whitlam's private office we worked very hard on the Whitlam-Wyndham proposals for party reform. There were five main objectives.

1. To get direct representation of the Parliamentary Leadership at the Federal Conference and Federal Executive.
2. To improve the policy-making processes.
3. To strengthen the national structure and organisation.
4. To reduce the power of paid officials.
5. To get direct national representation for the rank and file membership.

The first four objectives were broadly achieved; they constituted a major breakthrough for Whitlam. Despite the agitation and hopes for the fifth objective, it was stillborn. Today the ALP is still structurally a federation of six parties.

The main struggle at the 1967 conference was over representation of the parliamentary leadership on the Federal Conference and the Federal Executive of the ALP. Whitlam had only two 'leaders' in mind: the Leader and the Deputy Leader in the House of Representatives. Chamberlain and Cameron objected. A compromise was proposed by Mick Young, then an organiser of the ALP in South Australian.

Young circulated his compromise. I told him to 'stick it up his arse'. He chuckled but wasn't deterred. He was like that. So began a

30-year close friendship. He recalled much later our inauspicious first contact.

Mick Young was a much better political operator than either Whitlam, Wyndham or me. His compromise was adopted. The Federal Conference was increased from 36 to 47, with the four Federal Parliamentary Labor Party 'leaders', a Northern Territory delegate and an extra delegate from each state, with the qualification that every state delegation had to include the state parliamentary leader. The Federal Executive was increased from 12 to 17, by adding the four 'leaders' and a delegate from the Northern Territory.

Cameron and Chamberlain believed that by including the two left-wing Senate Leaders, Senators Lionel Murphy and his deputy, Senator Sam Cohen, it would neutralise Whitlam and Barnard. Cameron knew that this would irritate Whitlam, who had made well-known his view that 'there are not four leaders, there is only one, me'. The hand of God, however, was not too far away. In the 1969 election Sam Cohen died of a heart attack and was replaced by Don Willesee, a right-winger.

As a centralist Whitlam was very hostile to the delusions of senators about the powers of the Senate. In 1975 the ALP was to pay an enormous price for the role which Senator Murphy played, particularly through Senate committees, in building the authority and standing of the Senate. But in July 1967 in Adelaide, that cloud was not even on the horizon.

Whitlam settled for the primacy of the parliamentary party over the party organisation. Even today there is still no direct representation of rank and file Labor members on the national conference of the party, let alone Labor voters and supporters.

Only about one in 80 Labor voters are members of the ALP. The position is marginally better for the Liberal Party. No wonder party branches are so easy to stack. In the federal electorate of Sydney, where I live, about 50,000 people vote Labor but only about 300 party members choose the ALP candidate. But even figures do not really tell the sorry tale of unrepresentative parties. In both major parties national policy is largely determined by elites who choke off members' views through state conferences and steering committees. The party bosses throw a few bones to the membership to argue over, but not much more. They reward family, friends and acolytes. Our major parties need a strong infusion, at the national level, of direct grass-roots representation and participation.

I have never been attracted to citizen-initiated referenda as exist in some American states because they seem to play into the hands of extremists. I am certain that the two-party system is in the best interests of Australia but the ALP and the Coalition have both failed to engage their voter constituencies. Alienation from the major parties has occurred because of the ground shifting beneath them. They didn't respond. The media portray in a pervasive way what is happening in the world. We are bombarded with news and views. But with our interests aroused we find no effective way to influence the outcome. With our response frustrated it is no surprise that we feel powerless and alienated. Thus, while the major parties slept, Pauline Hanson sneaked in and occupied the ground.

The 1967 Adelaide Conference was also to see the release of further major policy revisions in health, education, transport, foreign policy and defence. For the first time the conference adopted an extensive policy on northern Australian development. It reflected Whitlam's own interests and campaigning in Queensland. It was his least successful policy innovation. The media widely commended the changes that were afoot. The ALP was on the way back. The 1969 conference was to take policy development even further. The party policy could then be reflected in the policy speech and not ignored or disowned. The foundations of the Labor victory in 1972 were being carefully laid, years in advance. Whitlam's policy speech of 1972 was a distillation of party conference decisions of 1965, 1967, 1969 and 1971.

One major problem, however, was not anticipated. The 1950s and the 1960s had been decades of relatively steady economic growth. Economic policy and economic management were not seen as major problems for western governments. So Whitlam developed social programs across a wide range with little concern for the pressures they would place on public finance and national resources, particularly in the face of the external shocks which western governments were to face in the 1970s. In the 1960s there were no such worries.

With the benefit of hindsight, I now think that those detailed policies carried within them the seeds of later difficulties in government as world circumstances changed dramatically. Members of Parliament were locked into policies which should have been much more open to discussion and re-evaluation. The platform provided mile posts, but it also became a millstone.

The ALP went to the other extreme after the defeat of 1996. If a truck hadn't crashed into Cheryl Kernot's house, Australia would hardly have known the 1998 conference was on. Well-considered policies were not developed for what turned out to be a winnable election later that year.

In advance of the 1967 Adelaide Conference, I discussed with Cynthia my plan to leave Gough Whitlam. She was quite adamant. 'If you feel it is time to move on, don't hang around.'

At the close of the conference I told Gough that I proposed to leave. It was impetuous. I didn't have another job to go to and we had three young children, a house mortgage and a car on hire purchase. I was only two months short of my long service leave after nine years and ten months in the Commonwealth Public Service. The mind and body tell you sometimes that a phase is over and that it is time to go. I had probably contributed all that I could have. I think it was the correct decision, both for Whitlam and for me.

He was surprised but not hostile. I took a couple of months to clean up my affairs and to give him time to make new arrangements. Race Mathews replaced me.

I was farewelled by Gough Whitlam and the staff at a dinner at the Carousel Restaurant at Red Hill, Canberra. I still reflect on Gough's words on my farewell card. Those 'seven lean years' were the greatest learning period of my public life—full of new people, new ideas and new opportunities. It was a remarkably stimulating and exciting time for me. Gough Whitlam encouraged me to learn and grow. He was the catalyst for an enormous change in my life and my outlook. For that I am ever in his debt.

Inside the front cover of his book, *The Whitlam Government, 1972–1975*, he wrote, 'John, my second appointment [Margaret being the first] … in gratitude and affection. Gough.'

Seeing what power is about
With Rupert Murdoch

*'Power tends to corrupt, and absolute power
corrupts absolutely' (Lord Acton)*

Afﬅer the Adelaide conference
in July 1967, I spoke to Brian Johns and Eric Walsh about my future.
Both great companions and counsellors, Johns was then leader writer
on the *Sydney Morning Herald* and Walsh was the Canberra correspondent
for Rupert Murdoch on the *Daily Mirror.* Eric thought that there might
be some opportunities with Murdoch and got in touch with him. They
both loved politics and political gossip.

After checking me out with some people in Canberra, Murdoch
offered me a job as his personal assistant in Sydney. Eric, however, was
the decisive influence. I don't think Murdoch really knew what to do
with me, but he wanted to be involved in the political process and my
background and contacts interested him. He was, and still is, a frustrated
politician. He can't leave politics alone.

In my seven years working for Murdoch I learned a lot about him
and the media. It was enjoyable. But I didn't learn much about myself. I
was absorbed into someone else's agenda.

At a distance, and much closer as I got to know him, I found
Murdoch attractive. He was not part of the business or media
establishment; he was a nationalist without colonial cringe and he was
politically to the left of centre or at least had more of an open mind than
many other businessmen. As a university student in Adelaide, I admired
what he and his editor, Rohan Rivett, had done in the *Adelaide News*—

thumbing their noses at the establishment, the *Adelaide Advertiser* and the Adelaide Club. As time went by, however, I became increasingly concerned about the way he used power. That concern increased after I left him when I saw his role in the Whitlam dismissal and his influence with ministers in aviation and pay television.

Working with him for seven years I saw what drove him. It was not making money, as useful as that was, but gaining acceptance by and then influence with people in positions of power. When he inherited the shareholding in News Limited Adelaide from his father, he felt very keenly that the Melbourne establishment, which his father was very much a part of, had denied him his rightful inheritance in the Melbourne Herald Group. The group then included the major metropolitan papers— the *Melbourne Herald* and *Sun News Pictorial* in Melbourne, the *Courier-Mail* and *Daily Telegraph* in Brisbane, the *Adelaide Advertiser* in Adelaide and the *West Australian* in Perth. From his father's inheritance he got the *News*, a small afternoon paper in a small state. He was effectively excluded from the Melbourne Herald Group.

Shy and reserved, he felt slighted by the establishment. He was dismissed as the 'boy publisher', the young bloke who had returned from Oxford in 1953, 'Rupert the chick', young and fresh-faced. At Geelong Grammar, which he had attended in the late 1940s, he was 'Red Rupert'. He wanted recognition and acceptance by senior business and political leaders in the way his father had enjoyed. Menzies and Holt had no time for him. Menzies was part of the Melbourne establishment and had been very close to his father. Menzies ignored Rupert Murdoch in favour of John Williams of the Melbourne *Herald*, Frank Packer at Consolidated Press and Warwick Fairfax at the *Sydney Morning Herald*.

The first politician who took him seriously was Jack McEwen, the Deputy Prime Minister and Leader of the Country Party. In the 1963 election campaign Murdoch was the only publisher to cover McEwen's campaign. Philosophically they had a lot in common: national development and a touch of rural socialism. McEwen helped him find the property that he bought at Cavan, just outside Canberra and Yass. Murdoch was very much part of the anti-McMahon push with McEwen effectively putting a veto on McMahon being prime minister after Harold Holt drowned in late 1967.

John Gorton was the first Liberal Party leader to take Murdoch

*(Top) John and sister
Beth at Bute, 1938.
(Centre) John, Elma and
Beth, Murray Bridge, 1944.
(Below) Four generations of
Menadues, Adelaide, 1964.
L to R: Peter, John, John
and Laurie.*

(Left) At sister Beth's 21st birthday, Adelaide, 1954. L to R: John, Beth, Elma and Laurie.
(Below left) In full flight, Adelaide University, 1953.
(Below right) John and future wife Cynthia, at Cynthia's Debutante Ball, 1955.

John revisits the Cowell Methodist Church, 1998.

*Up the steps at Parliament House, 1967. With Gough Whitlam
and other staff member, Kay Swinney.*

(From the top)
L to R: Graham Freudenberg,
commonwealth driver, Gough
Whitlam, John, Peter Cullen,
1967.
With Gough Whitlam at his
call on Israeli Prime Minister
Eshkol, Jerusalem, 1966.
Mr Dom Mintoff, leader of the
Maltese Labour Party, presents
Gough Whitlam to the
members of the National
Executive and Parliamentary
Group of the Labour Party,
Malta, 1967.

(Left) The candidate speaking in Tumut, 1966. (Below) Opening the Hume campaign in Yass with the 'Twilighters', November 1966.

With a soldier from Hume in Vietnam, 1966.

(Above) Celebrating the 1972 victory at the News Ltd party with Nugget Coombs, Mary Coombs and Mick Young.
(Below) Farewell party from News Ltd Board and senior executives, 1974. Rupert was overseas.

Up the front with Jim Spigelman and Liz Reid and, in the rear, the helmsman, Tahiti, May 1975.

Listening to US Secretary of State Henry Kissinger's view of the world, Washington, 1975. L to R: John Menadue, Lionel Bowen, unknown, Gough Whitlam, Henry Kissinger, Alan Renouf.

(Clockwise) With wife Cynthia at the Great Wall, China, 1975.
At Commonwealth Prime Ministers' Conference Jamaica, 1975, with Mrs Rowling (wife of NZ Prime Minister) and Harold Wilson.
Farewelling Prime Minister Whitlam, Fairbairn Air Base, Canberra, 1975.
At Premiers' Conference, 1976, with Prime Minister, Malcolm Fraser.

seriously. He benefited accordingly. The Liberal Party establishment never took Gorton to its heart. His larrikin behaviour, scepticism about American policy in the region, the Australian states and foreign investment were all applauded by Murdoch. Murdoch made something of the fact that both he and Gorton had gone to Geelong Grammar, although they were not contemporaries.

Murdoch loved to be part of the political game. He couldn't help himself. Perhaps he acquired it in his days with the Labour Club in Oxford. He spoke to me, half seriously, about becoming a Member of Parliament in Australia. We didn't ever really discuss what party he would run for but I assume it would have been for the Country Party in the seat of Hume, based around Yass where he had a home and property. But that seems hard to credit given Murdoch's subsequent career.

I commenced with Murdoch in Sydney in October 1967. After finishing with Whitlam there was no time for a holiday, mainly because we didn't have much in our bank account.

I spent the first few weeks doing research on submissions that Murdoch had to make on the book trade. Most of my time, however, was spent trying to learn about the production of newspapers, watching the processes in the days of 'hot metal', from journalists to editors, to layout, to typesetting, to composing, to reading, to stereotyping, to printing and publishing. It was all very new to me.

After a month, Murdoch offered me the position of general manager of the *Australian* newspaper, based in Sydney. It was a gamble for both of us. I had few obvious qualifications.

The *Australian* had been launched in 1964 in Canberra but the big markets were in Sydney and Melbourne and flying printing mats out of Canberra at night, often in bad weather, caused late deliveries. Facsimile transmission of pages was then very much in its infancy. So the head office of the *Australian* was transferred to Sydney, where Murdoch wanted to quarantine it with its computer typesetting, from the *Daily Mirror* and the *Sunday Mirror* which had bad work practices and old technology. Doors were kept locked between the two composing rooms. Ken Cowley was the production manager and did a very good job in quarantining the *Australian*.

Murdoch saw a market niche for a slightly left of centre newspaper, although he spent a lot of his life tugging it back from the left when he came under pressure from his business friends. He saw a broadsheet newspaper as a means of gaining political acceptance that his tabloids could not provide. He was also committed to national development and saw a national paper as essential to that. He didn't particularly care for state governments. Throughout his public life and also privately he was a nationalist and a republican. He never took British awards, despite the fact that he could have expected that they would be offered to him. In the end it was an Australian award that he accepted rather than a British award. Even though he later took American citizenship I always found him aggressively Australian.

It was a very courageous decision to launch the *Australian* and he lost a great deal of money over many years. When I was there we were losing about $20,000 a week, a lot of money in the late 1960s. On quite a number of occasions during industrial disputes Murdoch mused, 'What's the point of continuing; it's losing so much money'. But to his credit he hung on and the *Australian* progressively became a financially successful paper.

Working for News Limited appealed to me; I was close to the public issues of the day. I had enjoyed my quasi press secretary job with Whitlam. I found journalists lively people and Murdoch was not a conventional media proprietor.

It was to be an exciting time for newspapers reporting on public affairs. Domestically, it included the disappearance of Harold Holt and his replacement by the larrikin John Gorton and later the election of Gough Whitlam. Socially, women's issues were becoming part of the mainstream. Japan had replaced Britain as our major export market. The first cracks were starting to appear in White Australia. China was opening to the West and a Springbok tour brought to Australians, as never before, the real nature of apartheid. Underneath it all was of course Vietnam, which divided Australians as we committed troops and watched night after night on television the horror and futility of the US intervention with Australian complicity and cooperation.

Leaving Canberra, Cynthia and I had intended renting a house around Strathfield or Burwood, where I thought maybe one day there might be opportunities for ALP preselection. But we couldn't find anything suitable and finished on the North Shore at Lindfield. We built a Pettitt and Sevitt project house, the trendy thing to do in those days. We spent a lot of time clearing the battleaxe block of land and smoking the neighbours out by burning off. But we had only been in the house about four months when Cynthia and I both decided, almost on the same day, that we didn't like it. Neighbours were aloof and there was no sense of community. We decided to move to Balmain, pioneering yuppies. Elizabeth, our fourth child, was born that year. She had dislocated hips at birth but after months in splints recovered fully.

We bought a house cheaply in Louisa Road, Birchgrove (a small suburb on the Balmain peninsula) and later spent a lot of money in renovations. We never had enough money, at least initially, to do it up properly so we were always improvising. We had three goes before we were satisfied.

In 1968 the Balmain population was older and poorer than today but there was a sense of community. House prices were lower and the older residents were not being forced out with higher council rates and living costs. Many residents worked in the area, on the docks or in ship repair. Balmain was not yet fashionable for the aspiring baby boomers. In 1968 Balmain won the Rugby League Premiership. The 1999 team doesn't draw on locals much any more. The children of the newcomers are more likely to play Rugby Union and soccer.

ALP branch meetings were a sign of the change to come. On one side of the meetings in the Balmain Town Hall was the old 'Catholic right', and on the other the trendy left. The abuse was awful. One night the lights went out and the attendance book disappeared. Even in 1968 the Leichhardt Council had a whiff of corruption about it. These days, Balmain is like a large construction site as the gentrification proceeds apace with upgrades and extensions of houses in every street. The people in Balmain have changed even more than the buildings.

I always admired Reverend Alan Walker, so we joined the Central Methodist Mission in Sydney where he was the Superintendent. We went to church every Sunday morning and joined its social activities. I persuaded Gough Whitlam to speak at a breakfast meeting. Briefly I was on the board of the mission. The children went to Sunday School. Their teacher was Elaine Nile, wife of Fred Nile, the conservative fundamentalist who later headed the Call to Australia Party in the NSW Legislative Council.

The salary was quite reasonable as general manager of the *Australian*. It was not significantly greater than I was getting in Canberra. What made a difference was the overseas travel and 'plastic money'. Brian Johns, Eric Walsh and Mick Young look back with gratitude to 'Rupert's plastic' for excellent meals and good wines. So do I. We tried most of the best restaurants around Sydney.

I was confident that I could do the job although I had no real management experience whatsoever, let alone on a newspaper. I was responsible for five other staff when I worked for Whitlam. But I had developed a lot of contacts with business people. I saw how they operated. I didn't feel overawed. I had political contacts in Canberra. I had an economics training and background and an appreciation of government policies and budgetary issues, but in managing an organisation like the *Australian*, which had a staff of a couple of hundred, I had to play it by ear.

My job was to reduce the losses and to establish the *Australian* on a firm commercial footing as the leading national newspaper in Australia. I also knew that Murdoch would make an early change if I did not succeed.

I talked a great deal to him about public issues and editorial policies. He wanted to involve me because of my network but I had to tread carefully with editors. He was highly interventionist. I was that way inclined but he was the owner. So I had to achieve results through discussion and suggestion. Adrian Deamer, who came from a well-known journalistic family, was the editor. He was very good but was perhaps not always diplomatic, which is no great failing.

I spent a lot of time, at least in those early couple of years, on promotions, the serialisation of books, major features by international writers, selling Australian prints and Australian wine as well as big crosswords and quizzes. We had some dramatic surges in circulation.

I always found industrial relations hard. I felt pulled in opposite directions. On the one hand, unionists were concerned about a loss of jobs that would inevitably follow the introduction of new technology. On the other hand, we had to embrace more efficient work practices which were being adopted in large numbers of newspaper plants around the world, particularly in the US, but not as yet in Australia. We were falling behind.

I was attracted by Murdoch's strategic view of international media opportunities. He outlined to me on a quiet Saturday morning at Holt Street, Sydney, that to be successful, an English language newspaper group had to be established in each of the major English-speaking markets. He later followed that strategy into the UK and then the United States. He also believed that, increasingly, newspapers and the media were about entertainment and less and less about news. We have seen a lot of that strategy since: Twentieth Century Fox, Star Television and Super League. His strategy was clear over 20 years ago.

I was able to impress Murdoch early by a stroke of luck. He was concerned about $90,000 unpaid advertising from an advertising supplement on Japan. Several News Ltd executives from Sydney had gone to Japan to try to recover the money but without success. He asked me, maybe just to try me out, to go and see what I could do. Early in 1968 I went and saw the agent for the *Australian* in Japan and the agencies who placed the advertisements. It became very clear that the advertising agencies had paid the money to our agent but he had kept the money in his pocket. A well-connected American, he had been in the navy and stayed on after the war.

When I spoke to him he acknowledged that he had received the money and hadn't passed it on. I said, 'Can't we come to an agreement? You acknowledge the debt and we agree to repayment over eighteen months'. He agreed, never believing that I could enforce payment when earlier money collectors from Sydney had failed to do so. I also had doubts. I went and saw the Australian Trade Commission. They referred me to a large Japanese law firm.

I showed the firm the signed acknowledgment of the debt. When they saw the name of our agent there was a great sucking of teeth and embarrassment. We adjourned for about ten minutes. They came back and said, 'We have a difficulty. Your agent is a very good client of ours and we would find it very difficult to act on your behalf against him'. But I had sprung our agent with his highly respected legal advisers. They obviously spoke to him privately. Embarrassed, he paid the money within three months. It was a sheer fluke. That impressed Murdoch that I had financial acumen! It was nothing of the sort. That was my first visit to Japan.

In the early years my work very much involved contact directly with Murdoch. It was vertical reports to him rather than consultation amongst colleagues at a horizontal level in the organisation. As a newcomer and an outsider that was a great help to me. In a more formally structured company I would have had to wait many years for opportunities. That sort of structure produces people who are loyal and dependent upon him. In return they are well looked after. It doesn't, however, develop a core of independently-minded people who can manage the organisation when he is gone. Whether you were going up or down the escalator depended on whether you had Murdoch's support and whether you were in favour at any particular point of time. I played the game. I calculated what was in my career interest and didn't show my hand unnecessarily.

When someone fell out with Rupert Murdoch—and it was usually an editor—he would get that person out quickly. I don't think he ever left anyone in his organisation who was disaffected. He rooted them out, gave them a package and sent them on their way. He created a highly personalised business culture. But every king needs a knave, or a fool, to tell him the truth. There weren't many knaves or fools at News Limited in those days.

Murdoch travelled a lot and was stimulated by new people and ideas. That gave him much clearer perspectives and appreciation of changing global trends. He beat his rivals by seizing opportunities and changing quickly, cutting his losses if necessary. We launched the *Sunday Australian* and *Finance Week* in Sydney. They were closed quickly and without sentiment when difficulties arose. He was deeply suspicious of management consultants. MBA graduates need not apply for a job.

Murdoch had a very good financial reporting system that Merv Rich, the financial controller, developed. Rich never seemed to show any interest in the content of the newspapers. I thought that amazing. Using Rich's system, Murdoch could check quickly what was happening around the world in his business units. He was also a great telephoner, ringing any time of the day or night. He had a great telephone technique: long silences. We are usually frightened of silence. Following those long silences Murdoch was told a lot more than was ever intended. We blundered in.

In looking back on my relationship with Murdoch and, indeed, Whitlam, I keep asking myself, where was *I* in all this? I was making things happen for others, but what was happening to me? I could analyse figures much better than my own life.

This is something that women, who are so often cast in a supporting role, perhaps understand better than men. Cynthia often said to me that I was in danger of losing my identity to other people and confusing myself with the job. I ignored her advice. I was idealising others to make it easier to live with myself. I submerged myself and made personal compromises for the sake of my career and the esteem and recognition that came with that. The role became the man.

In *Rupert Murdoch, a Business Biography*, published in 1976, Simon Regan commented, perhaps with some perception, how I played the game.

The opinion in Holt Street is that John Menadue is the bright boy in the Murdoch camp. Not a lot is heard of him publicly and he seems to be a bit of a loner in Mahogany Row (the nickname for the executive part of the Holt Street building). He is a first-class and experienced in-fighter. Although he shows the customary loyalty to Murdoch, he is very much in command of his own tactics and claims he only refers to Murdoch on matters of great importance. He is not a typical Murdoch executive to be so high in the hierarchy. He is a new boy without the usual 'up through the organisation' back-ground. It was generally felt that the 'Adelaide Mafia' were unsure of him.

Before joining Murdoch, John Menadue was in Whitlam's 'bright young men team' and had built a fair reputation in this field. He combines a bit of whiz-kiddery with cool political judgement. He is concise and precise as a business-man and is first class at managerial decision-making. Within the intrigues of Mahogany Row he is a central character.

He is smooth and dapper, soft spoken and a bit of a charmer. He oozes an aroma of executive power and is extremely sure of himself. He has shining bright teeth and one gets the feeling he cleans them with razor blades. He has extraordinary eyes which have a softness to them around the edges while at the same time a penetrating glint screams out from the pupils.

There is a certain style to top executives which distinguishes them from others. The fact they are well fed and expensively clothed is not really it. Fat executive faces can have a lean and hungry look. It really is quite undefinable. But, whatever it is. John Menadue has it.

When I first read Regan's comments I quickly put them aside, but I never forgot them. The arrow was fairly much on target and it hurt.

It was ironic that whenever we had major industrial disputes on the *Australian* we made short-term profits. All the typesetting, layouts, stereotyping and printing were performed by secretaries and supervisors. At least for short periods we would be making profits because of the reduction of costs. It is something that we couldn't have maintained for long because people worked up to 80 hours a week. As soon as the industrial dispute was settled union members came back to work and we would be back into large losses again. I often asked myself, 'What are we in business for?'

In a report to Murdoch in 1971 on the financial viability of metropolitan newspapers I outlined the challenge:

> Union practices have severely restricted automation. Producing a product that has to be sold within a few hours of publication has rendered newspapers very vulnerable to union pressure ...
> The application of known technology to newspaper production could reduce by half existing production workforces in Australian newspaper houses. These high costs together with the growth of specialist and regional publications have resulted in the diversification of newspapers into radio, television, property and mining which ... has intensified the business emphasis of newspaper groups, rather than improvements in editorial product.

It was only a matter of time before the newspapers had to face up to inefficient work practices which seemed more appropriate to the 19th than the 20th century. For Murdoch this took its most extreme form at Wapping in England, where the reform of labour practices became, in fact, an attack of one class on another, with Margaret Thatcher baying on the sidelines. The signs were there, not just in Australia but around the world, that the big newspapers in the major cities were in trouble as a result of work practices. They were unable to persuade workers that by changing they could keep their jobs or at least be adequately compensated. Newspapers were unable to introduce new technology. Success was going to the smaller regional papers which had in some cases non-union shops, good work practices and the best technology. It was inevitable that unless the big metropolitan newspapers in New York, London and even Sydney faced up to that issue, together with the unions, they just would not survive. The big technology and work practice improvements came about a decade later with Wapping the catalyst for change in many countries. There were also newspaper mergers and closures, many for cost reasons and some because of the growing competition of television.

My relationship with Adrian Deamer, the editor of the *Australian*, was a good one, although there is always a tension between managers and editors. Responsibility is often blurred and it required a degree of confidence and trust in each other. Our differences were not over whether the editorial policy was right or wrong but whether, for example, there should be more promotional content within the paper. Perhaps we should be serialising this book or that book. Could there be more editorial support for competitions, puzzles and crosswords? We were blurring the difference between quality papers and tabloids and Deamer naturally resisted.

He was a very professional editor. I had one particular disagreement with him. Eric Walsh had been with the *Daily Mirror* a long time as bureau chief in Canberra. He was getting tired of tabloid journalism, although he was continually breaking stories. He needed to write for a more upmarket paper. I suggested to Deamer that he might like to consider him as the *Australian* correspondent in Canberra. But I couldn't persuade him on that one. He didn't think that Walsh was suited to a broadsheet newspaper, that his background was very much tabloid. Having me as a patron wasn't helpful either!

I was more successful in persuading Deamer and Murdoch that we needed our own correspondent in Japan. I persuaded them to appoint Greg Clarke in August 1969. Professional journalists were not keen on the appointment because Clarke wasn't a journalist, but he was very able and spoke excellent Japanese. He turned out to be a very successful correspondent of the *Australian* in Japan.

From Clarke my interest in Japan developed. He knew his way around so that whenever I visited Japan on business to buy newsprint or investigate technology, he went with me. With Cynthia and the four children we spent many holidays in Japan. Our first holiday was a two-week bus and walking trip around Hokkaido, which began with an overnight ferry trip from Yokohama to Kushiro. We stayed at *minshuku*—private family homes which take in a few guests overnight to supplement the family income. It was that personal introduction to Japan by Clarke that was a key factor in our enjoyment of Japan and a lifelong family interest.

Managers and editors will always have tension over editorial and advertising content, although, in the case of the *Australian*, in the early days we had so little advertising it wasn't a problem at all. Deamer was always resisting pressure from some advertisers, particularly in motoring or travel, for 'free' editorial in return for advertising. Some journalists were very close to advertisers with loans of cars for extended trial or travel offered by travel companies. Less discussed was the editorial independence which is eroded by dependence upon sources of information. There are arguments about whether the ABC should take paid advertisements and to what extent that might compromise the editorial integrity of those organisations. Equally important is how dependent a lot of journalists are on their sources of information. They trim and colour their stories, knowingly or unknowingly, because they do not wish to alienate contacts and sources. Packaged stories from reliable sources are much easier than painstaking research. I found later at Qantas how dependent aviation journalists were on us for information.

Deamer's departure as editor was a sad day for the *Australian*. He had transformed the paper. It was well organised with an excellent selection of international and local news and good columnists with opinions. Readers responded with sales exceeding 120,000; in one audit period they rose to 141,000. Mungo MacCallum provided satire on the federal political scene. Bruce Petty went to the Middle East to draw cartoons of Palestinian refugees caught in the Arab—Israeli dispute and Oriana Fallaci wrote about travels and her experiences in North Vietnam under American bombing. The *Australian* opposed the war in Vietnam in the early years, but Murdoch's support for Gorton in the 1969 election meant that the paper came around to back the government position. Then Douglas Brass in a powerful and moving piece attacked the United

States and Australian involvement in the war following the My Lai massacre in December 1969.

While Murdoch was in London buying newspapers, Deamer had more independence in Sydney. But on his return, after talking to a few of his business and political contacts, Murdoch invariably gave new directions to Deamer. Deamer later complained, 'Murdoch is an absentee landlord visiting Australia for short periods, three or four times a year and making snap decisions while he is here'.

In August 1970, as Murdoch was at Sydney airport returning to London after announcing plans for the launch of the ill-fated *Sunday Australian*, he instructed News Limited's chairman in Australia, Ken May, about editorial changes for the *Australian*. The Phillip Adams column was to be dropped, Mungo MacCallum was to be taken out of Canberra and Bruce Petty was not to draw about Palestinians. Murdoch had not personally given Deamer such instructions and he rejected them. But Ken May wisely worked out a compromise. Deamer stayed, although the battlelines were being drawn.

When the Springboks Rugby team arrived in June 1971, the *Australian* carried an editorial, 'Cynical use of Prime Ministerial power', after Prime Minister McMahon announced that RAAF planes would carry the South African footballers around Australia if the ACTU carried through with its proposed transport boycott of the players. The *Australian* editorial accused the Government of dividing Australians and giving implicit support for apartheid. Murdoch was furious. Back in Australia in July 1971, he decided that Deamer had to go. He spoke to many people including Ken May, Tom FitzGerald, the editor-in-chief, and me. Deamer was sacked and replaced by Owen Thomson as acting editor .

As a manager, my role was not to decide editorial policy and I did not participate in any editorial planning meetings. Further, my view would not have been decisive against Murdoch's clear determination. But I had influence and I didn't support Deamer as I should have. I have regretted it ever since. I was looking after my own interests, keeping on-side with the boss—the curse of many organisations.

By the 1960s the *News of the World,* in London, owned by the Carr family, was sinking in a sea of genteel incompetence and alcohol. It was a tawdry Sunday newspaper with a circulation of six million, the highest in the English-speaking world. Its readers got a diet of gossip, sex and scandal.

Murdoch's main competitor in 1968 for the *News of the World* was Robert Maxwell of Pergamon Press, who was associated with the Labour Party. The Carrs didn't want to sell their inheritance to a Labour-sympathising, anti-Nazi Czech who was thought to be a Jew. The editor of *News of the World* described his paper as 'as British as roast beef and Yorkshire pudding'. Murdoch, though a boy from the colonies, was clearly not Jewish and was educated at Oxford. So he was welcome; as Sir William Carr, the chairman of *News of the World*, somewhat pathetically put it: 'Thank God, you've come'.

It was a cheap purchase for Murdoch, with full control. Anything less was unacceptable. Jack McEwen put in phone calls to Prime Minister Gorton to ensure that Murdoch got approval to transfer funds to London for the purchase. Treasurer McMahon had refused but was overruled. McMahon was close to Frank Packer and would not want to be seen to be helping his competitor, Rupert Murdoch.

Fleet Street was in a sorry state of flabbiness and decline. So Murdoch was successful with the same gusto that he had shown in Australia. He took a few key staff with him. The formula was the same as in Australia: start with a down-market paper, promote it hard and break accepted tastes and standards if necessary.

There were strong reasons for Murdoch's passion to own a stake in Fleet Street. He was quite clear that a successful publisher in the English-speaking world had to have footholds in Australia, UK and USA. He saw Fleet Street as run-down and slothful, needing change, energy and competition. If he got it right, big profits could be made in turning around these British papers with their large circulations. He was also impressed with the great traditions and world status of the British newspapers. And he had a personal interest. Through his father he had got to know some of the household names in Fleet Street: Lord Beaverbrook of the *Daily* and *Sunday Express* and Hugh Cudlipp of the Daily Mirror Group. As a young man he had worked on the *Birmingham Gazette* and the *Daily Express*. He enjoyed storming the London citadel. In Sydney I was cheering from the sidelines. The boy from the colonies, 'the dirty digger', was getting up the nose of the English Establishment.

After purchase of *News of the World*, Carr the younger visited Australia to look us over. He was pleasant company on board Murdoch's yacht,

Ilena, on Sydney Harbour. He had a brief continuing role on the paper, but it didn't last long. There was no place in News Limited for failed English gentility.

In the United States, Murdoch's first interests were in San Antonio, Texas. He decided to test the US market in a small venture. He was also interested in *Look*, a glossy magazine sold on subscription rather than on the strength of its editorial content. Sales were inflated through subsidised subscriptions in order to charge high advertising rates. It had failed to get advertising away from television. I was sent to the United States for six weeks in 1970 to report on the magazine, editorially based in New York, with its printing and circulation centre in Des Moines, Iowa. I recall it was dreadfully cold there at that time of the year. When I came back through London, I spent a very pleasant weekend with Rupert and Anna at their cottage in the Cotswalds. Rupert cooked me eggs and bacon before church.

I advised him to leave *Look* alone. It was a very large, flabby organisation that would have required a great deal of effort to turn around. Not surprisingly, it closed shortly afterwards. He abandoned his interest in glossy monthlies. Subsequently, he bought the *New York Post*. It had strong unions and consequently reducing costs was difficult, but Murdoch enjoyed the politics of New York and the influence which the *Post* gave him.

The greatest successes though were in England. Following *News of the World,* which gave him a foothold but not victory in London, he acquired the *Sun*, which was owned by the Trade Union Congress. It was left-wing, broadsheet and struggling. Its circulation was just over one million compared with the *Mirror,* which boasted five million. He beat Robert Maxwell again and promised a 'straightforward, honest newspaper'. It was another bargain purchase.

With its core pro-Labour readership the *Sun* backed Harold Wilson in the 1970 election. When Wilson lost, the *Sun* showed Murdoch's flexibility. 'Well done, Ted Heath', it proclaimed. He changed it to a tabloid, took its circulation to over five million sales and, in the process, displaced the *Mirror*. It had a proven formula of cleavage, crime, voyeurism, gossip and lots of sport. Murdoch's defence was always 'Well, if the readers don't want it they can buy another newspaper', as if he was operating in a moral vacuum.

Murdoch was just too smart for the business brahmans and they hated him for it. In the end, he believed a cartel of Fleet Street proprietors and unions coalesced to stop him. The proprietors had had enough of competition, closures and mergers. The unions were also fed up with changes in work practices, new technology and reduced union membership. The Press Council disapproved of *News of the World* photographing and taping an English Lord in bed with a woman of easy virtue. Personally Rupert and Anna were shunned by 'good society'. Those business and personal factors forced him to the bigger market in the USA.

I had not then appreciated the damage that was to come from the media that Murdoch owned or influenced. I did not foresee how far 'infotainment' would go in persistent and unwelcome invitation to voyeurism and 'dumbing down'. There is no question of good or bad, right or wrong. In the world of market shares, everything is relative. It is all a matter of personal taste. To the Murdoch media now, talk of quality is snobbery.

The cultural and moral relativism of some modern media today reminds me of those lines of Dostoyevsky in *The Brothers Karamazov*: 'It's God that's worrying me. That's the only thing that's worrying me. What if he doesn't exist? Then if he doesn't exist man is the chief of the universe. Magnificent! Only how is man going to be good without God? That's the question. Without God all things are lawful. They can do what they like'.

I also had not appreciated how the media would become the cause of so much social envy and alienation. The media urge us daily to buy more and consume more. We are encouraged to 'keep up with the Joneses'. The lifestyles of the wealthy and famous, however vacuous, are flaunted before us. They are held up as our role models. Personal worth is confused with personal wealth. People who are doing it tough could be forgiven for feeling alienated when they see the good life of the famous and consumerism projected daily in the media.

The visual nature of the media also contributes to frustration and fear in a new way. It often seems that news does not occur unless there is a TV camera to cover it. As a result, the media is highly visual, with a heavy focus on violence and disaster. It provides dramatic pictures. No wonder old people particularly are fearful about crime as they watch commercial television.

I still had some time for electioneering in my personal time in Sydney in September 1970. Murdoch had no problems when I told him that I would be joining the Road Reform Group in its first campaign to challenge the old guard who year after year tied up the directorships of the NRMA. We were protesting that a large mutual association had been hijacked by bureaucrats and a coterie of worthy business suits. Other members of the Road Reform Group included David Landa, later NSW Attorney-General, Jim Spigelman, later NSW Chief Justice, Leon Fink, a prominent businessman, and Ted McBeatty, the Secretary of the Transport Workers' Union. But we were tilting at windmills. Only six per cent of members voted and we got 18 per cent of the formal votes.

I became general manager of the whole Sydney operation in July 1971, which comprised the *Australian*, together with the *Daily* and *Sunday Mirrors*. We operated the three of them out of the plant in Kippax Street, Surry Hills. The composing rooms were combined. Work practices sank to the lowest common denominator but there were overall benefits of larger scale. Total staff was about 2000.

Murdoch was back several times a year and always for the News Limited annual meeting in Adelaide. Senior executives trekked to Cavan to hear of his overseas triumphs and report on Australian activities. It was all very competitive, particularly on the tennis court. Murdoch was middling at tennis but played his heart out. One executive forgot his tennis shoes but, keen to impress, played in bare feet on clay. He hobbled for days with blisters. With a great deal of bravado Murdoch recklessly drove us around the hills of the property in his four-wheel-drive. It was really quite dangerous but we all laughed. We thought we had to.

Cavan is to Murdoch what Chequers is to British prime ministers or Camp David is to US presidents, although very Australian and much more modest. The *Yass Tribune* said that Murdoch had got European craftsmen to build and decorate the swimming pool, but the work was in fact done by Finnish migrant tradesmen from Yass. In summer its wide brown acres touched the dried-up Murrumbidgee River, upstream from the Burrinjuck Dam. Murdoch expected to find minerals on the property but was disappointed. To assist him in entertainment at Cavan his mother, Dame Elisabeth, came from Melbourne if wife Anna was not with him. It was usually an impressive line-up of the powerful to pay homage. Prime ministers in later years flew in by helicopter.

In the 1967 Senate elections, the ALP vote was the best for 12 years. It panicked and perhaps unhinged Harold Holt. Whitlam was on the way up. After Holt was drowned in December 1967, Bill McMahon was the aspirant for the prime ministership but Jack McEwen and Rupert Murdoch were waiting for him. Neither trusted McMahon. The *Australian* carried a story in the silly summer season, in January 1968, that McMahon had a close association with 'an agent of foreign interests who had sought to undermine Australia's tariff policy'. It was an awful beat-up directed by Murdoch. The so called 'agent' was Max Newton, the former editor of the *Australian*, who had a low-key consultancy with JETRO, the Japan External Trade Relations Office. McMahon was tarred with guilt by association with an 'agent of foreign interests'. There were other doubts about him as well. Gorton beat McMahon for the Liberal leadership ballot.

Murdoch found John Gorton very engaging. Gorton didn't have many friends in the Establishment and he was pleased to have Murdoch as a supporter. That personal relationship continued, even after the substantial loss of seats by Gorton in 1969, despite support from News Limited papers. That election showed further the groundswell behind Whitlam. The ALP won 18 seats and lifted its primary vote seven per cent and effectively reversed the 1966 landslide.

After being crippled in the 1969 elections, Gorton continued to lose support in the electorate and in the Liberal Party. He was not a well-bred Liberal and he was seen as erratic and indiscreet. He stood down as Prime Minister when McMahon tied a vote with him. He then voted against himself, inept to the very end. Gorton became Deputy Prime Minister and Minister for Defence.

After discussion with me and other senior executives, Murdoch mischievously made Gorton an offer he couldn't refuse. Gorton agreed to write three articles for the *Australian*, entitled 'I did it my way'. Murdoch, the frustrated politician, knew the damage it would do. And it did. The articles about Cabinet colleagues' lack of loyalty and leakages to the press created a furore. Gorton was forced to resign from Cabinet.

In mid-1972, in the lead-up to the December 1972 elections, Murdoch bought the goodwill of the *Daily Telegraph* and *Sunday Telegraph* for $15 million from Sir Frank Packer. It was very traumatic for the staff of those two papers; some got jobs with News Limited, but not many. Some journalists transferred to News Limited, on a fulltime basis, such as Buzz Kennedy, or as freelancers, as did David McNicoll. I persuaded Murdoch that Alan Reid was best left with Packer at the *Bulletin*.

I was responsible, as general manager of the Sydney operations, for the merging of the two *Telegraphs* with the two *Mirrors* and the *Australian*. There were some minor improvements in work practices but it provided an opportunity to use the equipment and the plant at News Limited on an extra shift per day. At News Limited we didn't have a morning newspaper, except the *Australian*, which had a very small circulation. So here was an opportunity with a major circulation paper like the *Daily Telegraph* to use the afternoon and evening shifts and more fully use the plant. There was sufficient capacity in News Limited to produce both the *Sunday Mirror* and the *Sunday Telegraph*.

But there was one loss. A few months earlier, in February 1972, we had launched the *Sunday Australian* with great fanfare. Bruce Rothwell, the editor, was brought out from London. We believed that there was a major opportunity for a quality Sunday newspaper in Australia. There still is. The launch went well but a new Sunday paper would have been struggling for a time. But what made its demise inevitable was the physical difficulties of producing three Sunday newspapers out of Holt Street: the *Sunday Mirror*, the *Sunday Telegraph,* and the *Sunday Australian*. The *Sunday Australian* was closed. Later the *Sunday Mirror* was merged with the *Sunday Telegraph*.

Purchase of the *Daily* and *Sunday Telegraphs* was politically very important. They had been traditional supporters of the Liberal Party under Packer. Their purchase constituted a major loss in newspaper support for the Liberal Party in New South Wales. Murdoch told us that on the Sunday when the purchase announcement was made he was having a drink at Frank Packer's house. When McMahon, in London, heard the news he rang Packer and complained bitterly about the sale of the *Telegraphs* to an unreliable self-seeker like Murdoch. Packer told McMahon that if he felt so strongly about the matter he should speak to Murdoch directly and he handed the telephone across. Murdoch said to McMahon, 'I can promise, Prime Minister, that we will be as fair to you as you deserve'. In the background Packer grumbled, 'If you do that you will murder the silly little bugger'.

Rupert Murdoch didn't have a high regard for Kerry Packer. He thought he would be easy meat. He had paid $15 million for the goodwill of the two papers and enjoyed telling the 'story' that Frank Packer called together sons Clyde and Kerry and said, 'Well, lads, I've got $15 million to distribute. Sit around and I'll divide it up. There's a million dollars for you, Clyde, a million dollars for me and a million dollars for—oh, for God's sake, Kerry, wake up.' I think Murdoch would believe that these days Kerry Packer is much more awake than that.

Developing a relationship between Murdoch and Whitlam was difficult. The chemistry was never there. Whitlam was uneasy and sceptical of people with power and money. He scorched their retainers as well. David McNicoll of the *Bulletin* opened his telephone call, 'David McNicoll here, Mr Whitlam, I'm speaking for Sir Frank'. 'David', Gough replied, 'I didn't think you ever did anything else'!

I had quite regular contact with Whitlam but I was working hard at News Limited and he was working even harder to become prime minister. My main link to the ALP was Mick Young, who became Federal Secretary in April 1969. I probably saw him, usually with Eric Walsh and Brian Johns, for a long lunch or dinner every two or three weeks.

The appointment of Mick Young was a stroke of good fortune. When Cyril Wyndham resigned as Federal Secretary it was expected that Tom Burns, the Queensland Secretary, would double as the Federal Secretary. The position was to revert to part-time to limit the growing influence of the federal office in Canberra. Senator Murphy and other left-wingers then went to work and over dinner in Canberra it was suggested that Joe Chamberlain and not Burns would again be Federal Secretary. Mick Young was appalled. He could see a repeat of the past. Whenever Chamberlain, 'the unwise man from the west', as we had called him in Whitlam's office, left Perth for a meeting of the Federal Executive he would create chaos and division. Having set the party back on each journey east he would then retreat to the fastness of Perth and watch others try to put the pieces together again.

Mick Young decided that he could not hold his head up in the ALP in South Australia or elsewhere if he did not oppose Chamberlain, even if he only got his own vote. He nominated. In the first vote the result was eight all. There was a tied second vote. And a third. Chamberlain then withdrew. Mick Young became Federal Secretary. A new and successful era in the ALP had begun.

I found the run-up to the 1972 election campaign very exciting. Media power could be used for a purpose that I could identify with: the election of Whitlam. More often my energies had been committed to Murdoch's goals.

I arranged a dinner with Whitlam when Murdoch was back from overseas in July 1971. The dinner was at the Hungry Horse restaurant in Paddington. Attendees were: Rupert Murdoch; Ken May, News Limited's managing director for Australia; Tom FitzGerald, who was editor-in-chief; Gough and Margaret Whitlam; and myself. Murdoch wanted to get on the political inside. Whitlam wanted to talk about newspapers. The dinner conversation was polite but always cool.

In September 1971, Gough and Margaret Whitlam were invited to Cavan as overnight house guests. I had higher hopes this time. But the reports I got, particularly from Gough, were that it wasn't successful either. He described the evening as one of the most 'excruciatingly boring' nights of his life. He is not good at small talk and again he was free with his advice about what he thought about Rupert's newspapers. He was putting Murdoch in the dock. Murdoch wanted to be the political confidant and Whitlam didn't want it; it was as basic as that. So the relationship stuttered forward in a fairly desultory way.

Mick Young and I couldn't see a great deal of progress. But we knew that Murdoch wanted desperately to support the ALP in 1972. Murdoch didn't like McMahon and he saw that Whitlam was a winner. For Mick Young and me it was like trying to arrange a dance with mirrors.

As the 1972 election got closer, Murdoch talked to me a lot about what the ALP had to do to win. He was concerned about how the Labor Party could present its economic credentials. It didn't have people with experience that could reassure the business community. It was at his suggestion that 'Nugget' Coombs was approached to be an adviser to a Whitlam government. Rupert felt that Coombs would give the ALP credibility in the big end of town. Mick Young and I sold the idea to Whitlam. The announcement worked to gee up the opening days of the 1972 campaign.

Murdoch was also very keen to have tax deductibility for housing interest repayments. He guaranteed extensive support for the proposal which Whitlam announced in his policy speech. Late in the campaign Murdoch proposed a competition for an Australian national anthem. Whitlam accepted and ran with that also.

But in very few instances were Whitlam and Murdoch in contact. It was usually done through Mick Young, Eric Walsh or me. In their book, *Making of an Australian Prime Minister*, Laurie Oakes and David Solomon described my role: 'The ALP's main contact inside the News Ltd organisation was Menadue ... He had not lost contact with Whitlam or his ties with the Labor Party and was in frequent contact with Mick Young in the months leading up to the election.'

About three weeks before the election, Mick Young and I spoke to Rupert about a social cruise on the harbour with Gough. He thought it a good idea. He was coming back from overseas and was in Australia for a few weeks before the campaign. He is always on hand for elections; he can't keep away. Mick and I organised the boat but weren't sure who was paying. But we couldn't get Gough to be in it. 'I'm too fucking busy to see Rupert, I'm too fucking busy.' We continued to press him but as a concession he offered, 'I'm not going, but will Margaret do?' I don't think Margaret had been consulted at all. We finally persuaded him that he had to come along for the boat ride. In the end it worked well, and Gough was courteous and relaxed. Rupert paid for the boat.

Murdoch was up to his ears in the campaign. Apart from some key people in the Labor Party, I don't think anyone was more active in the campaign than he. He was writing speeches and forwarding them, through Mick Young or me, to Whitlam. I remember one press statement that Whitlam put out about the release of conscripts from gaol. I was with Eric Walsh as he spoke to Mark Day, editor of the *Daily Mirror*. Eric said, 'It is a pretty good story that Gough's put out on conscription'. Mark said, 'Oh, it's old hat, isn't it? That's all been said before.' I remember Eric replying, 'You'd better believe it's new, because Rupert wrote it'. The story was carried.

In 1961 and 1963, when I was working for Whitlam, I saw that the campaigns of the parliamentary leaders were very often quite out of step with the state branches and what the advertising agencies were putting on television. In 1972, for the first time for the ALP, Mick Young directed a national campaign, 'It's Time'. The six state party machines, the national office, the advertising agency and the Parliamentary Leader were working effectively together.

During the campaign Murdoch used to get in very early to the office, sometimes write the editorial leader himself and see it down on to the 'stone' where the pages were made up under the old letterpress technology. One morning he dropped in to my office: 'Where's Mick and Eric?' I said, 'They've got a small office and apartment at the Park Regis', which Dick Crebbin from Marrickville Margarine had provided. He said, 'Let's go up and see what's happening'. He just wanted to be in the action. It was about 8.00 am. Mick and Eric were still in their shortie pyjamas. There were journalists eating peanuts and having a can or two of beer from the well-stocked fridge. The cleaner hadn't arrived. There was a mess. Rupert had a chat for a period and then we left. On leaving he said, 'I hope they run the country better than they run their apartment'. Ominous words.

Mick Young and Eric Walsh established 'Businessmen for a Change of Government'. It looked to be an independent business group that was opposed to McMahon and the Liberal Party. It was nothing of the sort. Sim Rubensohn, at the advertising agency, provided Patrick Sayers, a businessman from the Jewish community in Sydney to head it. Eric Walsh prepared press advertisements. They were very good and Murdoch was attracted both by the advertisements and the intrigue surrounding the front we were using. He agreed that he would run the advertisements in his own newspapers free of charge and would pay for their placement in other newspapers. It was all done through Hansen Rubensohn McCann Ericson, the ALP advertising agency. When Murdoch gave evidence in August 1975 in the Botany Council affair he confirmed that $74,257 for advertising was paid by News Limited. Approximately $59,000 of this was in News Limited's own newspapers.

As election day approached, News Limited papers progressively came on board, very destructive to the McMahon campaign and supportive of Whitlam. For the final rally of the 1972 campaign at St Kilda, Murdoch got Evan Williams, a very good writer and a staffer with the *Australian*, to write Whitlam's final speech. He didn't speak to Whitlam about it but I knew what was happening. I discussed it with Mick Young. 'We've got a bit of a problem here. Rupert wants the final speech to be his.' The speech was largely discarded, although there were a few ideas and lines picked up. Mick Young persuaded Whitlam to thank Murdoch for his input.

There was an expectation that Evan Williams would be Whitlam's press secretary after the election. Rupert Murdoch, Mick Young and I believed that Eric Walsh would be better. A day after the election result, I called at Whitlam's house at Cabramatta and persuaded him that Eric Walsh was the man. Eric got the job.

Murdoch really pulled out all the stops to support the ALP. It was partisan and highly interventionist. But sooner or later the people whom Murdoch supports pay a price. It was to come three years later for Labor, in November 1975.

On the Monday after the 1972 election, Murdoch was going over the ALP victory with me. 'How many seats do you think we won?'—'we' meaning News Limited. There was no doubt that he helped create momentum, but the biggest swing to the ALP (six per cent) was in Victoria where his newspaper base was weakest. There were special factors in Victoria: the Labor vote had come back after the Split and the sacking of the incompetent and sectarian ALP State Executive in 1970 had been warmly received.

Murdoch hosted a dinner in Sydney at the top of Australia Square to celebrate the Whitlam victory. We all enjoyed the night. Sir John Kerr and the first Lady Kerr attended. The Whitlams always enjoyed her company. With an eye to the future, Murdoch invited Katherine Graham, the publisher of the *Washington Post*. She would have been impressed at how Murdoch could whistle up a prime minister. Neither she nor Murdoch knew how difficult it had been to get Whitlam to turn up. 'Comrade', he said, 'I am not a national exhibit'—well, not then.

In 1972 our Christmas card from Rupert and Anna read, 'With best wishes for Christmas and a Happy New Year', to which Anna had added 'but nothing can beat the last, a Labor Government and a new baby. Next year will be an anti-climax'.

In his early days in business, Murdoch was content, like his father, to be close to those on the political throne. A direct telephone number was often sufficient. This changed in the late 1970s and 1980s when he came to believe that he could influence, or even better determine, who was on the throne, whether it was Whitlam, Fraser, Keating, Reagan, Thatcher, Major or Blair.

There was probably no better illustration of his powers than in July 1995 when he hosted a conference of News International executives at Hayman Island. Prime Minister Paul Keating attended and Tony Blair, the Leader of the Opposition in the UK, flew halfway around the world to attend and ingratiate himself. He was rewarded; Murdoch supported him against John Major in 1997. When Major was asked, 'Were [you] upset by the [London] *Sun's* defection?', he replied, 'I could feel that one coming. You can't expect the mercenary to be consistent'.

I do think that Murdoch's powers are overestimated, particularly by politicians. Murdoch's papers are influential but, more importantly, he can pick public moods and trends and reinforce them. He will back political winners who he thinks can be made kings. Whosoever wins, Murdoch is determined not to be a loser. It didn't need a king-maker to conclude that Whitlam would win in 1972, Fraser in 1975, Reagan in 1984, Thatcher in 1987 and Blair in 1997. Murdoch's political power is that politicians think he can make or break them and they are not prepared to chance their careers on a gamble to find out. The perception is enough. Politicians now fall over themselves to advantage or at least not to disadvantage Murdoch. He often does not have to ask for favours; they are offered. With Keating he didn't even have to pay his respects at the Lodge. Keating called at Murdoch's Red Hill residence.

Murdoch certainly believed that he had played a major part in the 1972 election result and that something was due to him. What he asked for was that he be appointed as Australian High Commissioner to London. He wasn't seeking business favours. He wanted acceptance and recognition, and what could be better than a prestigious position in London where he could thumb his nose at the English Establishment, which had not accepted him?

Murdoch raised the appointment with me and explained that if he was the High Commissioner he would put his newspaper and television interests in a trust so there would not be a conflict of interest. He believed also that he could influence other Australian media proprietors and avoid media flak for the new government over the appointment. He has since denied that he sought the High Commissioner's job.

I raised it with Mick Young. The absurdity of it amused him. I put it to Whitlam on the phone. It was the Sunday morning a week after the election. We had a lengthy discussion. Whitlam had made a commitment to John Armstrong to appoint him the High Commissioner. Armstrong had been a Labor senator since 1937 and a former Chifley Government minister. He was very successful in London. But Whitlam was adamant about Rupert for London. 'No way', he said.

After 12 months a person with Murdoch's energy and ambitions would have become bored with the job. But that was what he was after at the time. As far as I could tell, he carried no grudge for the knockback. In the cold light of day he may have come to the view that the request was a bit rich. Setbacks, though, never slowed him down.

After the 1972 election, Whitlam was very busy and it was difficult once more to keep him and Murdoch in contact. Mick Young and I talked with Eric Walsh about doing what he could to keep the relationship in repair. In Easter 1973, Whitlam was in London but a meeting with Murdoch proved difficult to arrange. In January 1974, in New York, a dinner was set up but when Gough saw David Frost in the foyer of the Plaza Hotel he went to dinner with him and cancelled the Rupert engagement. Eric Walsh was able to get the two together for breakfast at Rupert's apartment two days later, but Gough Whitlam did not do so with good grace. He didn't feel it necessary to share his thoughts with Rupert Murdoch. He was wary and cautious as to where the relationship might lead!

The Botany Council Affair and its aftermath took a lot of energy and wasted a lot of my time in late 1973 and 1974. News Limited had acquired land for newsprint storage at Botany. It had been zoned industrial but subsequently came under an interim development order to rezone it residential. In August 1973, Neville Wran, the Leader of the New South Wales State Opposition, came to lunch at News Limited with Ken May, the *Australian*'s Managing Director, Frank Shaw, the Editorial Manager, and News editors. I attended. Discussions were mainly about state political issues. The point was put to Wran at the end of the lunch that it seemed unusual, when all the container and shipping activities were being shifted from Port Jackson to Botany Bay, that the Botany Council seemed to be going in the opposite direction in rezoning commercial land to residential.

Subsequently Frank Shaw was in touch with Neville Wran in more detail. Neville Wran spoke to Laurie Brereton. What Neville Wran said or how Laurie Brereton responded or interpreted it, is not clear. But at least some councillors believed that if Botany Council would change their decision, there would be a financial contribution or other support from News Limited to the Labor Party. That was never, to my knowledge, ever proposed by News Limited. As was so often the case with Murdoch, more seemed to be offered than requested or expected. I spoke to Geoff Cahill, the State Secretary of the ALP. No money or other inducement was discussed. It was quite an open and legitimate viewpoint which News Limited had: this seemed an unusual zoning decision and shouldn't it be examined? I am confident it went no further than that but other people obviously put a twist on it. There was protracted political controversy and charges laid but the outcome was inconclusive. The affair stalked Laurie Brereton for years.

As the economy ran into difficulties in 1974, Whitlam and Murdoch gradually parted ways. In the 1974 election, Murdoch played it down the middle in the *Australian* editorial pages, one senior journalist writing 'Why I will vote Liberal' and the other 'Why I will vote Labor'. Increasingly Murdoch and the Labor Party drifted apart.

Meanwhile, back at the newspaper there was plenty to do. The *Telegraphs* had been taken on board and the *Australian* was beginning to make good progress. Murdoch was increasingly overseas with his growing business interests. But the 1972 election was the high-water mark in the emotional energy and excitement that I had in the relationship with Murdoch and in doing something that I regarded as beneficial.

It was probably time to think about other things, particularly after the 1974 election. I had worked close to seven exhausting but exciting years for Murdoch. But I thought that my position would be increasingly uncomfortable with his moving politically to the right. More importantly I came to the view that to be my own person I had to move. There was more to life than working to his agenda and seeking his approval.

I must admit that my views on Murdoch hardened over the years. Working with him, I was like a frog in a pot of slow-warming water: I was becoming conditioned to the News Limited environment and too self-centred to sense the rising temperature and the dangers ahead. It was a great learning experience, but years later I could see that I jumped out of the pot just in time.

I was also keen to get more directly involved with the Labor Government. A sea change in Australian politics was under way with Whitlam as Prime Minister. For most Australians, as it was for me, it was a very exciting time. But I was something of a bystander in Sydney.

Mick Young took a sabbatical in Adelaide and then came back to Whitlam's staff when it became clear that there were clouds on the horizon. Like others, I became worried at the difficulties the government was running into. Rex Connor was stopping a lot of mineral development. The Government was spending heavily. Whitlam, who had written so much of the platform, was ticking off the monuments one by one but there didn't seem sufficient appreciation of the changing global economic circumstances. There was a need to slow down the pace of reform and explain policies better. I had itchy feet to get back to Canberra.

It had been a very intense workload at News Limited. There was always more to be done: reports, phone calls, meetings. My activism was often at the expense of Cynthia and the family, although Cynthia was included in social functions with leading advertisers, balls, parades, presentations of medals and sports awards. I enjoyed it but it was tiring.

My father, Laurie, died of a heart attack in 1971, aged 67. I am sure he was content with his life and not at all resentful of the struggles he had had. He had realistic hopes for himself and was not disappointed. He had higher hopes for me. My regret now is that I discounted so much of his rich experience. As a young man I thought I knew it all.

I was active right through my Murdoch days in church activities, in a formal sense. But my life was quite compartmentalised. Church was a parade, not an experience. With effort I was able to keep the world of money apart. Ethics was for Sundays only. My spiritual life was in hibernation. I shut out personal reflection with hard work. I was strong, controlling and successful—at least in public terms.

A replay of Murdoch's association with the Labor Party came in 1984, with the Hawke Government and Keating as Treasurer approving his acquisition of the Melbourne Herald Group, the inheritance he had been denied 30 years before. He now effectively has ownership of about 70 per cent of morning newspaper circulations in Australia. I spoke to Mick Young, then a senior Labor minister, objecting to the Melbourne Herald Group being acquired by News Limited. He said, 'Well, Jack, the old Melbourne Herald Group was always against us; Rupert's with us sometimes'.

Working for Murdoch, I learned about business and networks. Most starkly I saw power and the way it is exercised. It left an indelible impression on me. The need for decentralisation of power, not just politically but in the economic and social fields has stayed with me ever since. Today there is not a significant politician who will raise his or her hand against Rupert Murdoch. That says a lot about politicians. Secure people with strong core values would not want to ingratiate themselves in this way.

After I left I could see more clearly his power at work and I was confident that I knew what made him tick. In the early days it was recognition by the person on the throne. Later, as he became bolder, it was to be influential or even instrumental in deciding who sat on the throne.

In the years to come, when I was CEO of Qantas and, later, a Telstra director, I was to see at first hand the sort of influence that Murdoch could exert on the Hawke and Keating governments. He was also an active participant in the dismissal of the Whitlam Government.

Born to rule and jobs for the boys

With the Whitlam Government

' In the generally undistinguished and often tawdry atmosphere of Australian national politics, it is impossible to deny the Whitlam Government a certain grandeur' (Clem Lloyd & Gordon Reid)

From the beginning, the cards were stacked against the Whitlam Government. By the time I arrived, in September 1974, most of the cards had been dealt.

One card was the external economic shock caused by huge US budget and trading deficits to pay for the war in Vietnam. President Johnson found that even the US could not fund the Vietnam war and eliminate poverty at home at the same time. This was followed in 1973 by the Arab oil embargo and a 70 per cent increase in OPEC oil prices. The first OECD survey of the Australian economy, in December 1972, reported that Australia had had 15 previous years of smooth economic sailing with few external shocks.

The second card was the unwillingness of conservatives, seduced by 23 years in power, to accept the legitimacy of a twice popularly elected government. It was spiteful and unfair. Because of that the Government was always distracted and under threat from the Senate.

The third card was the weaknesses at the centre of the Government: disunity and inexperience in a 27-man Cabinet. By 1974 Gough Whitlam was turning his attention to how he could better handle this third problem.

If the ALP had won in 1969, before the oil shock, it would have been better able to learn from and overcome its internal difficulties.

The core of any government is the Cabinet. How the Cabinet performs, month in and month out, determines how the government as a whole performs and whether or not it will be re-elected. Good Cabinet performance requires leadership, talent, hard work, patience, good judgment, a feel for the electorate and a strategic view about where Australia is headed. The early Hawke governments had more of these qualities than the Whitlam governments.

Among those close to Whitlam in 1974 there was a growing view that the Department of Prime Minister and Cabinet (PM&C) was too passive and reactive; it was seen as a 'post office', sorting and posting mail between departments. It provided the Cabinet Secretariat, organised Cabinet meetings and wrote and distributed the minutes of Cabinet decisions. But it played a limited role in advising the Prime Minister on priorities or helping him supervise the performance of 27 ministers and their departments.

As put to me, the Prime Minister was also concerned about Treasury's performance and loyalty. Treasury gave dogmatic advice. If its proposals were not accepted it took its bat home. There was concern too that senior bureaucrats promoted in the Menzies era were unsympathetic to the Labor Government: Sir John Bunting, Head of the Department of Prime Minister and Cabinet; Sir Arthur Tange, Head of the Department of Defence; Sir Frederick Wheeler, Head of the Treasury; and Allan Cooley, Chairman of the Public Service Board. He was later knighted. They all lunched regularly together at the Commonwealth Club.

In early 1974 my name was put to Whitlam as a possible head of PM&C. So was Peter Wilenski's, a medical doctor and former student activist who was on Whitlam's private staff. Eric Walsh, also on his private staff, was a good advocate of mine. Not surprisingly, Whitlam was cautious about an appointment from outside the Public Service.

The first two days of the April 1974 election campaign, however, changed that. With the economic indicators not looking good, the media talked of Billy Sneddon's impressive start to the campaign. Whitlam then raised the issue of his Public Service support with his private staff. He made up his mind while campaigning in Perth that a change in PM&C would be made if he was returned as Prime Minister.

Whitlam probably didn't read more than the newspaper headline but he would not have been surprised by a speech I made to the Australian Institute of Management in Canberra, in October 1973, about government policies and how their implementation was perceived in business.

> It is clear that the business community is concerned—some would say beside itself—about its relationship, or lack of it, with the Australian Government ... Business success requires opportunities for growth, investment and confidence about where the Government is heading ... There is no doubt that relations are in worse shape than for a long time. If business would be more politically literate we could also do with business literacy from our politicians ... A major barrier, I suggest, is an ambivalent and often hostile attitude by the Government, or at least some of its Ministers, towards profit ... One of the early and major misconceptions was a belief among some Ministers that the best way to improve the well being of the community is by increases in wages and improvements in conditions of employment. To date, we have seen a sound policy on minerals and energy thrown into public confusion. Developing Australia's resources in the overall national interest has been clouded and almost lost sight of through a failure to explain what the policy is about and how the development and exploitation of our energy resources will proceed.

Bringing in an outsider to such a senior position, who was personally associated with him and into a Public Service which was supposedly politically neutral, was risky. It wasn't politically neutral in my view. With its service to conservative governments for 23 years it was steeped, however unwittingly, in traditional ways of thinking and doing things. It was culturally, if not politically, conservative. But I had a label on me. There was an assumption that senior public servants were neutral and I wasn't. The difference as I saw it was that I was open about my position. Furthermore, I have always been sceptical of the person who says 'I am non-political'. A person who is non-political accepts the status quo and is not attracted to political action to change it. That person, in my view, is conservative and should acknowledge it.

With the benefit of hindsight, the Whitlam Government, on election in December 1972, would have been better served if it had focused on administrative arrangements: how to make the Cabinet and the Public Service better coordinated and effective. Instead there was a flurry of new policy decisions in those early heady days. A slower start would have been better. It sounds dull to focus on administrative arrangements but it would have minimised so many later problems. The new government was inexperienced and too impressed with the reputations of heads of major departments who found change hard. It should have replaced them on day one.

For several months I was confident that a job offer was coming. Whitlam probably had doubts, but he finally rang me in Sydney. Just as it happened 14 years before when he made me a job offer, I quickly said yes.

My appointment as Secretary of PM&C was announced on 23 August 1974. I was 39 years old. I didn't tell Murdoch until the day of the announcement. I rang him in the United States. He was generous and considerate. He subsequently had discussions with Whitlam and told him that if I wanted, I could come back and work again for him. Clearly having a confidante close to the throne would be useful!

The response by conservatives to my appointment was a shrill chorus of 'jobs for the boys'. The *Australian* poster next day was 'New Man to Head The Whitlam Staff'. Laurie Oakes's story in the *Melbourne Sun Pictorial* was headed 'Whitlam Picks Ex-Aide For Top PS Job'. But other newspapers were hostile. The response of the Liberal Party was bitter. My appointment was followed by other 'jobs for the boys'; Peter Wilenski, as Head of the Department of Labour and Immigration; and Jim Spigelman, as Head of the Media Department. Phil Lynch, the Shadow Treasurer, said that we would all be sacked by a future Liberal-National Party government. The Shadow Minister for the Public Service, Vic Garland, confirmed that we would all be removed. Those born to rule believed that jobs should go to their boys, not boys like us. Alan Reid in the *Bulletin* referred to Wilenski, Spigelman and me as the Whitlam 'palace eunuchs'. We had been 'raised from poverty and obscurity by our patron and we could not become his rivals because we could not generate a line of succession'.

I commenced as 'Secretary designate' of PM&C on 23 September 1974 but was in effect in charge in the department. Cynthia stayed in Sydney with the four children until school holidays in December. Susan and Rosalie were then attending Methodist Ladies' College, Burwood.

Peter was attending Newington College, the Methodist college at Stanmore, and Elizabeth was attending the local Birchgrove Primary School. I rented a small apartment in Canberra for a few months and Cynthia came down from Sydney for occasional visits. Kerry Packer offered me the use of his Canberra house and car but I declined. Late in 1974, we bought a house in Deakin. By normal custom ASIO 'swept' the house to detect any listening devices, insisting that Cynthia leave the house while they did their work. Welcome to the world of spies. The children speculated that ASIO was installing listening devices to spy on me rather than to protect me from 'unfriendlies'.

There was clear resentment from many senior public servants in Canberra to my appointment. This was not the way to do things. With the media deluge, I felt on trial as never before or since. I was still a member of the ALP but let my membership lapse. I never rejoined. Party membership seems so pointless.

I had support from some department heads who resented the clique that lunched at the Commonwealth Club. Those who had suffered at their hands welcomed my appointment but they were in a minority. I joined the Canberra Club and not the Commonwealth Club.

The strength of the Secretary of PM&C is that he is at the centre of government. I could draw on the Prime Minister's authority. I had to be careful in the way I used that authority but it was a great help to get things done. Sitting in Cabinet meetings I had a better view than any other public servant on what was happening across the range of government.

As the recorder of Cabinet decisions it also served as a useful lesson for me on the importance of proper records on major and perhaps controversial issues. Coming from the private sector it was not a skill I had acquired. From those Cabinet days I have always laid an 'audit trail' on matters in which I was involved that might be of later significance. Years on, a colleague who headed a statutory corporation under a Labor minister was put under pressure by the minister and the head of department to resign to make way for the minister's favourite. He asked for my advice. I advised him to make records of all discussions over a couple of months and then present them to the head of department and ask him to confirm his recollection of the discussions. He did that. Suddenly the harassment stopped. Bullies thrive on secrecy.

In the first few days at PM&C I learned very quickly how Treasury, the department I had always admired, was distrusted. I got a disturbing account from the Prime Minister on Treasury's role in the preparation of the 1974 budget. In July 1974, Treasury seriously underestimated the deteriorating state of the Australian economy. It proposed to Cabinet a deflationary package, 'a short, sharp shock'. It was rejected by Cabinet. In August, Treasury presented a similar package to the Labor Caucus. It was unconcerned that its proposals would be rejected again. Caucus endorsed an alternative proposal put forward by Jim Cairns, chairman of the Caucus Economic Committee. The Treasurer, Frank Crean, gave up any effective presentation of the Treasury case. As Whitlam described it to me: 'Treasury sulked and determined not to serve the Government'. Treasury refused to offer advice on the Cairns package and how it might be improved. Then Michael Keating from the Department of Urban and Regional Development and later Head of PM&C discovered that Treasury calculations of the domestic budget surplus for 1974/75 were understated by $1 billion. Then it was revealed that Treasury's unemployment 'projections' were in serious error. One outcome of this Treasury mistake was that the Australian Bureau of Statistics, which was then part of Treasury, was put on a separate statutory basis. On budget night, Treasury presented a perfunctory budget speech draft and refused to cooperate in explaining the budget to the press. Not surprisingly, the budget of August 1974 lacked clear direction and purpose. Step by step, Treasury was forfeiting its opportunities to influence the course of events.

Hostility from Treasury was calculated and pointed towards me. Within four weeks of my arrival at PM&C, there was a leak about a likely devaluation of the Australian dollar. Treasury pointed the finger at me through their media contacts. In fact the leak came from the Treasurer's office. I found that it is a reliable rule of thumb that 90 per cent of government leaks come from ministers' offices.

One of the first things that Whitlam asked me to do was to draft an Economic Statement for him to deliver in Parliament to try to repair some of the damage that had been done in the 1974 budget. A statement was prepared in PM&C, principally with the help of Ian Castles, who had recently joined the department from Treasury. An excellent economist, he later became Commonwealth Statistician. Together with Professor Fred Gruen from the Australian National University and Austin Holmes from the Priorities Review Staff working with the Special Minister of

State, we developed a new statement. I coordinated the work but I was relying on professional economic advice.

The statement was presented in November 1974 to the Parliament by the Prime Minister. It was the first public signal that Whitlam was taking economic advice from other quarters and was not dependent on Treasury. The statement was designed to encourage private expenditure, promote profits and keep government expenditure under control. Personal tax concessions were seen as necessary because of the slowing of the economy and also as a means to reduce wage pressures. Treasury didn't like the statement and privately ridiculed it and briefed the press accordingly.

Late in November 1974, Whitlam established an Economic Council to try and further break the Treasury monopoly on economic advice. The council, chaired by the Prime Minister, included the Governor of the Reserve Bank, Sir John (Jock) Phillips, and Bill Hayden, the Social Security Minister. It had few meetings and no staff but was indicative of the scepticism about Treasury's performance and its advice.

Early in 1975, I was asked by the Prime Minister whether I was willing to become Head of Treasury, perhaps a sign of how desperate he was with Treasury's performance. He was encouraged by Sir Lenox Hewitt, a former senior Treasury officer. I said 'Thanks, but no thanks'. Whitlam then asked me about moving Hewitt to Treasury. I advised against that also.

Whitlam never really had confidence in Treasury from 1974 on. On a personal level he was particularly irritated that Wheeler would bring a large team of Treasury officers with him for meetings: the 'Wheeler caravan'. Wasn't he confident enough to come on his own? Was he under pressure from John Stone, one of the deputies? Why did they always hunt in packs? This suspicion of Treasury laid the basis for the mistakes that occurred on loan raisings when Treasury advice was ignored. They had been unprofessional and disloyal and wouldn't be listened to. There was disaster ahead.

On top of the external economic shocks and Treasury disloyalty, there were serious problems within the Government, with 27 ministers all members of Cabinet and many running their own races. Having been in opposition for 23 years, many ministers were unfamiliar with the bureaucratic machine or, worse, intensely suspicious of it. Some ministers had been captured by their departments. They projected departmental interests at the expense of the Government as a whole. The Government as a single entity was always under threat, particularly by the determination of some ministers to appeal to Caucus if they lost their argument in Cabinet. The competing interests and loyalties within the Government were not well managed. None of the ministers had been in a federal government before and only two, Fred Daly and Kim Beazley senior, had been backbenchers in Labor governments in the 1940s.

Whitlam was brilliant as Prime Minister but not so much at ease leading a team, something I had learned as his chief of staff in a small office in Opposition. In three years he had three Treasurers and three Deputy Leaders and reshuffled his Cabinet four times. Seldom was political strategy discussed in Cabinet. It was submission after submission, most of them promoted by public servants who, not surprisingly, did not know what the political strategy was. Graham Freudenberg rather tenderly described the reactions of some staffers to the Government's problems: 'we were rather given to tears in the Whitlam Government'.

One thing I learned above everything else working with Whitlam in the Department of Prime Minister and Cabinet was that execution of policy was just as important as, if not more important than policy itself. Wise and effective execution must go hand in hand with good policy. Whitlam was a remarkable policy innovator, but the means to execute policy were often an afterthought.

In April 1975, we established new Cabinet procedures or reinforced old ones to improve coordination. The Prime Minister directed that Cabinet submissions had to be lodged seven days before they would be considered for inclusion on the Cabinet agenda. This would provide opportunities for better reflection and judgment of policies coming forward from ministers. Under these new arrangements, ministers had to spell out the financial implications of policies. There also had to be in the submission an indication of how the proposals related to the ALP platform that Whitlam had largely written. These new Cabinet procedures, which now seem so trite and obvious, provided better prime ministerial oversight and direction.

The Prime Minister agreed that every morning before question time there would be departmental officers, together with his private staff, to brief him. I initially attended those meetings but increasingly I left it to Geoff Yeend, my deputy, who had a very good political and policy touch. Whitlam had initially been sceptical about Yeend because of his earlier close associations with Menzies in the Petrov Affair. Whitlam found, as I did, that Yeend was very professional and trustworthy. Brian Johns, whom I appointed to PM&C from the *Sydney Morning Herald*, also attended these briefings. He had a good journalist's nose for news. Whitlam was always dominant in the House but this briefing innovation gave him additional support.

On 28 January 1975, we took a major step to start to bring ballooning government expenditure under control. It had increased by 20 per cent in 1974/75. Whitlam established the Cabinet Expenditure Review Committee. By the following year the Government expenditure increase had been reduced to five per cent It took many budgets to bring expenditure under control and the process is still continuing. But the new committee did provide a means for more effective oversight of spending by ministers. I had discussed it with Wheeler from Treasury. Wherever possible I was trying to include Treasury in the process rather than have it on the outside and potentially disloyal.

I saw the curbing of expenditure increases as probably my most important contribution. I have always believed and still do that the community would and should support higher taxes to help people in need, provided the expenditure is carefully targeted and spent. So many of the Government's spending programs were worthwhile. After years of neglect they were improving the life of many Australians. Whitlam was the greatest social reformer in Australian history and the last Australian prime minister to seriously pursue full employment. The problem was that too much was being attempted too quickly. So much was being lost by an inability to slow down, consolidate and communicate effectively.

On arrival in Canberra I had learned at first hand what I suspected: minerals and energy exploration and development was practically a 'no go' area for the Prime Minister and most of the Government. It was the exclusive domain of the Minister, Rex Connor, and the Head of the Department, Sir Lenox Hewitt. Connor was from Wollongong, an Australian nationalist par excellence, suspicious of foreigners and with a great love of the mining industry. He spoke about coal with knowledge and passion. A great resource was being plundered by the Japanese.

He was a burly and physically intimidating man, nicknamed 'the strangler' from his rough and tumble days in New South Wales ALP politics. Like Whitlam he was a loner. Hewitt gave Connor unswerving support. He intensified Connor's suspicions. Hewitt told me when I went to visit him after I became Head of PM&C, 'I won't allow interdepartmental committees to get their fingers into this department'. It was a very clear warning to keep out of his department's territory, but at least I knew where I stood.

There was a serious impediment to resource development. I made no secret of my view. Importers and investors in Europe, Japan and North America were confused about Australia's policy and intentions. Projects were dying on the vine.

To get around the logjam, Whitlam agreed to my proposal in August 1975 that there should be a Resources Committee of Cabinet. It consisted of Whitlam, Connor, Hayden, as well as public servants such as Wheeler, Hewitt and myself. I chaired the Officials Committee to advise ministers. The Connor-Hewitt axis was being outflanked. As a result, the Government did start to get important resources developments under way. The new crude oil pricing policy provided encouragement for explorers and developers. The foreign investment guidelines were liberalised to get dormant mining projects started. New coal projects in Queensland received the green light. It all flagged to the business community that, on terms which advanced Australia's interests, resource projects would go ahead.

With others, I also persuaded Whitlam that Hewitt should be offered another job. Whitlam was never willing to take on Connor. It was easier to move Hewitt. Ministers decided that Hewitt should be appointed chairman of Qantas. Jim Scully became the new Secretary of Minerals and Energy in August 1975.

A more hazardous change to improve the Government's performance and standing, which I strongly supported, was the replacement of Clyde Cameron by Jim McClelland as Minister for Labour and Immigration in June 1975. The ACTU agreed. While Whitlam paid a heavy price in earning the undying hostility of Cameron, even to this day almost 25 years later, it was a sensible decision to move him and start bringing industrial relations back under the Government's collective supervision and to support the Government's economic objectives. Cameron had been allowed very much to run his own race. The economy was suffering from excessive wage demands, partly as a result of the early decisions of Cameron to make the Commonwealth Government a pacesetter in wages and conditions of service. In Clyde Cameron's last year, average weekly earnings increased by a staggering 29 per cent In the next year they were 15 per cent, but still too high.

As with Connor, Whitlam was uneasy and uncomfortable in confronting someone with the political and personal skills of Cameron. Super-confident and extrovert in so many ways, Whitlam was diffident in tackling people. Cameron refused to resign and several ministers spoke privately to him to try and persuade him. The advent of Jim McClelland as the new Minister for Labour and Immigration was a real fillip for the Government even though Cameron's departure was messy.

The greatest turnaround in the public perception of the Government was the replacement of Jim Cairns by Bill Hayden as Treasurer. George Harris, President of the Carlton Football Club and a friend of Phil Lynch, the Shadow Treasurer, had a letter from Treasurer Cairns authorising him to undertake loan raisings. Cairns claimed that he didn't know that he had signed the letter and wrongly denied that the letter offered Harris a commission. He was forced to resign, although, as with other ministers, Whitlam had let him run too much before pulling him into line. Whitlam had also been concerned but took no action about Cairns's relationship with Junie Morosi, his 'office coordinator'. Cairns had declared a 'kind of love' for her.

Hayden's budget in August 1975 was well received. The growth in expenditure was reined in. Medibank was introduced. Personal income tax deductions which benefited high income earners were replaced by a flat rate tax rebate regardless of income. Once again Treasury was needlessly reluctant to cooperate on this reform and the work was done mainly by PM&C staff, particularly Ian Castles and Professor Fred Gruen.

The budget strategy was described by Hayden as 'a line along which we can achieve sound, substantial and sustainable growth which at the same time will bring inflation down gradually over perhaps two or three years'. There were signs of improvement in the economy.

In the second half of 1975, the Government's performance was starting to improve. Hayden brought strength as Treasurer. He had the confidence of Whitlam and he quickly won the support of Treasury. If the Government had been able to hang on until early 1977 when an election was due, I have no doubt that its performance would have continued to improve. It was starting to remedy its problems. That improvement influenced Malcolm Fraser to move early. It is highly unlikely, however, that Whitlam could have won the next election, whenever it was held. But the retreat would have been in good order and would not have been such a rout.

After I had had 12 months in the job Paul Kelly, in the *Australian* of 5 September 1975, described my role.

> John Menadue has been a prime mover in Labor's efforts to curb its own spending, stimulate the private sector, install economic management as Labor's first priority and try to limit the previously unrestricted power of the Minerals and Energy Minister, Mr Rex Connor, and get mining and development projects working again.

A special report in the *Australian* of 18 October 1975 also gave an account of my performance.

> The survival of Menadue's reputation may be due to his short tenure in the job. It was a blatantly political appointment with Sir John Bunting, in many ways the lynch pin of the 'old boys' structure which still survives at the top of the Public Service, being shunted off to London. Given this it is noteworthy how quickly the tremor died down. The reason is that [Menadue] has succeeded at the bureaucratic level where the Government has failed on the political plain. In short he has managed change. His considerable achievements have been made largely within the existing structures and in cooperation with the people who might originally have regarded him as their rival. He knows what he wants to do but if he cannot do it within the system then he won't, is how one colleague described it.

That last sentence told me more about myself than I knew. Staying on side with the system was more ingrained in me than I had realised.

Two years later, in 1977, Michael Sexton in *Illusions of Power* described the way I worked with the system.

> [Menadue did not have] the background of most of Canberra's permanent heads, and the appointment drew the traditional criticism that it aimed to politicise the public service. All of this could have been a severe handicap in dealing with older and

more experienced counterparts in other departments but Menadue had a number of natural advantages. Firstly, he had established a significant reputation in business. Secondly, he had a relationship with Whitlam so close that it assured him the opportunity of carrying out his designs. Thirdly, he was determined to go about his tasks through traditional public service channels. His access to the Prime Minister alone would have guaranteed him respect, even as an outsider, by his public service colleagues who all appreciated just what a unique source of power that was. But the style in which he let it be known he would exercise that power won the co-operation of, and ultimately acceptance by, the mandarins who under other circumstances could have obstructed him almost indefinitely. An important element of this style was, from the beginning, to discourage the use by the government of outside advisers and consultants and, in his own dealings with the Prime Minister, to bypass Whitlam's staff wherever possible.

But cutting the ground from under private staff didn't all go smoothly, as Sexton pointed out,

> The stormy public departure of Whitlam's adviser on Women's Affairs, Elizabeth Reid, in 1975 was a victory, if a rather bloody one, for Menadue in his efforts to have her policy function based entirely in the department, in the newly-established Women's Affairs Section.

I had advised the Prime Minister, in September 1975, to transfer women's affairs activities out of his private office and into the department. Liz Reid did a great job despite the personal attacks on her as the Prime Minister's 'Super Girl' and the trivialisation and distortions in the media about what she was doing. The electorate was only beginning to get used to equal opportunities for women. The same was probably true of me.

My view was that in the long term women's affairs would be more secure in the department than in Whitlam's private office. Prime Ministers and private offices come and go but Prime Minister's Departments stay. It is also easier to influence policy and practices in other departments from the vantage point of the Prime Minister's Department with its strategic and coordinating roles. Whitlam agreed and I wrote and spoke to the Public Service Board, which said that it would approve a branch structure and positions for women's affairs within the department. Both Whitlam and I spoke to Liz Reid about what was planned and informed her that she would have a job within the department. I told her that Public Service positions would have to be advertised and that she would have to take her chance in competition with others for any career position. I said, however, that I was confident that I could find a way of employing her as a consultant if a career position was not possible.

We had a small women's affairs section within the department, with Sarah Dowse in charge. I spoke to her about the proposed changes. She went away and came back in a couple of hours and said that the women's section was opposed to Liz Reid joining the department. I asked Sarah why, but was not persuaded by her answer. I then had to go to Liz Reid and explain that there were difficulties. She was very upset and let fly publicly at both Whitlam and me for dudding her, saying that it was an attempt to silence her. The transfer of the women's function to the department proceeded and the Women's Affairs Branch was established. Some of the sisterhood was not impressed with what I had done and sent a lot of male chauvinist pig cards through the post.

Later, in 1976, Sarah Dowse and I advised Prime Minister Fraser to make the Women's Affairs Branch the nucleus of a network of women's policy units to be established in other departments. In 1976 a Minister Assisting the Prime Minister on Women's Affairs was appointed. In 1977 the Women's Affairs Branch was upgraded and renamed the Office of Women's Affairs. At the end of 1977 the office was moved to the Department of Home Affairs. In 1982 it was renamed the Office of the Status of Women and returned the following year to PM&C, where it has remained. In 1975 the new government machinery arrangements on women's affairs did not proceed as smoothly as I had hoped but they were long lasting.

Overall I was impressed in PM&C and later in other departments with the professionalism and honesty of middle and senior officials. Having worked in both the public and private sectors in my career, I found public officials much smarter in marshalling information, analysis and recommending action. Their intellectual horsepower was impressive. I found them, however, much more risk-averse than their private counterparts, both as to career choices for themselves and what they would recommend. A predictable career path in the remote and privileged Canberra environment does not lend itself to risk taking.

One issue on which I devoted a great deal of time in the Whitlam Government and, as it turned out, with very little success, was in trying to improve relations with the states. Whitlam was a centralist in unremitting struggle with the states, Labor as well as non-Labor, particularly over Section 96 specific purpose grants. These grants to the states were the new vehicle for the Whitlam Government's activity in fields from education to health, transport, cities and the arts. On Whitlam's staff in opposition I had devoted enormous time to developing the programs. Between 1972/73 and 1975/76, general purpose grants to the states declined from 6.0 per cent of GDP to 5.8 per cent. But specific purpose grants increased from 2.1 per cent to 5.4 per cent of GDP. This assertion of national priorities through specific purpose grants was anathema to the states. They were an intrusion into their affairs. They wanted the money but without conditions. In those three years, commonwealth payments to local government also trebled. The states were under attack from two sides: commonwealth and local governments. Given that the media generally reflect state, even capital city interests rather than national interests, we were under an incessant barrage in the execution of the new policy.

In the South Australian election in July 1975, Don Dunstan, after discussion with Whitlam, publicly disowned his association with the Whitlam Government. Whitlam didn't enjoy it but he accepted that Dunstan had no alternative. Dunstan survived the election. The relations with Joh Bjelke-Petersen in Queensland were the worst of all, despite the fact that Whitlam's standing there ten years before had been so high that it had saved him from expulsion from the ALP. But he didn't lose his sense of humour. He was invited to meet the teams at a World Cup Rugby League match in Brisbane. He went out to do the kick-off and was booed from one end of Lang Park to the other. He turned to Ron McAuliffe, who was a Labor senator and a very popular president of the Queensland Rugby League, and chided him: 'Don't you ever bring me here again if you are as unpopular as this'.

Brian Johns headed the division in charge of State Government relations to try to improve relations with the states. But with Whitlam's views about premiers and the states we didn't make a great deal of progress in dousing the flames of commonwealth–state hostilities. Whitlam was just so determined and committed in that area. I don't think his policies were wrong but the states won the political battle. My hope has always been to get rid of state governments and distribute their powers to the national government and larger regional authorities. But it is a herculean task.

In February 1975, the Whitlam Government appointed Mr Justice Hope, from the New South Wales Supreme Court, to conduct an inquiry into Australia's intelligence and security activities, particularly the Joint Intelligence Organisation (JIO), the Australian Security Intelligence Organisation (ASIO) and the Australian Security Intelligence Service (ASIS). The Hope Inquiry reflected Whitlam's scepticism about these organisations and a general view of many in the ALP that the intelligence and security services, through the long years of the Cold War and conservative governments, had become politically partisan and were not very competent. Operating in secret, they were not subject to effective review and checks. In the lead-up to the dismissal in 1975, we discovered, for example, that the Australian Defence Department headed by Sir Arthur Tange, an ex-Department of Foreign Affairs Secretary, knew of CIA personnel in Australia who had not been declared to the Department of Foreign Affairs. By custom, undercover agents were identified to the Commonwealth through Foreign Affairs. Tange knew of a CIA agent, Richard Stallings, but had not identified him to Foreign Affairs. The Prime Minister knew nothing of Stallings either.

The Hope Inquiry resulted in the removal of the Director-General of ASIO, Peter Barbour. In its exaggerated concerns about the security of Australia, ASIO had been careless about threats to its own security. I suggested that Barbour be replaced by Mr Justice Xavier Connor. He was approached but declined. Mr Justice Woodward got the appointment. Whitlam liked appointing judges.

Whitlam's wariness about intelligence and security operations went back to his days as Deputy Leader of the Opposition. On the instruction of Prime Minister Menzies and with the connivance of Arthur Calwell, he was refused briefings on ASIS and the Defence Signals Department. Whitlam had learnt about them from Tun Abdul Razak, the Prime Minister of Malaysia, during visits we made in the early 1960s, including visits to Razak's home. The refusal of briefings reflected the paranoia of the Cold War and the view by the intelligence community that the ALP was not to be trusted. Calwell had his own reasons to keep his ambitious young deputy in the dark.

My experience with people in the intelligence and security community over twenty years taught me to be very cautious. They seriously deceived me twice without any apology or seeming regret. Deception of friend as well as foe was all in the game. I found many of them brittle and not all that smart or well balanced. They are, however, adept in doling out juicy bits of information that are often untested but draw one into the inner circle of people with privileged information, a twilight world of secrets and gossip. Perhaps we all read too many spy thrillers and vicariously want to be part of the action. Few are immune.

Very few things during Whitlam's prime ministership, however, attracted as much criticism as his overseas travel. He loved travel. The trips were never junkets; they recharged his spirits and refreshed his mind. It is not at all surprising that in retirement he and Margaret would lead overseas tours. For a visit to India and Pakistan, the department suggested that Allan Cooley be included. Whitlam queried, 'Why would you include the Chairman of the Public Service Board on a visit to the Indian subcontinent?' It was explained that it was an opportunity for a senior public servant like Allan Cooley to get to know the Prime Minister. He mused and then agreed. 'I guess when you go to India you should always take a coolie.'

The most celebrated overseas visit was at the end of 1974, when Whitlam spent 30 days visiting 13 countries. As the new Secretary of the Department, I decided I should stay in Canberra. I even thought by declining to go, I would discourage Whitlam's travel, setting an example. It had no effect whatsoever.

The Darwin cyclone hit on Christmas Eve. Whitlam was, as the newspapers described it, surveying the ruins of the Mediterranean when he should have been surveying the ruins of Darwin. Actually on Christmas Eve he was listening to Christmas carols in King's College, Cambridge.

On Christmas Day 1974, I went with Jim Cairns to Darwin. He was the acting Prime Minister. We got into Darwin at about 1.00 in the afternoon. It shocked me before we landed to see the awful power of nature. Galvanised-iron roofing sheets were strewn all over or wrapped around telegraph poles like crumpled silver foil.

From England, Whitlam spoke to Cairns and me about whether he should return from overseas. The emphatic and unanimous advice of everyone he spoke to was that he should come back urgently. I awaited his arrival in Alice Springs on 28 December, by RAAF plane from Perth. At the Alice Springs airport he received a very hostile response. It shook him. The extent of the animosity at his being overseas when Darwin was shattered was palpable. The next day we went up to Darwin. Brigadier Stretton was in charge of the restoration and did a very good job, although he was frustrated by the many Federal ministers who came to Darwin making decisions in their own portfolio areas. Stretton complained and I recall Whitlam saying to him, 'Well, they give me the shits as well. Do what you have to do. If you have any problems give me a ring and I will fix it'. The evacuation and the restoration of Darwin went very well. Towards the end of the emergency Stretton wanted a ceremony to hand back his authority. I consulted the Attorney-General's Department which advised me that there was no authority to hand back. People cooperated because of the emergency and Stretton did not hold any emergency powers at all.

After Darwin we came back to Sydney for Cabinet meetings at Kirribilli House. Decisions were made for the restoration of Darwin and Sir Leslie Thiess was appointed to head the restoration effort. He was followed by Clem Jones, who had been Lord Mayor of Brisbane for 14 years. But Whitlam was determined to resume his overseas trip. Many of his ministerial colleagues and friends urged him to stay home. When I tried to persuade him he was relaxing on a plastic li-lo beside the swimming pool at Kirribilli, annotating his Hansards. I suggested to him that he stay in Australia; that as it was a holiday period he could stay at Kirribilli quietly and relax. 'But stay in the country.' I could see that I wasn't impressing him, so foolishly I pressed my argument several times. He sat up, looked me in the eye and said, 'Comrade, if I am going to put up with the fuckwits in the Labor Party I have got to have my trips'. Off he went to resume his trip. It did confirm to a lot of people the self-indulgence of the Government. Over twenty years later I came more to appreciate his view. The ALP and so much of domestic public life was suffocating and parochial. Outside reference points and experiences are invigorating.

My work in the department was to try to improve the Government's domestic performance. I spent little time on foreign affairs. But relations with Indonesia and the impending American defeat in Vietnam were never far away.

In the Department of Prime Minister and Cabinet, we were only marginally involved in the Indonesian military build-up and subsequent takeover of East Timor. Whitlam worked almost exclusively to the Department of Foreign Affairs on the subject, or more particularly to some people in that department.

The future of Portuguese rule in East Timor was discussed when Whitlam and Soeharto met at Townsville in April 1975. I was not present but I was briefed later. There was not the slightest suggestion then, to my knowledge, that the Australian Government encouraged the Indonesian takeover of East Timor. The Australian position was consistent. East Timor should have self-determination and that Portugal should facilitate it. That position, however, was brought undone by the Portuguese military fleeing East Timor in August 1975 and leaving their arms to Fretilin. It was hardly the act of a responsible colonial power. Instability ensued.

Whitlam was also certain that the United States would not lift a finger to oppose Indonesian actions, just as it had not opposed the Indonesian incorporation of Dutch New Guinea in 1963. The US would not put Australia's interests or concerns ahead of its relations with Indonesia. Whitlam was adamant that in any dispute with Indonesia, Australia would be on its own. The US would side with or turn a blind eye to Indonesian actions. On 6 December 1975, a week before a change of government in Australia and against a background of media speculation and diplomatic cable traffic that an imminent Indonesian invasion of East Timor was likely, President Gerald Ford and Secretary of State Kissinger were in Jakarta. The next day Indonesian forces landed at Dili. It would be difficult for the US to make its encouragement of Indonesia any clearer.

The Whitlam Government was correct in its assessment of the *Realpolitik* of the Indonesian takeover. It showed, however, little concern for the victims, the East Timorese people. Their plight was not sympathetically considered.

With the fall of Saigon, I was also distressed by the Government's reluctance to help orphans in Saigon who had been fathered by servicemen. Whitlam was influenced by experience with refugees from the Baltic States. They had come to Australia and represented a hard core of bitter opposition to the Labor Party. He anticipated that another group of refugees from communism would do the same. In the end he was reluctantly persuaded and a couple of B747s went to Saigon. Bill Morrison went on the aircraft and several hundred orphans were evacuated to Australia. The refugees from Indo-China are not anti-Labor as Whitlam had feared.

For me the treatment of East Timorese and Vietnamese refugees was a low point in the Whitlam Government. The Fraser Government retrieved the situation on the Vietnamese refugees, but the harshness towards East Timorese asylum seekers is still with us over 20 years later.

While the Government obviously contributed to its own problems, there was also a spiteful conservatism in the country that would not accept the Whitlam Government. One of the great successes of the Hawke Government, eight years later, was that it did demonstrate that a Labor government was a legitimate force in Australian political life and must be accepted as such.

After 23 years in government, many conservatives would not accept that they had been fairly beaten by Whitlam in 1972 and 1974. The petulance of some, particularly senior shadow ministers in the Country Party, was like that of small children who had lost their toys.

The reaction to the appointment of Attorney-General Lionel Murphy to the High Court was an illustration of the different standards that were applied in public life. Four Attorneys-General had been appointed to the High Court before: Isaacs, Higgins, Latham and, more recently, Garfield Barwick, a 'capital "C" conservative'. But, whereas a Barwick appointment was regarded as proper, the Murphy appointment was roundly attacked as improper. Barwick, who was Chief Justice, was caught up in the anti-Murphy campaign.

The Secretary of the Attorney-General's Department at the time, Clarrie Harders, described Barwick's attitude to me:

> Attorney-General's Department believe that the appointment of Senator Murphy to the High Court was a very significant factor in turning Sir Garfield Barwick against the Labor Government. He had expressed concern before about Senator Murphy in his

position as Attorney-General, but apparently became
particularly upset about the appointment to the High Court …
He had reacted so unfavourably that he was unlikely to give any
judgement in favour of the Labor Government, unless he had
publicly expressed a contrary view beforehand on the issue.
According to Attorney-General's, Sir Garfield Barwick believed
that the reign of the Labor Government should be brought to
an end as quickly as possible. Sir Garfield had hoped that the
Labor Government would have been defeated in May 1974, and
had spoken of the likelihood of Mr Ellicott (his cousin)
becoming Attorney-General in a Liberal Government.

Barwick was waiting for an opportunity, in the High Court or
outside it, to destroy the Government. He didn't have long to wait.

In that hothouse environment of prejudice, gossip and double
standards, it was easier for people of birth, power and money to start
breaking the rules and conventions which had underpinned parliamentary
life in Australia. A social class believed that the accepted rules of political
conduct did not apply to it. Trust was unimportant. With two casual
vacancies in the Senate, conservative premiers in New South Wales and
Queensland broke the convention that new senators should be from the
same party as the outgoing senators. Labor lost two senators as a result.
Without that break of convention, deferral of supply in late 1975 would
not have been possible.

The unwillingness by conservatives to accept the legitimacy of the
Whitlam governments was the reason for the impasse in the Senate
which led to the dismissal on 11 November 1975. It highlighted Gough
Whitlam's worst appointment: Sir John Kerr as Governor-General.

A job on the line
John Kerr's or
Gough Whitlam's?

*'I think a Governor-General should never be worried about
the security of his job. I think that is always on the line and I think
John Kerr was not prepared to put it on the line. I think he
intentionally meant to deceive Whitlam' (Sir Roden Cutler,
on 'Four Corners', 6 March 1995)*

T he Government's loan-
raising ventures were to be the pretext for Malcolm Fraser's attempt to
bring the Whitlam Government down. Neither he nor political life in
Australia ever fully recovered. It was the most dangerous undermining
of trust in institutions in my lifetime and it was done by people who
particularly espouse the need for stability and public confidence in
institutions. At a personal level the dismissal was even more tragic: a
Governor-General, the representative of the Head of State, deceiving
his Prime Minister, his constitutional adviser, to save his own job.

The background to this crisis needs to be revisited. Oil prices had
increased dramatically in 1973 and petro-dollars were being lent by oil-
rich Middle Eastern countries from their newfound wealth. Rex Connor,
the Minister for Minerals and Energy, and Lenox Hewitt, his departmental head, were attracted to possible loan raising from the Middle
East for two reasons.

The first was that the Government's major social programs didn't
leave funds for large national resource projects. Connor and Hewitt were
looking for alternative ways of funding such projects. They were also
looking for ways that didn't forfeit Australian ownership and control;
they were interested in loans rather than equity.

Connor had a vision of a major gas pipeline grid linking gas fields and particularly the North West Shelf to consumers across Australia. Twenty years later, that pipeline grid is near completion but its development took a very different path to the one Connor envisaged. Connor had many other 'big ticket' projects in mind for use of the funds: petrochemical plants, uranium mines and milling plants, railway electrification, coal hydrogenation and coal export. Connor always thought big.

The second reason was that neither Connor nor Hewitt trusted Treasury, which had administrative responsibility for loan raisings and was very jealous of its turf. Money had to be found that Treasury couldn't get its hands on. In July 1975, Whitlam complained to me, 'We are the victims of a power struggle between Wheeler [the Secretary of Treasury] and Hewitt'.

Through Clyde Cameron, Connor met a Pakistani middleman, Tirath Khemlani, in October 1974. Khemlani claimed that he could raise large loans in the Middle East. Cameron approached Connor because he thought the proposal was more saleable to Connor than Whitlam.

The first proposal I heard of for a substantial, 'unorthodox' loan raising was to be through the Atomic Energy Commission (AEC) of which Hewitt was chairman. It became clear, however, that such a borrowing would not be within the powers of the AEC. Hewitt then approached Sir Roland Wilson, who was chairman of the Commonwealth Bank Board. Wilson was quite close to Hewitt, as both were former senior officers in Treasury. Hewitt had hoped to succeed Wilson as Secretary of Treasury. The Commonwealth Bank would do the borrowing and then on-lend to the Commonwealth Government for projects. But in the end the Commonwealth Bank also decided that it was not appropriate to do so, though Wilson was supportive. That he believed it was worth a try influenced me more than anyone else. Perhaps I attributed to him more support for the proposal than I should have.

Throughout all these discussions, the Department of Minerals and Energy was being advised by merchant bankers, Darling and Company. With the failed attempts through the AEC and the Commonwealth Bank, senior ministers decided that the Government should consider borrowing directly on its own authority and were interested in what Khemlani might have to offer.

From 6 December to the fateful Executive Council meeting on 13

December 1974, there were at least five meetings to discuss a loan raising through Khemlani. Those meetings variously included Whitlam, Connor, Cairns (Treasurer), Murphy (Attorney-General) and senior public servants Fred Wheeler and John Stone from Treasury, Lenox Hewitt from Minerals and Energy, Clarrie Harders and Dennis Rose from Attorney-General's, as well as the Solicitor-General, Maurice Byers. I attended most of the meetings. It was not until the fourth meeting that Treasury was included at my suggestion. Whitlam feared, correctly, that Treasury would not keep the matter confidential.

An Executive Council meeting was held on the evening of 13 December, at the Lodge, where there was also a meeting of the Federal Executive of the ALP. Under Section 62 of the Australian Constitution, 'there shall be a Federal Executive Council to advise the Governor-General in the Government of the Commonwealth ...' It gives legal force to government decisions, appointments and similar matters. By convention, only members of the current government attend meetings of the Executive Council.

It was a hectic and confused night. Whitlam and Cairns ducked back and forth between the ALP meeting and the Executive Council meeting. Whitlam was also under additional pressure as he was leaving next day on a 30-day overseas tour. His party included Hewitt and Harders. Cairns would be the acting Prime Minister. He had been Treasurer only two days.

I was a new boy on the block, only three months into the job. I wasn't as alert as I should have been to the risks the Government might be running.

After much discussion and many drafting changes, an Executive Minute was signed by four Ministers: Whitlam, Cairns, Connor and Murphy. It authorised Connor 'to borrow for temporary purposes $US4 billion and to determine the terms and conditions for borrowing'. Connor could in turn authorise other people in writing to borrow the funds on behalf of the Australian Government. The explanatory memorandum attached to the minute which explains the purpose of the proposal said:

> The Australian Government needs immediate access to substantial sums of non-equity capital from abroad for temporary purposes, amongst other things to deal with exigencies arising out of the current world situation and

international energy crisis, to strengthen Australia's external financial position, to provide immediate protection for Australia in regard to supplies of minerals and energy and to deal with current and immediately foreseeable unemployment in Australia.

It was envisaged that the loan would be for 20 years.

The strong oral advice of Attorney-General Lionel Murphy was that the Commonwealth Government could borrow the funds for 'temporary purposes' under the terms of the Constitution. There was a major world crisis in energy, with large increases in oil prices, and Australia needed to make provision to protect its interests through the development of its own mineral resources. The loan was for 'temporary purposes' to avoid taking the matter to the Loan Council. Murphy said it was important to distinguish between temporary loans and loans for temporary purposes. Loans to achieve a temporary purpose, such as the short-term problem brought about by the increase in oil price, need not be temporary or short-term loans.

The advice of Solicitor-General Byers was that a loan for 'temporary purposes' was 'arguable'. I interpreted this to mean that the Commonwealth had a good case. He subsequently interpreted to the Attorney-General's Department that what he meant was that at least he could argue the case before the High Court Bench sat him down. Whether the bench would sit him down after one minute or one day would be a matter of debate. But certainly on the advice of the two senior law officers of the Commonwealth, Murphy and Byers, it was believed that the borrowing was legal and would probably be sustained in the High Court. In any event it is common practice for governments to test the bounds of constitutional power. Prime Minister Whitlam thought the 'temporary purposes' argument was drawing a 'long bow' but was persuaded by Murphy and Byers that it was worth a try.

Subsequently, as I described in my personal note of 11 December 1975, the Governor-General 'expressed to me his concern about the legal advice tendered by the Attorney-General and the Solicitor-General' that night. I will return to that later.

In explanation I should mention that in the period from the dismissal on 11 November and before the election on 13 December, I made detailed personal notes on the events leading to the dismissal. There was time to recall and reflect on the momentous events that had happened and while they were still fresh in my mind. One day I might want to tell my own story! I quote from those notes, dated 11 December 1975, quite extensively in the following pages.

In addition to the legal advice from the Attorney-General and Solicitor-General, there was also a political view that if the borrowing and developmental projects went ahead, no one would quibble about constitutional niceties. If the Snowy scheme could be built under the defence power of the Constitution, why couldn't loans be raised for major energy projects? And if the states received some of the money, they wouldn't challenge anyhow.

But the Government's reach exceeded its grasp.

Whitlam attempted to ring the Governor-General to say that an Executive Council meeting was proposed that night but John Kerr was in Sydney at the ballet viewing *Romeo and Juliet*, so he didn't know about the meeting. There are numerous precedents for Executive Council meetings being held without the Governor-General being present. There were 97 meetings of the Executive Council when Sir John Kerr was Governor-General and Mr Whitlam was Prime Minister. Twenty meetings were held in Sir John Kerr's absence. In his absence, 13 of those meetings were presided over by a senior minister (for example, Whitlam, Hayden, Crean); at another seven the Vice-President, Frank Stewart, presided. The Vice-President is appointed by the Governor-General on the advice of the Prime Minister for the specific purpose of presiding at Executive Council meetings when the Governor-General cannot attend. Ministers can also constitute a quorum for Executive Council meeting. If the Governor-General is not present at a meeting the minutes and the schedule from the meeting are subsequently submitted to him for signature. It certainly was always the practice and a matter of courtesy, however, that the Governor-General was informed if a meeting was held in his absence.

So the meeting went ahead with the four key ministers: Whitlam, Cairns, Connor and Murphy. The Executive Council Minute was signed just before midnight authorising Connor to undertake the $US4 billion borrowing. Wheeler argued that Treasurer Cairns should not be authorised to undertake the borrowing. Whitlam was only too pleased to give authority to Connor. He commented to me: 'We've decided to give Rex [Connor] the authority; it won't be Treasury; we can't trust them'.

The next morning the Prime Minister spoke to the Governor-General and briefed him about the Executive Council meeting. According to the Prime Minister, the Governor-General expressed no concern. Subsequently, in discussions which he had with Kerr, Whitlam said that Kerr was quite excited about the prospect of major developments proceeding with the loan raising. Never at any stage did he 'advise and warn' his Prime Minister about either the processes of the Executive Council meeting or its substance.

The Executive Committee Minute was taken to Admiralty House by the Secretary of the Executive Council, an officer from PM&C. The Governor-General duly signed it next morning, 14 December. Without that signature the minute could not be put into effect.

Later the Governor-General cast doubt on the propriety and the processes that were involved in that Executive Council meeting on 13 December. My note of 11 December 1975, written a year after the Executive Council meeting, recalled:

> [the Governor-General] was concerned at the Executive Council decision in the first place and expressed concern to officers and me and I suspect also to Mr Whitlam about the nature of the loan raising and particularly the circumstances in which the first meeting on 13 December 1974, was held.

Whitlam, however, is adamant that any concern Kerr might have expressed about the 13 December 1974 meeting occurred much later and only when pressure was exerted on him by legal and business associates as the momentum for dismissal gathered force. Mr Whitlam's view is consistent with my file note of 11 December 1975:

> I do not think an Executive Council meeting was held in [the Governor General's] absence over the *last three or four months* [my emphasis].

From my own notes and recollections, it is clear to me that Kerr's concern about Executive Council processes came well after December 1974, that is, when the loan raising became a public and political issue.

Whitlam is on the public record that Kerr never raised concerns about the 13 December 1974 meeting with him. In any event the $US4 billion authority was cancelled 25 days later, on 7 January 1975. Another authorisation for $US2 billion was considered on 28 January 1975 by the Executive Council. The Governor-General had notice of the meeting, was present, raised no problems and signed the Executive Council Minute. The authority for that $US2 billion loan raising was revoked on the 20 May 1975.

Treasury was quite right to warn the Government about what it was proposing and the risk of putting itself in the hands of 'funny money' people like Khemlani. But Treasury was ignored. It had lost credibility on a range of matters. In the department I insisted that Treasury be copied in on correspondence. But I have no doubt that the Treasury was the major source of leakages which, in the end, became a torrent. The first question in the Parliament on loan raisings was by the Shadow Treasurer, Phil Lynch, in February 1975.

Day after day I found leakages in the newspapers even before I had a chance to read my incoming memos and briefs. The Opposition was often better briefed than ministers. I spoke to Wheeler about specific leakages that I could trace to a senior officer in Treasury. Wheeler rejected my information. I am certain I was correct.

Two other senior officers in Treasury, known as 'Mr Williams', were the key links from Treasury into Phil Lynch's office and by extension into Malcolm Fraser's office. The Labor Party was paying a heavy price for its estrangement from Treasury. The Government's lack of confidence in Treasury was a reason why it went on this unorthodox loan-raising escapade. It was Treasury that now returned the favour in spades by doing all it could to discredit the Government. The information pouring out of Treasury was extraordinarily damaging to the Government.

Treasury was defending its turf in an international network of government treasuries, central banks, brokers and financial institutions such as the IMF. It was a club, exchanging information and people and supporting the business interests and ideology of one another. Treasury was opposed to loan raisings outside the club. It proved to be most effective in helping bring down the Government.

A loan-raising venture of A$3 billion by Sir William Gunn, in April 1975, received little attention. Gunn was a member of the Reserve Bank Board and chairman of the Wool Board. Whitlam rang me in August 1975 to say that Gunn had been in touch with him from London to say that he could raise A$3 billion from the Saudi royal family. Gunn had enquired whether the Australian Government was interested. Whitlam told me that he had said two things to Gunn. The first was that there would be no consideration of the matter until about ten days time when Hayden, the new Treasurer, and Crean, the Deputy Prime Minister, would be consulted. There was a parliamentary recess at the time. Secondly, the Prime Minister told Gunn that any communication should only be with Sir John Bunting, who was the High Commissioner in London, and with me. The Prime Minister was still determined that Treasury was not to be informed. I conveyed the message to Gunn.

Subsequently Gunn rang me and reiterated that he could raise A$3 billion. He also commented that Khemlani had done a lot of damage to the reputation of Australia. That I could believe. The Melbourne *Sun Pictorial* ran a story on Khemlani, the whiz money man, sleeping on a camp stretcher in a London cellar. I discussed the Gunn matter further with the Prime Minister. I had persuaded him that there was no point continuing to exclude Treasury from the process, and of the damage that could cause. I rang Gunn back advising that any proposal should be put to Treasury and that any contact should be with Wheeler.

I called Wheeler and told him of Gunn's activities. He was appalled that a member of the Reserve Bank Board, part of the Treasury family, was on an escapade like this. Now the matter was with Treasury and communications would be with Wheeler. Bill Hayden was also across the issue. I cabled John Bunting in London and informed him that any further approaches from Gunn were to be referred to Wheeler. Within a few days a message was sent informing Gunn that the Commonwealth Government was not interested.

The Gunn loan-raising venture never received any publicity. It didn't suit Treasury to publicise it. The international financial club, however, did all it could to help the Australian Treasury publicly nail Khemlani and by implication the Australian Government.

There was a great deal of media speculation and questions from February 1975 suggesting that the Government was involved in unorthodox borrowings and inferring that at least some of the four ministers who signed the 13 December Executive Council Minute might be taking illegal commissions. There was nothing that I saw which would give any grounds for that rumour. I was regularly advised on the point by the Attorney-General's Department. One could question the commercial and political wisdom of what was attempted but there was certainly no illegality that I saw.

In the end, with all the hostile comment, Connor was a beaten man. He had a great vision of developing Australian's energy resources without 'selling the farm' to foreigners. He lost his judgment and he was not frank with the Prime Minister, even when he was told to stop his borrowing activities. Whilst the formal loan raising authorities were withdrawn on 20 May, there is no doubt that Connor continued to make unauthorised contact with possible lenders, including Khemlani. It was very sad, Connor sleeping in his office at night hoping that he would get confirmation of a borrowing to demonstrate to all his critics that this wasn't some desert mirage. Night by night his vision of big national projects was crumbling. Bob Sorby, Connor's principal adviser, told me of Connor waiting by his teleprinter night after night for the message that never came.

Clarrie Harders, Secretary of the Attorney-General's Department, and I both expressed concerns to the Prime Minister that there was a lot of correspondence around that Connor had not disclosed despite numerous requests. The responses from Connor were unsatisfactory. I was sent by the Prime Minister to get from him all copies of correspondence, telexes and other information concerning any continuing loan activities after 20 May. Our concern was to protect the Prime Minister and ensure that there could be no possible legal claims against the Australian Government.

On 8 October 1975, I went with the new Treasurer, Hayden, to see Connor at his Canberra home to put before him the evidence of his continuing loan enquiries. He was sick and looked anything but a 'strangler'. His explanations were again unsatisfactory.

Despite a very difficult political situation the Prime Minister decided that Connor had to go. I was instructed to go and see him on 14 October in his office and to ask for his resignation. I said to Whitlam that I didn't really think that was my job, but he told me that I had to go. He was intimidated, as others were, by Connor.

I went downstairs in the old Parliament House and spoke to Connor and told him that we were preparing papers for his resignation. He told me to 'piss off'. I was not surprised. I reported the discussion to the Prime Minister. He then spoke to Connor himself, and he resigned.

The resignation of Connor didn't save the situation. The damage was enormous. It gave Fraser the pretext to move in the Senate. There was a widespread impression that the Government was perhaps racked with corruption and scandal, not just incompetence. The public mood was prepared for Malcolm Fraser to act. He had found his 'extraordinary and reprehensible circumstances'. The next day, 15 October, he announced that the Opposition in the Senate would defer Supply.

There had been speculation a year and a half before, in early 1974, that the Government could have problems with its budget or supply bills. But the Government resolved that problem with a pre-emptive strike, by calling an early election which it won. In 1975 that political option was not on. The Government's standing was low and it would have lost an election, so the Prime Minister chose to fight the Senate for its obstruction and on the convention that governments are made and unmade in the House of Representatives and not in the Senate.

Senator Reg Withers, Leader of the Opposition in the Senate, had developed the tactic not to reject the supply bills but to defer them. Even with the corruption of Senate numbers caused by the breach of convention on the filling of Senate vacancies, the Opposition did not have the numbers to reject the supply bills. Further, some Liberal senators felt easier with deferral rather than rejection. Deferral meant that the bills could then be brought forward for vote at an appropriate time.

The ALP had also contributed to a view about an expanded role for the Senate. Senator Lionel Murphy promoted an increasingly activist Senate, particularly its committees. In Opposition, led by Murphy, the ALP had attempted to block supply on numerous occasions. It would come to rue the day.

In the lead-up to the 1975 budget in August and the debate that followed, there was continuing speculation that the Government might face difficulty in the Senate on its supply bills. It was part of the prevailing view that the Government was illegitimate and wasn't entitled to govern. In 1973–75, more bills were rejected in the Senate (93) than in the first 73 years of Federation (68). With the continual threat of elections, good government was well nigh impossible.

With a possible deferral of supply in prospect even before 15 October, we were involved in the department with advice to the Prime Minister. My note of 11 December 1975 highlights the advice we gave, which with the benefit of hindsight could have stymied the Opposition's plans.

> By being able to restore the Appropriation bills to the Notice Paper almost at will, the Opposition was placed in a position,

they believed, of ensuring Supply to the Governor-General if he had asked. This, incidentally, was a major point which was raised early by Mr Whitlam in discussions with the Attorney-General, Solicitor-General and PM&C. Mr Whitlam asked was it possible in any way to prevent the Opposition in the Senate being able to resurrect the Appropriation Bills and ensure Supply? The final advice which was given to Mr Whitlam on this point was that the only way the House of Representatives could be certain of its position would be to insert clauses in the Appropriation Bills, insisting that the Bills be returned from the Senate to the House of Representatives before they were presented to the Governor-General for assent. The view was expressed by some members of the Government, and particularly Senators James McClelland and John Wheeldon, that this might only provoke the Opposition into refusing Supply. At the time there was still optimism that the Opposition would not proceed with the rejection of Supply and in order to encourage this view it was decided that these clauses in the Appropriation Bills would not be inserted. As it turned out this was the greatest mistake the Government made. If it had been able to deny Supply to a Fraser Government it is most unlikely, in my opinion, that the Governor-General and Mr Fraser would have contemplated the action that was finally taken. The advice from Attorney-General's Department on this question is on file.

Early in the crisis, as my note of 11 December 1975 shows, Whitlam did consider the possibility of the Governor-General dismissing him but,

as time passed he became less concerned with the question. On a couple of occasions I asked him if he had considered the mechanics of contacting the [palace] if he had to move quickly. He merely said that he would have to ring Martin Charteris, (the Queen's Personal Secretary) but believed that this was a hypothetical possibility which he did not consider likely. I suggested early after the Opposition had moved to refuse Supply that perhaps Sir John Bunting [the Australian High Commission in London] should be briefed on the subject and, if necessary, I could go to London for this purpose. He thought that this would be quite unnecessary.

His view was that it was inappropriate to involve the Palace in an Australian dispute. 'It will be resolved politically within Australia', he said.

We suggested that the Prime Minister invite the Governor-General to address the Senate or perhaps both Houses of Parliament, urging the passage of the supply bills. My note of 11 December 1975 referred to

> many suggestions made by the Department about how advice should be given to the Governor-General, including letters to him setting out the Government's position. (See file for copies.) The advice given by Mr Whitlam (to the Governor-General) was oral in the expectation that the Opposition would give way.

The Prime Minister did not believe it was correct to involve the Governor-General in such a political enterprise. In retrospect that might have flushed the Governor-General out, but the Prime Minister was always very conscious of the proper role of the Governor-General and that he should not involve him politically.

Everything that the Governor-General said to Gough Whitlam, Jim McClelland and to Attorney-General Enderby and others, indicated that he was supportive of the Government's position. I put it this way in my 11 December note:

> There is no doubt from the conversations I had with Mr Whitlam, that the Governor-General viewed with disfavour the proposal, or suggestion, that the Opposition would refuse Supply. Mr Whitlam acted on this assumption, I believe, right throughout the crisis that developed. Mr Whitlam said to me that the Governor-General had offered, quite early in the year (I would expect some time in April/May 1975), and later, that he would be prepared to sign Appropriation Bills on the advice of his Ministers, even if they had not been passed by the Senate. Mr Whitlam told the Governor-General that he would not be prepared to advise this course because he was sure that if the Governor-General did sign such Bills a challenge in the High Court was certain, which the Government would lose. This could precipitate a general election, and the Government would

be forced to campaign in an election on what would be widely interpreted as an illegal act. This was an offer made by the Governor-General and was not proposed by Mr Whitlam. I think that this confirmed more than anything else the belief by Mr Whitlam that the Governor-General viewed with considerable concern the proposed course of the Opposition, and that he was willing to take what, on the surface of it, was a very drastic step to resolve the position in favour of the Government with a majority in the Lower House. On several occasions Mr Whitlam referred to the Governor-General as being somewhat indecisive, but overall there was no doubt that Mr Whitlam believed that the Governor-General was sympathetic to his position and the problems with the Senate.

Robert Ellicott, the Shadow Attorney-General, produced an opinion which he widely circulated, on 16 October, that the Governor-General should dismiss the Government. To Prime Minister Whitlam, John Kerr described the opinion as 'bullshit'. In the department we received a colourful briefing from the Prime Minister on what John Kerr thought of Ellicott's opinion.

Later, in discussion with Harders, Kerr tried to backtrack on his 'bullshit' comment, as I recorded in my note of 11 December.

In speaking with Mr Harders (Secretary of Attorney-General's Department) today (December 11) he recalled the discussion which took place when Senator Greenwood, Mr Byers and he called on the Governor-General several days after 11 November. This was at the request of the Governor-General, in view of the leakage of the (ex) Attorney-General's and Solicitor-General's opinion. In the course of discussion the Governor-General raised the question of his earlier comments on Mr Ellicott's opinion. Mr Harders recalled to me that the Governor-General had earlier told him that the Ellicott view was 'bullshit'. (The same phrase was mentioned to me by Mr Whitlam earlier.) In justification on this occasion, and with Senator Greenwood present, the Governor-General said that his comments on Ellicott's opinion had only related to that part of the opinion that suggested that the Governor-General should act quickly or immediately in the situation. The Governor-

General said that he did not reject Ellicott's total view that, in the end, the Governor-General would have to intervene. Mr Harders' view, expressed to me, was that he had no doubt at all, at any time, that the Governor-General rejected Mr Ellicott's view completely and that he was embarrassed at having made the earlier comment, and attempted to justify his action by saying that he was only referring to a part of Mr Ellicott's opinion.

I had quite a number of discussions with the Governor-General in the lead-up to the dismissal, although when the crisis became more critical I deliberately stayed away so that the Governor-General could not get any conflicting signals from me. He should be getting advice directly from his Prime Minister, his principal adviser. So I didn't see the Governor-General, except socially, after 12 September. Supply was deferred on 15 October. My note of 11 December reads:

> In conversation with me, the Governor-General gave the very clear impression that he regarded the course proposed by the Opposition as being quite improper. This arose during discussions I had with him at briefing sessions in the months leading up to the crisis ... The Governor-General's views were expressed mainly in connection with his proposed overseas trip in November and December 1975. There were a considerable number of arrangements to be discussed. I got the impression that the Governor-General did not expect Mr Fraser to adopt the course that was finally taken. He said that Mr Fraser was considerably influenced by the views of Sir Robert Menzies on the role of the Senate and that, as Sir Robert was in fairly regular contact with Mr Fraser, he (the Governor-General) believed it was most unlikely that Mr Fraser would adopt the course that was finally taken. There is no doubt in my mind that the Governor-General believed that the action proposed or suggested by the Opposition was most improper.

Kerr quoted to me, approvingly, that Menzies had said that Fraser was 'wet behind the ears', to try to defer or block supply.

To me the Governor-General always seemed genuinely concerned for the Prime Minister and how he was faring. He certainly never gave any indication that he would be anything but supportive of the Prime Minister.

Several factors influenced John Kerr. He was under pressure from his new wife and from business and professional colleagues to be his own man. He was upset by the constant public statements by the Prime Minister that the Governor-General would do what he was advised by his Prime Minister. That must have wounded his pride. Knowing Kerr's weakness and vanity Whitlam never took the time to massage his ego. Intellectually very bright and active, Kerr was seeking a role for himself. He discussed it with me as my comments in my note of 11 December reveal:

> He was an able, articulate man, still quite young, and did not see himself as a person retiring to Yarralumla. He was seeking to make and find a role for himself. He asked [me] on many occasions what his role should be in speaking engagements and the extent to which he should discuss public issues in a way which, whilst not causing embarrassment to the Government, demonstrated that the Governor-General had a view of his own. He asked my advice on whether he should hold press conferences and how he should respond to press queries. He was also most anxious to travel and to project the role of the Governor-General abroad. I said to him that this did raise problems as he was the Queen's representative in Australia but it might be difficult in some countries to explain, particularly in countries which did not have a British background, what a Queen's representative in Australia was when he was travelling overseas. We discussed these issues at considerable length. In his trips to Asia he had meetings with Prime Ministers and Heads of State. He believed that he could play a useful role. In feeling for this new role for himself he must, in the end, have been affronted by the suggestion by Mr Whitlam that the Governor-General would do as he was told—that he must accept advice from Mr Whitlam and from him only. This must have deeply offended the Governor-General and was quite contrary to the view of the position which Sir John had been trying to develop. Furthermore, it is highly likely that the Governor-General was increasingly embarrassed by what he may have thought was his

complicity with Mr Whitlam in the course that Mr Whitlam was pursuing. He knew that Mr Whitlam took him for granted and expected that he would do as he was told. He may, therefore, have felt that he had to extricate himself from what he regarded as an intolerable personal position. For most Governors-General this would not have arisen, because they did not see the wider role for themselves.

The Prime Minister was very cautious about an expanded role for the Governor-General. The previous Governor-General, Hasluck, was 'Commander in Chief, in and over the Commonwealth of Australia'. Whitlam insisted that Kerr's role and aspirations be more limited. From the beginning of his term on 11 July 1974 he was 'Commander in Chief of the Defence Force of Australia'.

When pressures came from business, legal and media associates, John Kerr was indecisive. My 11 December note reads:

> As for the reason why His Excellency sought the advice of the Chief Justice, I can only suggest that it reflects the indecision of the Governor-General. He was quite clearly seeking reassurance in the course that he was contemplating. In the events leading up to the sacking of the Whitlam Government the Governor-General had spoken to a number of people, asking them their views on the constitutional issues and the likely outcome of the whole controversy. To what extent the Chief Justice may have participated, directly or indirectly, before the Governor-General made up his mind is not clear, although he said that he only consulted the Chief Justice after he had decided on the course of action he would take.

Kerr was particularly concerned that the High Court on 24 June 1975, with reasons given on 30 September 1975, had decided that, in the view of the majority (Barwick, Gibbs, Stephen and Mason), Governor-General Hasluck should not have granted a double dissolution in April 1974, in respect of the Petroleum and Minerals Authority (PMA) Bill. Kerr was very concerned about the implications of the PMA decision in the use of the Crown discretion which would be necessary to dismiss a government. That is why he went and saw Sir Garfield Barwick on 10 November, to make sure that Barwick would be on-side on his proposed action against the Government. He was lobbying the High Court in advance. As we know, Barwick, quite improperly, showed his opinion supporting the proposed dismissal of the Whitlam Government to Justices Stephen and Mason because Kerr was concerned that these other two High Court Justices in two other cases, the Senate (Representation of Territories) Act and the Australian Assistance Plan Act, had moved away from Barwick. Barwick was confident that Gibbs would support him. Barwick had what Kerr lacked. He was tough and single-minded. I found in my discussions that Kerr had enormous respect for Barwick. It is not surprising he wanted to see him for reassurance.

Kerr also directly sought advice and reassurance from Harders, as my note of 11 December indicates:

> On 28 October 1975, the Governor-General had drinks at Government House for participants in a Public Service Board seminar. At this gathering, Sir John apparently raised with Mr Harders the question of the reserve powers of the Governor-General. Mr Harders expressed the view that he did believe that there was reserve power, but it could only be used in the most extreme, extraordinary circumstances. The Governor-General apparently expressed the view that if there was fighting in the streets it might be necessary for him to intervene. Mr Harders passed this to me and I, in turn, mentioned it to Mr Whitlam, whose reaction was that if the Governor-General thought that there would be fighting in the streets over the refusal of Supply, which might force him to act, there would be even more fighting in the streets if he dismissed a Labor Prime Minister.

Pressures on Kerr were also coming from the Murdoch organisation. George Munster in his book about Rupert Murdoch, *Paper Prince*, recalls a visit which Kerr made to Murdoch's home at Cavan, as far back as late 1974. Murdoch knew Kerr reasonably well but they were not close. I recall a News Limited luncheon at which Kerr, the New South Wales Chief Justice at the time, was the guest. Murdoch was impressed by him and privately suggested after the lunch that if he were ten years younger he would be a good editor for the *Australian*.

The account which George Munster gives of that meeting in Cavan in late 1974 is very similar to an account which Ian Fitchett, who was also present, gave to me. Fitchett was political correspondent of the *Sydney Morning Herald* and doyen of the Canberra Press Gallery.

Kerr's first wife had died and he was quite lonely. He had been invited by Murdoch to drop in at Cavan for a drink and perhaps a meal. Murdoch was holding one of his soirees with his editors from around the world. Kerr, over several drinks, embarked on a very detailed and elaborate outline of the various possibilities that the Whitlam Government might face in the future if the Senate blocked or deferred supply.

According to Fitchett and Munster, all the options were laid out in front of Murdoch. There was probably no one in Australia better briefed than Murdoch as to how the Governor-General might act. He was very privileged; the Governor-General never gave his Prime Minister such a briefing. Kerr was very indiscreet. That was a briefing that Murdoch tucked away for future reference, a year later. Just as importantly, Murdoch, who was always a great judge of people's strengths and weaknesses, knew how and when to apply pressure to Kerr.

Murdoch's organisation played a major role in the events leading to the dismissal. The Murdoch papers focused very clearly and directly on Kerr's vulnerabilities as Murdoch knew them. After all, he had had a detailed briefing twelve months before. The headline of 20 October 1975 in the *Australian* was 'Fraser says Kerr must sack Whitlam'. Then there was a three-part editorial series entitled 'Stalemate and Sir John', focusing on Kerr and how he should act. The last in the series was headed 'The decision rests with Kerr'. Murdoch was putting all the heat that he possibly could on Kerr. Feature writers of the *Australian* referred to Kerr as the 'Man in the middle'. Kerr rang Whitlam and objected to the vituperative and the high pressure way that Murdoch was mounting pressure on him through his newspapers. No newspapers focused on Kerr like the papers in the Murdoch organisation. Again I quote from my 11 December note:

> Mr Murdoch used his papers as far as possible to produce (the dismissal) as can be clearly seen in the editorials and news stories leading up to the dismissal. In retrospect, the papers were uncannily correct about predicting the outcome and what the Governor-General should do. It is also true that Mr Murdoch was in direct contact with Mr Fraser for many weeks before 11 November. This was admitted in the House of Representatives

and I am aware of it from other quarters as well. The fact is that Mr Murdoch cannot keep off the telephone and has a great desire—almost a compulsion—to talk to politicians, and particularly people in power.

I had kept in touch with Rupert Murdoch but we had gradually drifted apart. However, I did have lunch with him and Ken Cowley on 7 November 1975, in Canberra at a Kingston restaurant. I had a few words to say about the coverage of the *Australian* and the News group in the crisis. There were stoppages by journalists at News Limited for the partisan way in which Murdoch was using his papers. Labor had been a beneficiary in 1972. A price would now be exacted. I told him I had cancelled my subscription to the *Australian*. That didn't put him off his lunch.

In my record of 11 December about that lunch with Murdoch five weeks earlier I wrote:

> Rupert Murdoch told many of his friends that Mr Fraser had informed him that the Governor-General had given him [Fraser] an assurance that if he hung on long enough there would be a general election before Christmas … although I have no direct information. He did tell me, however, on 7 November that he was quite certain there would be an election before Christmas, and an election specifically for the House of Representatives. I suggested to him that a half Senate election was the only possibility. He rejected this view and said that he believed that there would certainly be a House of Representatives election before Christmas, and that he would be staying in Australia until this occurred. He was very confident of the outcome of any election, and even mentioned to me the position to which I might be appointed in the event of the Liberal victory— Ambassador to Japan.

Murdoch denies my account of our lunch. I stand by it. Murdoch was intimately involved with Fraser in the dismissal. His whole record shows that he can't help himself in such events. I had seen it at first hand three years earlier in the 1972 election. It is like an addiction.

Murdoch knew Kerr's feeling of insecurity. That insecurity was reflected in Kerr's concern about his own possible dismissal, shown particularly in his agitation over the Queen's termination of Governor Hannah's 'dormant commission'.

The practice is that the senior State Governor holds a 'dormant commission' and becomes the Administrator of the Commonwealth in the absence of the Governor-General. Colin Hannah from Queensland was the senior State Governor. He had made a speech at a long lunch in Queensland on 15 October which was extremely hostile to the Whitlam Government. He had caught the Bjelke-Petersen infection as many in Queensland had. Whitlam decided immediately that Hannah's dormant commission should be withdrawn so that he could not become the Administrator in the Governor-General's absence. At Whitlam's direction we drafted a letter in the department for the Prime Minister to sign to go to Buckingham Palace via Sir John Kerr, terminating Hannah's dormant commission. Kerr received the letter but decided that the letter should go direct from the Prime Minister to Buckingham Palace. It was sent on 17 October. Hannah's dormant commission was terminated on 26 October. That action put Kerr on notice that if he misbehaved, a similar fate might befall him. The mechanics and time delay in Whitlam sacking Kerr in a crisis made it a most unlikely possibility. It may not have been in Whitlam's mind but it was certainly preying on Kerr's mind, as the following clearly shows.

In Paul Kelly's *November 1975*, Senator John Wheeldon, a Whitlam minister, is quoted as saying, 'After the dismissal I said to Kerr, "Why didn't you talk to your ministers? You could have told us that unless the ministry obtained supply that you might have to dismiss us". But Kerr said to me, "If I'd done that Whitlam would have sacked me".' Precisely.

Kenneth Gee, an old friend of John Kerr's, recalled on 'Four Corners' on 6 November 1995 that at a dinner at Government House for Tun Abdul Razak, the Malaysian Prime Minister, on 16 October 1975, 'Gough Whitlam said in a joking but not very sensitive way, "It could be a race between me getting to the Queen to get you dismissed and you terminating my commission as Prime Minister". Everybody laughed. Kerr saw the danger to him'. Roden Cutler, who was Governor of New South Wales and held the dormant commission to be Administrator in the absence of the Governor-General after Hannah was terminated, recalled on the same program that at an Admiralty House dinner during the crisis on 26 October 1975, 'I said that he, Kerr, should talk to Whitlam. That after all is the requirement. Kerr had not discussed it with Whitlam.

He had made it fairly clear he didn't want to. I said, "Well John, of course the PM could move beforehand to have your commission withdrawn". He became quite animated and said, "Yes, I know, I know!" Cutler added, 'I think the Governor-General should never be worried about the security of his job. I think that is always on the line and I think John Kerr was not prepared to put it on the line.'

On 4 November 1975, when presenting the Melbourne Cup, the Governor-General said, 'The horse is the same, the jockey is the same and, thank goodness, the Governor-General is the same'.

During the supply crisis, Kerr's office contacted Buckingham Palace to find out the procedure for a Prime Minister to dismiss a Governor-General. That he was afraid of dismissal could mean only one thing: he was considering acting against the only person who could dismiss him, his Prime Minister. The evidence is overwhelming that he was obsessed about losing his job. As Paul Kelly put it: 'In power terms Kerr had decided to dismiss Whitlam before Whitlam had a chance to dismiss him. It was that elemental, that primitive. But Kerr sought a loftier motive than merely saving his own job. His justification was to preserve the reputation and importance of the Crown'.

Most importantly, he conveyed his fear of dismissal to Fraser. It was conveyed at their first meeting on 21 October at Yarralumla. Kerr gave Fraser the vital clue and the encouragement that he needed.

In *The Unmaking of Gough*, Paul Kelly commented that after that 21 October meeting 'The Opposition changed its public stand … Fraser announced (on 22 October) that "The Opposition Parties will abide by any decision reached by the Governor-General"'. Kelly, in *November 1975*, highlights the significance of that 21 October meeting: 'From the time Fraser left that meeting he never wavered in his belief that Kerr would intervene, finally, on the Opposition's behalf if Whitlam refused to call a general election'.

I had two discussions with Malcolm Fraser, which taken together were very significant in confirming a clear impression that he had got from the Governor-General on 21 October that Kerr was fearful of dismissal by Whitlam. The first was at a dinner at Government House for Princess Margaret on 22 October 1975, the day after the critical first Kerr-Fraser meeting. My note of 11 December 1975 reads:

Almost at the conclusion of the evening he—Fraser—drew me

aside and said that he was concerned about the Governor-General and steps should be taken to 'protect' him. I interpreted this to mean that, with the political temperature rising, extra security should be ensured for all public figures, including the Governor-General. Mr Fraser said, however, that that was not what he was referring too. He felt that the Governor-General would be under enormous pressure in the coming weeks and that special action and attention must be given to ensuring that his Excellency should be fully protected in the exposed position in which he could be placed.

With the benefit of hindsight, I now take that to mean that Fraser believed that Kerr was in fear of dismissal. Further confirmation that Kerr had revealed to Fraser his insecurity was given to me by Fraser in a discussion on 28 January 1976. My file note reads:

> Governor-General encouragement to the Opposition. On 28 January this year—1976—Mr Fraser said—on the street outside West Block—that on his first meeting with the Governor-General during the Supply crisis—21 October—the Governor-General had said that he could not give Mr Whitlam any inkling of what he had in mind or Mr Whitlam would be immediately on the telephone to London seeking the Governor-General's dismissal.

Malcolm Fraser has denied saying this to me as reported by Paul Kelly in *November 1975*. Kelly reported, 'When I asked Fraser about Menadue's account of his note he insisted that he (Menadue) was wrong. Fraser says that during the crisis he was aware that Kerr felt his position was at risk from Whitlam but Fraser is adamant that Kerr did not act improperly by saying this to him during their talks'. I stand by my account.

Kerr in effect was saying to Fraser that he could not discuss the options with Whitlam or he would be sacked. It was a critical clue.

Fraser came back to this issue of the Governor-General's insecurity in an article in the *Australian* on 25 October 1995, which was about Kerr's fear of dismissal. 'While it will certainly be disputed, I have no doubt that if he—Sir John Kerr—had attempted to have such discussions with Mr Whitlam and his colleagues, he would have been sacked.' Precisely. He had no doubts because Kerr had given him the nod.

The withdrawal of Governor Hannah's dormant commission made Kerr doubly alert that he had to withhold any clues from Whitlam of what he might do. In short, he had to deceive his Prime Minister to save his own job.

I am not here suggesting that Kerr told Fraser on 21 October, or subsequently, what he was going to do, but Kerr indicated or inferred to Fraser that what he had in mind could result in his own dismissal. That was very significant encouragement for the Leader of the Opposition. He didn't need to spell out the details. Kerr was afraid of dismissal by Whitlam and Fraser knew it.

Certain of Kerr's obsession about Whitlam dismissing him, Fraser put on the pressure even more. According to Paul Kelly, on 6 November, in what Fraser described as his 'most important meeting with the Governor-General', Fraser said, 'I now told the Governor-General that if Australia did not get an election the Opposition would have no choice but to be highly critical of him. We would have to say he had failed his duty … to the nation'. Fraser was doing more than addressing the Governor-General, he was threatening him. He knew the state of Kerr's mind, and his insecurity, much better than Whitlam.

On the night before the dismissal Whitlam was in Melbourne to speak at the Lord Mayor's banquet. Fraser and Lynch were also guests at the banquet and hitched a ride back to Canberra that night on Whitlam's VIP aircraft. I had stayed in Canberra but met Whitlam at the airport with some papers. I heard Lynch say to Fraser, 'Do you think he knows?'. Those words meant nothing to me at the time. Knowing what was in store, perhaps Lynch was bemused that Whitlam would generously offer them a ride back to Canberra.

On the morning of the dismissal I attended a meeting with Whitlam, Crean and Daly, together with Fraser, Lynch and Anthony. It was hoped that from this meeting some resolution of the impasse might be possible. In particular, Fraser hoped that the Government would call for an election for the House of Representatives. Whitlam gave no ground whatsoever and told him that he intended recommending to the Governor-General later that morning that there should be a half-Senate election only. The 'casual' Senators (Field and Bunton) would be replaced and there would be senators elected, for the first time, from the Australian Capital Territory and Northern Territory. But the meeting produced no result. Fred Daly said afterwards how confident he thought that Malcolm Fraser and Phil Lynch were. Doug Anthony was much less confident.

On the steps of Parliament House after the meeting I met Eric Walsh. He grabbed me and said, 'Jack, are you still sure that Kerr is on-side? I am hearing otherwise'. I told him not to worry.

Later that morning I got a telephone call from Frank Ley, the Commonwealth Electoral Commissioner, who told me that he had received a telephone call from Fraser asking him the last date that was practical for a House of Representatives election to be held before the school holidays. The advice given by Ley to Fraser, which he conveyed to me, was that any decision on a pre-Christmas election had to be made quickly, perhaps that day or early next week at the latest. This was obviously very valuable advice for Fraser as to when the Governor-General should make a decision. I passed the information from Ley to the Prime Minister. He said that he was going out to see the Governor-General to recommend a half-Senate election. But the Governor-General had other plans.

Fraser arrived at Government House earlier than requested by the Governor-General. He was shuffled into an anteroom to wait for the Governor-General to see Whitlam first. The Governor-General then sacked his Prime Minister and commissioned the leader of the minority party on the condition that Fraser guarantee supply and recommend a double dissolution of the Parliament.

I was eating a sandwich in my office at West Block, waiting for a call from Whitlam that the Governor-General had agreed to a half-Senate election. That would have destroyed the Opposition campaign and probably damaged Fraser irreparably.

I got a different sort of phone call, at about 1.45 pm. David Smith, the Governor-General's Official Secretary, told me that the Whitlam Government had been dismissed and that Fraser had been commissioned to form a government. I was stunned. I turned to doing rather than thinking. I rang Fred Wheeler at Treasury and Allan Cooley at the Public Service Board to inform them of what had happened. I then had a phone call from Whitlam's driver, saying that Whitlam wanted to see me urgently. I went to the Lodge.

Whitlam was in the sunroom eating a steak. The words he used to me as he used to others were 'The bastard's done a Game on me', referring to the dismissal of the Lang Government of New South Wales in 1932 by

Governor Philip Game. I don't think that is strictly correct. Game had at least had open discussions with Premier Lang before dismissing him.

Progressively other people were arriving: Fred Daly, Frank Crean, and John Mant and Graham Freudenberg from Whitlam's office. Whitlam said to me, 'Get Harders', who was Secretary of the Attorney-General's Department. I said I didn't think that was appropriate, and that he should get Enderby, the former Attorney-General, because it was no longer a government matter but a party matter. Kep Enderby came.

There was a lot of confusion as to what should be done. Gough Whitlam started to draft resolutions for the House of Representatives.

I received a telephone call at the Lodge from my secretary, Elaine Miller. She said that Mr Fraser wanted to see me. I said, 'Tell him you can't find me'. She rang about 15 minutes later and said, 'This is a message from Mr Fraser. Could you please tell John Menadue that the *Prime Minister,* Mr Fraser, wants to see him urgently'. I was still stumbling to understand what was afoot. I considered what I should do. I then took my leave of Whitlam and his colleagues. In retrospect I have often thought that I should have said more. Perhaps 'Malcolm Fraser has called me and this is my situation and this is, I believe, what I should do'. I regret that I didn't give more explanation of the predicament I was placed in and what, professionally, as Head of the Prime Minister's Department, I should do. I don't think it would have made any difference but in retrospect I felt quite strongly that I hadn't taken the time—it might have taken only 30 seconds—to explain more adequately the situation I was in and what I proposed to do. So I said very briefly that I was being called by Mr Fraser and I was sorry, I had to leave. I left with a heavy heart. As I got in my car I thought, 'Should I go back in and explain myself more fully?' I didn't.

I went back to Parliament House and called in Geoff Yeend. Clarrie Harders also came. We provided advice on the dissolution of the Parliament. Attorney-General's Department had a proclamation ready. It was ironic that the grounds for dissolution were the 21 bills of the Whitlam Government which the Senate had rejected. Kerr did not make it a condition of his commissioning of Fraser that he attempt to have these bills passed.

I got caught up in the momentum of the day and didn't fully appreciate until later the gravity of what had happened. I was in overdrive. I recall coming back from Parliament House to West Block mid-afternoon and Cynthia and our first daughter, Susan, were scurrying across the car park. I said to them 'Where are you going? What are you doing?' Cynthia said, 'We are going to Parliament House to demonstrate against that bastard Fraser'. She never used language like that. Those words riveted me like nothing else that day. Briefly I was forced to stand outside the maelstrom. She really brought me down to earth more than anyone or anything else. It was like pouring a bucket of ice-cold water over me. There was a lot of family discussion later that day but there wasn't time mid-afternoon outside West Block on 11 November.

In the department I had to get on with the preparations for the swearing-in of the caretaker Ministry and the preparations for an Executive Council meeting next day at Government House. Late in the afternoon, Fraser went off to the Commonwealth Club, where he stayed. I had some documents that had to be signed that night so he asked me to come over to the Commonwealth Club. I did this and he asked me whether I would like a drink. I had a red wine. He asked me if I would like to stay for a meal. I decided that that would be just too much. I couldn't share a meal with Fraser at the Commonwealth Club on the night that Kerr dismissed a Labor government. I went home wounded that night, but others had been wounded much more than me.

At the beginning of the day, the outcome seemed clear: Gough Whitlam would take his recommendation for a half-Senate election, Kerr would agree to it, and the Opposition would be exposed and defeated in its breach of constitutional convention.

With Cynthia and the children we were a stunned household in Deakin that night. What had happened was outside our contemplation. The conventions had been broken in a way that would change public life in Australia forever. Cynthia was angry and upset. I was more stunned. What could this mean for the future?

In later years I was able to articulate better how I felt that night. It was that governments can't legislate for trust and decency. Those values are not anywhere in the Constitution. But they underpin the whole foundation of how we operate in a civilised community towards each other. Those values are the glue that holds us together. On 11 November, what was expedient became more important than doing what was right. Trust in ourselves and our institutions was dealt a severe blow.

We felt a great hollowness. There was something quite unfair and dangerous about it all in a way that I could not accept then or now, almost 25 years later. An accelerating decline in trust in politicians, the political system and public institutions began in 1975. Conservatives had damaged state parliaments in NSW and Qld by refusing to follow the convention that casual Senate vacancies were filled by a member from the same party. Led by conservatives, the Senate broke a convention of centuries that governments are made and unmade in the 'people's house'. The High Court, through the political intervention of its Chief Justice, was compromised. The media, through News Ltd particularly, abused its power. The Governor-General's Office was damaged more than any other institution. I never again felt the same confidence in our institutions.

The sun came up on 12 November but only just. One thing which still stands out vividly in my mind about that day is the swearing-in ceremony at Government House and how agitated the Governor-General was in explaining why he had refused to see the Speaker of the House of Representatives the previous afternoon. The Parliament was then still in session. The House of Representatives had passed what could only be described as a momentous resolution: 'That this House expresses its want of confidence in the Prime Minister [Fraser] and requests the Speaker to immediately advise His Excellency the Governor-General to call the honourable member for Werriwa [Whitlam] to form a government'. Speaker Scholes went to Government House but the Governor-General refused to see him. Kerr said next day that he was very conscious of the House of Representatives resolution and that the Speaker was waiting to see him. But, as I noted at the time, he explained clearly and with much emotion 'that once I decided on the course of action to be pursued [I] had to see it through'.

His carefully laid plan of deception of his Prime Minister to ensure his position had looked as if it could unravel. So he pressed on regardless of the Parliament. So much for constitutional convention. He had locked out a Speaker reporting the defeat in the Parliament of the new Prime Minister whom he had just installed. Seeing the Speaker in such circumstances is the most important duty it is possible to imagine a monarch or vice-regal figure ever having to face. He refused to do his duty.

The Palace was not amused by what Kerr had done. I learned of this later from a note from Tim McDonald, the Official Secretary at Australia House, London, who relayed to me a discussion he had had with Sir Martin Charteris, who was personal secretary and political adviser to the Queen at the time. The discussion that McDonald had with Charteris was within a few weeks of the dismissal. Commenting on the Whitlam dismissal, Charteris said to McDonald that 'the Palace shared the view that Kerr acted prematurely. If faced with a constitutional crisis which appeared likely to involve the Head of State, my advice would have been that [the Queen] should only intervene when a clear sense of inevitability had developed in the public that she must act. This had been Kerr's mistake'. A clear sense of inevitability had not been arrived at.

In considering whether Kerr acted prematurely in a political dispute it is important to consider three points: first, the Opposition was clearly losing momentum. Whitlam was dominating the parliamentary forum and on the deferral of supply, opinion polls showed 70 per cent favoured passing the budget and the Government had dramatically improved its political standing to be running neck and neck with the Opposition. Secondly, supply would not run out until at least 30 November. The Governor-General could have waited almost three more weeks. It is noteworthy that President Clinton continued to govern in 1996 when Congress led by Newt Gingrich in the House of Representatives 'shut the government down' by not passing the budget. It was also the beginning of Gingrich's political demise. Some US public servants didn't come to work and some facilities were disrupted. It was inconvenient but not much more. Thirdly, newspapers were full of speculation at the time and confirmed afterwards that some Opposition senators were ready to break. Senator Reg Withers, the Leader of the Opposition in the Senate in 1975, is quite clear. Ten years later in the *Australian*, on 6 November 1985, he said:

> For all I know, my blokes might have collapsed on the 12th. I don't know. You just hope day after day you would get through until the adjournment ... There were two Senators who told me they were prepared to go ... I reckon we had another week. If I had got through that week then you would look at the following week. I would have lost them some time about 20 November onwards. I know I would have lost them in the run up to 30 November, but it wouldn't have been two then, it would have been ten.

Murdoch was also concerned that the Opposition might break: Paul Kelly, in *November 1975,* reports Murdoch as saying, 'My concern at that time was that Malcolm Fraser, having taken the country to the brink, might lose his courage and back off. Maybe if the *Australian* hadn't been so firm on the Constitutional issue then Fraser might have lost his courage'.

I recall speaking to Margot Anthony, Doug Anthony's wife, in February 1976. She said that the Country Party had become so discouraged and disillusioned in the days before 11 November that she had arranged a social get-together for the night of 11 November, to try and boost morale and keep spirits up. As it turned out it was a celebration rather than a wake.

Clearly Kerr's premature intervention saved Fraser from certain defeat in the Senate.

The Governor-General misled many people in the events that led to the dismissal. Or did we mislead ourselves? I don't think we did. Were we too trusting? Yes, we were, but we thought the Governor-General was a trustworthy person. I think we were part of that innocence which Patrick White describes in *Flaws in the Glass:* 'Australians of all classes, levels of education, of the best intentions and integrity are prey to their native innocence. Even a man of Whitlam's intellect and wit and capacity was brought down by precisely that strain of Australian innocence ...'

John Kerr was driven from office, a sad and beaten man. Malcolm Fraser had a prime ministership of lost opportunities. Gough Whitlam was eventually taken to the hearts of the Australian people who knew that an injustice had been done. The public verdict on the three protagonists of 11 November 1975 now seems clear.

An outsider
With the Fraser Government

'An alien in a foreign land' (Exodus 2:22)

Working for Malcolm Fraser helped me to understand that coming to terms with being an outsider can be liberating.

Hunkered down in Canberra after 11 November with the 'caretaker' conditions imposed by the Governor-General on Fraser, there was a sense of unreality and nagging doubt about the future. The political and social fabric of trust had been torn. Would it keep tearing?

Some of my senior Canberra colleagues, conservative and privately Liberal Party supporters, were appalled by the turn of events. I received sympathetic support from them in the situation in which I was placed, which was unique because of my long association with the sacked Prime Minister. I was his personal appointment to the most senior position in the Public Service. Would I want to stay if Fraser was elected? Should I stay? Would I be asked to go? I knew the questions were being canvassed. I thought the gossip was beside the point. Not for one moment did I consider resigning.

In the Department of Prime Minister and Cabinet, we turned to briefings for the new Government after the election. One normally has a number of months to prepare. In this case we didn't have much time. It was made more difficult because the Liberal Party had not given a great deal of thought to policy development. A Liberal Party government would be a natural return to the pre-1972 order. We hoped that Fraser's election policy speech would give us guidance on what we should prepare for, but it was stronger on politics than policy. We had long discussions with the Public Service Board about major departmental changes that Fraser had flagged.

In the unlikely event of Whitlam being returned as Prime Minister we also made preparations. We expected that Kerr would resign rather than be sacked. I also knew that Whitlam had privately speculated that he might make a symbolic point of switching the residence of the Prime Minister from the Lodge to Yarralumla and oblige the new Governor-General to move into the Lodge. He would have enjoyed that. I knew that we might also need to be ready for possible impeachment action against the Chief Justice. Mick Young privately raised it with me, although I never heard Whitlam mention impeachment. Under Section 72 of the Constitution a Justice of the High Court could only be removed by the Governor-General in Council 'on an address from both Houses of the Parliament in the same session praying for such removal on the grounds of proved misbehaviour or incapacity'.

With the help of colleagues in the department, I wrote extensive notes under the title 'The Labor Government: lessons to be learnt'. I thought that perhaps some time in the future they would be useful for a new Labor government. The notes have languished unused in my filing cabinet ever since.

My first meeting with Fraser after his landslide victory on 13 December 1975 was in his office in Parliament House on the afternoon of Monday 15 December. It was very matter-of-fact; just the two of us. There was little small talk. There were awkward silences. I congratulated him on his election victory. He modestly acknowledged the success and said he appreciated my assistance in the difficult period from 11 November. He then asked me to continue as Head of the Department. That didn't surprise me, but if he had said please go, I wouldn't have fallen off my chair either. He said that I had behaved professionally. More importantly, although he didn't say it, he was looking for continuity, which I supplied.

In his book, *The Unmaking of Gough,* Paul Kelly wrote:

> Three days before polling day Whitlam received a phone call from John Menadue, who was now head of the Prime

Minister's Department under Malcolm Fraser. Menadue was anxious to stay on in the job if Labor was defeated but thought he should clear this with Whitlam who had originally appointed him. Whitlam told Menadue he could see no problem with this and said later he regarded it as a vindication of Menadue's appointment in the first place.

Much as I would have appreciated Gough Whitlam's encouragement, such a discussion never took place. I didn't even think of clearing it with him.

Peter Wilenski and Jim Spigelman, the other two departmental heads who had been tagged with me as being recipients of 'jobs for the boys', were shifted, and quickly the Fraser Government proceeded to make its own political appointments, but mostly from within the Public Service. The two 'Mr Williams' in the Treasury were never disciplined. In the early weeks of the new Government, Fraser seriously considered splitting Treasury to break its monopoly of economic advice. He didn't tell me why he didn't act but my view was that he had been too much the beneficiary of Treasury disloyalty to the former Government to take them on so soon.

Later Fraser commented in the *Age* of 6 February 1978 on how he found the Prime Minister's Department: 'The quality of the Department is noticeably good. It has been from the beginning [of my Prime Ministership]. With John Menadue I certainly had no complaints at all with the way the Department was servicing the requirements of Government'. Under Fraser I continued to build up further the activist role of the department that I had started with Whitlam. It was necessary to be able to respond to Fraser's wide-ranging interests and energy.

I had not known Fraser much at all before we worked together for 12 months. Our worlds did not intersect. I had met him first 20 years before, when as the new and young Member for Wannon he came to speak at Lincoln College in Adelaide. The relationship between Fraser and me worked reasonably well considering our different backgrounds but I didn't think for a moment that it would last. On the personal side he was quite easy to work with. He was considerate to me and my family. He went out of his way to include Cynthia wherever possible in dinners at Parliament House or the Lodge or travel. He was more predictable than Whitlam, but didn't generate the same level of excitement. I was kept well informed and had quick access when necessary.

Despite the bitterness of the dismissal, I found little vindictiveness in Fraser towards the Public Service—quite unlike the Howard Government years later. People were more likely to be judged on their ability and honesty rather than what side of the political tracks they came from. To properly inform him about the people he would be dealing with, I insisted that he be told of their party activities if it was possibly relevant. His answer, with his chin sticking out, was invariably, 'So?' He wasn't interested. He won the respect of a wide range of senior officers in PM&C and I would include myself in that category.

But inevitably in a position like that I got involved in discussions on the fringe of Government with Liberal Party officials and business people. I increasingly felt that my home wasn't with those people and that, inevitably, I would want to go or be asked to go. As Secretary of Cabinet I was in regular contact with ministers. Although polite, some were suspicious of me, particularly the new-money Liberals out to prove themselves. Ministers from longer established wealthy families, particularly families on the land, like Tony Street and Doug Anthony, were more relaxed towards me. Fraser covered for me as best he could.

I was able to assess and interpret more maturely what it meant to be an outsider. As a son of the Methodist manse, I had often felt an outsider in socially conservative country towns when I'd tried to establish relationships with other boys and later girls, in school and after school. I found acceptance at school through sport. As a university scholarship holder I also felt different. I had to study harder. At the age of 41, under Fraser, I was an outsider again. But by that time I found I didn't really care.

I vividly remember a lengthy discussion at the Lodge, in the early days of the new Government, with Malcolm Fraser, David Kemp, Dale Budd and other members of the private office. The evening was informal and quite friendly but I had a strong sense that I didn't belong. But I didn't feel perturbed as perhaps I expected. Belonging was no longer so important. It was transforming to realise that if push came to shove I could survive as an outsider; not comfortably, but I could manage. That realisation was assisted by Malcolm Fraser's personal consideration for the predicament in which I was placed, amongst people most of whom bore me no ill will but whose backgrounds and attitudes were different to mine. It was a turning point for me. Until then I was much more anxious to work the system, to be an insider. From this time on it was less appealing.

Some of the business community who were apoplectic about the Whitlam Government clearly wanted me to go. A Liberal Party official in Sydney, a knight of the realm from the insurance industry, leant on Fraser to remove me. A very senior Melbourne Liberal business leader asked me over a lunch, 'Is it true that after the dismissal your Department was shredding and burning files?' It was hard to accept the prejudice and ignorance of so many of those people. The same business leader later had to resign his company directorships.

Some commentators speculated that because of my Methodist origins and my 'fierce detestation of idleness and extravagance in Government' I was a natural ally of Fraser in cutting waste. This was partly true. The same journalist, Peter Samuel, reported five months into the new Government that 'Menadue remains a strong and vocal critic of the Governor-General's action in dismissing Whitlam'. That was very true.

Early in January 1976, with senior officers in the department, I organised drinks for Mr Whitlam to wish him well. He was without bitterness, despite the injustice that had been done to him. It was important to thank and farewell him, to underline the civility and continuity of public life.

With the smell of blood in their nostrils, some ministers were determined to pursue further four of the outgoing ministers—Whitlam, Cairns, Connor and Murphy—involved in the attempted loan raisings.

On 21 October 1975, a few weeks before the dismissal, Ellicott, the shadow attorney general, had presented a petition from Danny Sankey, a solicitor and constituent of his, to the House of Representatives stating that he wanted to prosecute the four ministers involved in the 13 December 1974 meeting of the Executive Council and asked for leave to subpoena certain loan documents. It was refused by the Whitlam Government.

On 20 November, in the middle of the election campaign, Sankey launched a private legal action against the four ministers for allegedly conspiring with each other to contravene the financial agreement which regulates loan raisings. Furthermore, he alleged that they had conspired to deceive the Governor-General. When Sankey's prosecution came on in the Queanbeyan Court in the week before the December 13 election he asked that warrants be issued for the arrest of the four ministers.

Then in the early months of the Fraser Government there was a bolt from the blue. Billy McMahon privately approached the Secretary of the Executive Council, David Reid, who was based in the Department of Prime Minister and Cabinet. Reid reported to me that the former Prime Minister had approached him to provide copies of the Executive Council minutes. He refused. McMahon was quite persistent and suggested that if Reid left the documents in the letterbox at his home he would arrange for them to be collected. After discussions with Clarrie Harders, the Secretary of the Attorney-General's Department, we decided not to call in the police to investigate McMahon's actions. I thought it better that the matter rest.

Ellicott was determined that the Government take over the prosecution. I advised Fraser not to because, to the best of my knowledge, there was no corruption or illegality in the attempted loan raising. The four ministers had acted legally at every step. Fraser didn't take much persuading that that was the case. He was also persuaded that it was unwise for one government to be raking through the documents of another government and that if the matter came to court the Commonwealth Government should refuse to release them. But Ellicott was single-mindedly determined to continue. At the end of the day, Fraser said that Ellicott should not proceed. He had wrung everything he could politically out of the loans affair and the Executive Council meeting and to proceed further would be fruitless or even counterproductive.

As a result of Cabinet's decision not to proceed, Ellicott later resigned as Attorney-General in September 1977. In his view, he was being blocked from what he saw as his duty as the first law officer of the Crown. Ellicott's actions were puzzling. He was a lay preacher who had been personally welcomed to the Parliament and praised by Whitlam, although he was joining the other side. When he entered Parliament in 1974, Whitlam said that the institution of Parliament needed more men like Ellicott.

On Ellicott's resignation, some media thought that he had resigned on the principle of not interfering with a previous government's records.

In fact, it was the opposite—he resigned because he was not allowed access. The adversaries of 1975 were toppling one after another.

Kerr requested that I resume the regular conversations that I had had with him during the Whitlam Government. It is common practice for the Head of PM&C to have such conversations with the Governor-General. I spoke to Fraser and he agreed. As before, Kerr was eager to get a briefing on a wide range of government activities. Security, intelligence and foreign affairs were always top of the list.

At the second and all subsequent meetings, we were joined by Lady Kerr. She would stay for the full meeting, often an hour or so. She didn't join in the conversations except for the normal courtesies. She was there to listen and support. In those discussions, Kerr conveyed very starkly his concern about his physical safety. He asked me several times to review security at Yarralumla and, to a lesser extent, at Admiralty House in Sydney. He was afraid that protesters might scale the walls and attack him. He felt very insecure. We made some checks and decided that security was adequate.

He also continually sought my view whether Labor hostility would blow over. I could not advise him what the Labor movement was likely to do but I had a pretty good idea. From Mick Young and other friends, as well as what I could read in the newspapers, I was aware of the extent of the hostility. I gave Kerr no encouragement whatsoever that the hostility was only a passing phase.

Perhaps as a thank you to Kerr, Fraser, unknown to me, wrote directly to the Queen in April 1976, proposing that the Governor-General receive the honour of Knight Grand Cross of the Order of St Michael and St George (KCMG)—'Kindly call me God'. I got a rebuke from Sir Martin Charteris, the Queen's Official Secretary in a 'Dear Menadue' letter, indicating that it was unwise for the Prime Minister to be sending such a formal letter requesting a KCMG to the Queen. The letter was leaked. Charteris suggested that whilst I might think it was 'mumbo jumbo', it was useful to first do some preliminary informal soundings. Only in informal discussions would it be proper for the Queen to indicate whether she agreed with the proposal or not. Once it came as a formal proposal from the Australian Prime Minister she really had no choice but to approve. Charteris said, of course, that '[the Queen] had no reluctance in approving this award'. But the message was clear. The Queen had reservations.

Increasingly Kerr became an embarrassment to Fraser, with his extravagant public lifestyle and overseas travel. He claimed he couldn't holiday in Australia because of protests. Fraser finally cut him adrift in July 1977, glad to be rid of an embarrassment. By that time I had gone to Japan. For a period, however, Kerr was a useful fall guy for Fraser. Kerr, rather than Fraser, was the focus of scorn and derision.

Fraser never really got away from the fact that in coming to power he divided the country. That division was mirrored in his own person. Soft on issues such as welfare, he was tough in the way he grabbed power. In his awkwardness, he tended to push people apart. He was socially privileged but believed passionately in racial equality.

If the Whitlam Government was over-prepared for Government, the Fraser Government was under-prepared. In the three years in opposition it did little rethink on policy. It was a matter of reclaiming its rightful position in government and performing competently. At a discussion at the Lodge early in 1976, with his senior political colleagues and his own staff, Fraser commented that despite the brilliance and the glamour of Whitlam in 1972 against an 'old dope like McMahon', the Labor Party had won by only nine seats. In his view, if the Labor Party was anything like a natural party of government in Australia it would have won handsomely in those circumstances.

The lack of preparation for government and any clear direction had been highlighted in his 1975 policy speech to 'give Australian industry the protection it needs', but also claiming that a Liberal government would 'make Australia competitive again'. The political rhetoric was there, but it lacked a core philosophy. Contrasting himself with the Whitlam Government, Fraser was committed above all else to managing his ministers, the Public Service and the economy and removing from government all waste and extravagance: 'Life was not meant to be easy.' To highlight the end of extravagance, Fraser instructed that expenditure on the reception for the new Parliament be cut. Instead of champagne we had orange juice. Fraser also tried to lower the political temperature after the frenetic days of the Whitlam Government. He told us in the department that he wanted to take politics off the front page of the newspapers.

We are all wise after the event but the Fraser Government missed the opportunity, with a strong Prime Minister and with a record majority, to initiate reforms, particularly in industry structure. Business was protected and inward-looking. Australia had to become part of the global economy and develop its economic relations with Asia on a competitive basis. Nothing much changed, though. Hard-nosed policy development in opposition, free of the burden of government, should have better equipped the Liberals. There was no coherent framework in government.

Fraser toyed with monetarism, the Treasury fad at the time; inflation could be broken by controlling the money supply. It didn't work. In the Fraser years, demand was not controlled through the budget and large wage increases resulted in high inflation and rising unemployment.

In fairness, however, it should be said there are convenient lapses of memory by the critics. At the time no ministers, policy advisers in the Liberal Party or business or media commentators were seriously espousing any credible alternatives. The dumping on Fraser for failed economic policies came well after the event.

The manner of the Fraser Government seizing power sapped its confidence and resolution from day one. I thought a nagging doubt was always there. It was tentative on tough issues. Government spending was a clear example. Ten years later, Fraser acknowledged to his biographer, Philip Ayres, that 'he should have undertaken more radical surgery on the public sector in his first year'. He believed that Treasury gave him bad early advice on spending cuts. Most important of all, he was nervous about creating further social division and hardship with large expenditure cuts.

He went to great pains to try to build a consensus with the ACTU and Bob Hawke. Tony Street, the Minister for Employment and Industrial Relations, was the most reasonable person in the Cabinet and close to Fraser. They went to school together. As a result, in the early months of the Government there were compromises on Medibank, the abolition of the Prices Justification Tribunal and secret ballots in trade unions.

Fraser was interventionist across all ministerial portfolios but Treasury resisted. It paid the price. We briefed Fraser on the regular quarterly Treasury forecasts and monthly Reserve Bank reports. He instructed Treasurer Phil Lynch that Treasury should send copies directly to him. It delayed. I wrote to Fred Wheeler confirming the Prime Minister's requirements. Reluctantly Treasury complied but invariably the reports arrived at the last moment and too late for proper consideration. Fraser was angry with this continued defiance. The outcome was that in November, just after I had left the department, Fraser split Treasury into two: Treasury and Finance. It was for one purpose: to reduce Treasury influence. Treasury was always slow to learn that its first duty was to serve the Government.

On economic affairs Fraser was not a Thatcherite. He didn't have any truck with 'rational economics' or the 'radical right'. As a Western districts grazier he saw the world differently. People who had privilege and opportunity had responsibilities, particularly towards the underprivileged. There was a sense of *noblesse oblige* and of an important role for the public sector to play.

Whitlam had mistakenly left his ministers to run their own affairs. Fraser was determined not to make the same mistake. He did it by his own strong personality and the much stronger position that Liberal leaders traditionally hold in Liberal Cabinets. He curbed ministers and restricted the number of their private staff much more than ever before. Most ministers were refused press secretaries and leakages were investigated by the Federal Police. Ministerial decisions were brought under his control. It infuriated his colleagues but they scarcely said 'boo'. Former ministers who now say they stood up to him must have attended different meetings to the ones I attended.

Matters came to Cabinet that really should have been left to ministers or perhaps attended to in private consultation with the Prime Minister. He was concerned about reinforcing his own authority, in a party and government that had a record majority. He was never under threat but always seemed wary.

The Whitlam Cabinet had been active and interventionist, but in this Fraser put Whitlam in the shade, as the public record shows. In the first year of the Whitlam Government, 1973, there were 1700 Cabinet submissions. In the first year of the Fraser Government there were 1900 and, at the peak in 1978, they had risen to 2700. There was an explosion in Cabinet business, whereas by all expectations the Fraser Government was going to be less interventionist and make fewer decisions. It was frenetic. Cabinet meetings were called at very short notice. Ministers did not get sufficient notice. The workload that we had in the department in that first year with Fraser was far more than anything we had known with the Whitlam Government. He would ring at any time of the night. Years later when I spoke to Tammy Fraser about Malcolm's future plans, perhaps relaxing and spending more time at Nareen, his family property in western Victoria, she commented, 'John, at Nareen he is bored shitless'. Seeing him in Cabinet and with his ministers I knew exactly what she meant. He wanted to relax but wasn't sure how to. It was work, work, work. Outside politics he had few real interests.

I saw at first hand his great affection for black Africa. He was queried by a colleague about support which the Australian Council of Churches was providing for 'guerrilla movements in Africa'. I was flabbergasted by Fraser's response. He said that 'the liberation movements in Southern Africa should be supported—Ian Smith [in Southern Rhodesia] is mad. I don't just mean politically stupid. I mean he is clinically mad and the sooner he is got out of the way the better'. I was gasping. This was not what I had expected of a conservative Prime Minister.

A senior PM&C colleague later described to me how in a visit to South Africa in 1986 as a Co-Chairman of the Eminent Person's Group (EPG), Fraser called on Nelson Mandela in gaol. The EPG had been established by the Commonwealth Heads of Government to encourage a process of political dialogue to end apartheid in South Africa. Fraser described Mandela, to my colleague, as the most impressive man he had ever met. After 23 years in gaol Nelson Mandela asked Fraser if Don Bradman was still alive. Fraser sent him a bat autographed by Bradman.

In the caretaker period after 11 November there were continuing and well-sourced reports about Indonesian troop movements which suggested a likely Indonesian attack on Dili. It came on 7 December 1975. Before the attack, however, Fraser had discussed the position in Timor and Indonesia with Tony Eggleton, who was the Federal Secretary of the Liberal Party, and myself. Eggleton had been a press secretary to three Liberal Prime Ministers and the Director of Naval Public Relations. Fraser asked me to prepare a paper on the possibility of Australian military intervention in Timor against the Indonesians. He outlined two possibilities: either that Australia would intervene under a United Nations flag; or that Australia would do it unilaterally. He wanted information about the physical capabilities of the Australian defence forces to mount such a military operation against the Indonesians. Fortunately,

Tony Eggleton was also opposed. He didn't describe it as a madhatter idea but I think that is basically what he thought. I suggested it would be wise for Fraser to sleep on it before we did anything further. No further action was requested.

Later Fraser asked Alan Renouf, the Secretary of the Department of Foreign Affairs, to raise the Indonesian annexation of Timor in the United Nations. The department, however, was reluctant to intervene between Indonesia and Portugal. Renouf recruited Arthur Tange, the Secretary of Defence and former Foreign Affairs head, and respected by Fraser, to try to dissuade him. The problem was overcome by Portugal itself taking the matter to the United Nations.

In June 1976, Cynthia and I travelled with Fraser to Japan and China. At the last moment Susan Peacock, wife of the Foreign Minister, Andrew Peacock, could not make the trip and Cynthia was invited in her place. It was a great opportunity to be in Japan again and to see our oldest daughter, Susan, who was a Rotary student in Okayama in western Japan. In Tokyo, Fraser signed the Treaty of Friendship and Cooperation between Australia and Japan, which Whitlam had first proposed to Japanese Prime Minister Tanaka, three years earlier. It was pleasant to see it signed after long years of bureaucratic delay on both sides. On the instructions of Fraser, I gave the Secretary of our Foreign Affairs Department a deadline for completion of negotiations.

In China, Fraser received a tumultuous welcome, very similar to the welcome Whitlam had received in 1973. In Whitlam's case he was welcomed following the establishment of diplomatic relations. In Fraser's case his anti-Soviet stand won him points with the Chinese.

The visit proved very eventful. By accident, the record of discussion of Fraser with Premier Hua Kuo-Feng was distributed by our Embassy to the media in error. The record highlighted Fraser's criticism of the Soviet Union. That was bad enough but real turmoil was created by the leakage to the Melbourne *Herald* of a late-night discussion which Fraser held with his visiting party at the hotel. The story alleged that Fraser had proposed a 'four power pact' comprising the United States, China, Japan and Australia, to contain the Soviet Union. On the Great Wall the next day, Peacock, the Foreign Minister and now Australian Ambassador to USA, almost out of breath waved a cable and yelled, 'Prime Minister, Prime Minister, have you seen this?' It was a cable on the Melbourne *Herald* story. I was under suspicion. Warren Beeby in the *Australian*, referred to 'unreconstructed Whitlamites' who were leaking to embarrass the Fraser Government. Fraser went out of his way to tell me that he did not suspect me. He didn't need to do that but he was very aware of my difficult position, under pressure and in hostile territory.

On the return from Beijing, Fraser was irritated by the pretensions of the British in Hong Kong. Hong Kong police impounded the pistols of the Australian Federal police officers who were guarding him. In response he cancelled a visit to Governor Macelhose and rejected a cruise on his yacht around Hong Kong Harbour the next day. Steve FitzGerald, the Australian Ambassador in Beijing, and I, with our wives and staff had no problem taking over the cruise and sampling the Governor's wines. When senior Hong Kong officials came later to Australia, Fraser had pleasure in instructing that the pistols of their police were to be impounded.

In the United States in July, I attended with Fraser his discussions with President Ford and Secretary of State Kissinger. In Kissinger's world of *Realpolitik* there was no place for waverers. You were either on the United States' side or against. He detested the non-alignment of India. He said that he always arranged his itineraries to avoid any possibility that he might have to visit India. He adapted an old schoolboy story: 'If you meet an Indian or a death adder on the jungle path at night, which do you kill first?' For the Secretary of State of the most powerful nation on earth that was really something.

Fraser took a lively interest in all sorts of gadgets, especially the newest cameras and the radio telephone on his VIP aircraft. At a meeting of officials and private staff in the Hotel Okura in Tokyo, he brought in an amateur listening device he had acquired and, as a joke, placed it on the table. As the meeting started, ASIO officers dashed in shouting, 'There is a listening device in here emitting a signal. Stop talking. Stop'. The toy was taken out to wry amusement. The meeting resumed. He was infatuated with intelligence and security gadgets.

His interest in intelligence gathering included checking on Whitlam's abortive $500,000 fund-raising from the Ba'ath Socialist Party in Iraq at the time of the 1975 election.

The go-between for the ALP and the Iraqis to raise the money was Henry Fischer, a Sydney businessman of central-European background and with contacts in the Middle East. Fischer took the story, unsolicited, to Murdoch in London. From my knowledge, a reliable account of what then transpired is in *Oyster*, written by Brian Toohey and William Pinwell, and published in 1989. After action by the Commonwealth Government in the Federal Court in 1988, the text of the book was vetted by and negotiated with the Department of Foreign Affairs.

Having got the Iraqi scoop from Fischer, Murdoch swung into action. According to Toohey and Pinwell, Murdoch tried to get Fischer to persuade Whitlam to go to London to pick up the money personally, and be secretly photographed in the act. Whitlam didn't oblige. When Laurie Oakes broke the Iraqi story in the *Sun News-Pictorial*, Murdoch was scooped. In catch-up, he dictated his story for the *Australian* under the byline 'A Special Correspondent'.

After the election of the Fraser government, the London ASIO representative was tasked from Canberra to interview Fischer. The ASIO reports distributed in Canberra made it clear that their primary information source was Murdoch. Fischer couldn't be found. Murdoch was simultaneously playing the game from both ends: the source of the London ASIO reports that Canberra was reading, and writing for the *Australian*.

But that was only the beginning of the story. Foreign Minister Peacock and his department were instructed to open an embassy in Baghdad as a cover for the posting of an ASIS agent, with the task of investigating Whitlam and his connections in Iraq. Alan Renouf, Secretary of the Department of Foreign Affairs, and his Deputy, Nick Parkinson, together with Ian Kennison, Head of ASIS, were, to say the least, disturbed that this was not a legitimate intelligence-gathering exercise.

As head of Fraser's department, I spelled out my concern to Kennison and others and told him that he should refuse to open an ASIS office. If he felt he couldn't refuse, he should at least insist on a written direction from Peacock, his minister. The written direction was given, the Baghdad post opened, including an ASIS agent. The post was closed within 12 months.

Years later the Hawke government appointed Justice Hope to undertake a further judicial inquiry into intelligence and security matters. I briefed Hope on the extraordinary role of ASIO and ASIS in a party political dispute over attempted fund raisings in Iraq.

Before I leave this episode I should say that I believe Whitlam's attempted fundraising from Iraq was out of character. Except for this one incident, I found him, almost to a fault, sceptical of people with money and mindful of the compromise that might be involved in accepting party donations from them. 'Comrade, I will be beholden to no one.' Bill Hartley, his partner in the venture, a leader of the sectarian left in the ALP in Victoria, was as unlikely a collaborator as it was possible to imagine. In 'normal times' it would have sent all sorts of warning bells ringing and lights flashing in Whitlam's mind. I can only conclude that after 11 November 1975, Whitlam was so distressed that his old caution and judgment on fundraising was thrown to the wind.

Prime Minister Fraser was an inspiration to work with on immigration and multicultural affairs. The contradictions in the man kept multiplying.

His commitment to non-discriminatory immigration was deep-seated. He buried White Australia as no other prime minister had. In 1966, the Holt Government had begun marginally changing White Australia. The Labor Party in Government in 1972–75, endorsed the policy of non-discrimination in immigration. But the immigration intake under Labor was so minimal that the new policy was never put to the test. In 1975, population growth due to immigration was the lowest for 30 years and the lowest this century if we exclude the Depression and war years. It was Fraser who was responsible for accepting a large number of Indo-Chinese refugees after the fall of Saigon in 1975. Those refugees, supported by the generous Australian community response, were the decisive turning point in moving Australia away from White Australia.

Fraser picked up the migrant resettlement programs of the Whitlam Government, particularly the English-learning programs, and ran hard with them. Petro Georgiou, on his staff and now the Liberal member for Kooyong, was very influential, as was Frank Galbally from an old Irish Catholic Labor family in Victoria. Funding for English language programs was greatly increased, along with programs for part-time ethnic schools.

The Fraser Government extended ethnic radio and established SBS television. Petro Georgiou and Brian Johns, who remained a senior officer in the Department of Prime Minister and Cabinet under Fraser, were the key drivers for SBS. Fraser got on well with Brian Johns. He saw him as professional and straight. Years later, Johns was to head SBS and the ABC. Fraser encountered a lot of opposition from within the Liberal Party and the ABC and its supporters over the establishment of SBS, but he believed, correctly in my view, that the elitist ABC should have better served the non-English-speaking section of the Australian community. What was required was a specialist, more focused broadcasting service to meet the needs of those who were being neglected by mainstream media. The Broadcasting and Television Act of 1977 provided for the establishment of SBS to provide multicultural radio and TV services. SBS was an important achievement of the Fraser Government.

The origin of the Fraser Government's legislation on Aboriginal land rights was the Woodward Royal Commission, established by the Whitlam Government. The implementing bill was awaiting introduction into the Senate on 11 November 1975. I did what I could in the department under Fraser to advance bipartisanship on Aboriginal affairs. In the first year of the Fraser Government, Parliament passed the Aboriginal Land Rights (NT) Act 1976, which allowed traditional Aboriginal land in the Northern Territory to be granted to Aboriginal Land Trusts. This gave Aborigines freehold land outside reserves. Three Land Councils were established and the office of Aboriginal Land Commissioner was created. Ian Viner was the Minister.

These were all significant achievements in immigration and Aboriginal affairs by Fraser. It was something which he believed in passionately. I found it a very pleasant surprise. As Prime Minister, he would certainly have said sorry to the stolen children.

I didn't expect that my job with Fraser would be long term. I provided some useful continuity for him after the dismissal. At the same time I was certain that I would want to move on, to recuperate and get my bearings again after the searing events of 1975 and 1976. I wasn't at home with the hard men of the Liberal Party.

My interest in Japan was well known. So much so that Murdoch had told me on 7 November 1975, four days before the dismissal, that I would be posted by Fraser to Tokyo after the election.

Within the bureaucracy I pursued my interest in Japan, particularly the establishment of an Australia-Japan Foundation. Mick Shann, the Australian Ambassador to Japan 1975–77, had proposed to the

Department of Foreign Affairs such a foundation to promote the non-economic relations between the two countries. The department sat on the proposal. It would encroach on its territory, despite the fact that cultural relations was always a 'cinderella', and an afterthought in the department. I persuaded Whitlam as Prime Minister that he should legislate to set up the foundation. It was one of the bills on the notice paper when Kerr dismissed him. It was one of the first bills introduced by the new Fraser Government in 1976. The second reading speech we had prepared for Whitlam to make on the afternoon of 11 November 1975 was almost identical to the second reading speech that Fraser delivered on 19 February 1976. The foundation was established a few months later. I was appointed to the first board of the foundation. Because of earlier obstruction by the Department of Foreign Affairs, the new Board reported to Fraser and not to the Minister for Foreign Affairs, Peacock. With his antipathy to Peacock, Fraser would also have had his own reasons to keep the hands of the Department of Foreign Affairs off the foundation.

In public speeches about Japan, I spoke of the need for people-to-people ties to augment economic relations, build linkages between non-government organisations, improve media coverage by both sides, and of the promotion of Japanese language studies in Australian schools and lowering airfares between Australia and Japan. I was practising my new agenda.

I sensed from Fraser's office that my departure was imminent. I started getting curt responses to memos. A bit of static was coming through. So when Fraser raised the possibility of me going to Japan, on the afternoon of 9 September 1976, I wasn't surprised. I welcomed the opportunity to move from the position which, for over two years, had been very exhausting and difficult. It had involved a lot of work, some criticism and, I hoped, some achievements as well. Here was a chance to do other things and not be as dependent as I had been as chief adviser to two prime ministers or a newspaper proprietor.

In the statement on 17 September 1976, about my appointment to Japan, Fraser kindly referred to my 'competence, impartiality and discretion' and that I 'had given unstintingly of [my] energies and managerial skills in serving as the confidential adviser to the Prime Minister and Cabinet in the important transitional period of the Liberal/National Country Party Government as [I] had done for its predecessor'.

I didn't hang around and left the department on 12 November. I had four months before I commenced in Tokyo, spent mainly on leave and briefings in preparation for my new assignment.

Since my two and a half years as Head of Prime Minister and Cabinet we have seen continual changes in the Commonwealth Public Service, and in particular to the status and tenure of heads of departments to make them more responsive and accountable. My appointment had been the first major break from the traditional 'non-political' career service with its permanent tenure.

In more recent times debate has continued as to whether all these changes over the years have affected the capacity and willingness of departmental secretaries to provide 'frank and fearless' advice. Do better salaries and contract appointments rather than permanent tenure promote honest advice? Frankly, I don't think they do. Neither am I convinced that appointments from outside the Public Service are inherently better or worse. The evidence doesn't seem compelling either way.

In my experience as a CEO in government and business and as a board member, the issue is one of personal authenticity and experience rather than one of tenure or money or even management training. By personal authenticity I mean being publicly true to one's private values. I am confident that it is within that authenticity that frank and fearless advice is most likely to be found. It is true of both the public and private sectors.

Learning about Australia and myself

Japan

'The true grandeur of Mt Lou is not seen by only remaining on the mountain itself' (Eleventh-century Chinese poet, Shu Shi)

It was to be a rich experience of life, learning about Japan and the Japanese, but much more importantly for me, it informed me about Australia. From outside I saw Australia with a clarity I had never experienced before.

Japan was also a means to help bridge the gap between my private values and my public roles. Ironically, career, status and public esteem were to become less important for me where, as an ambassador, status, title and rank were so apparent.

It is exhausting work living in separate worlds of the private and the public. Conflict between what you privately think is right and what you feel you have to do publicly, or what Thomas Merton calls the struggle between the true self and the false self, saps the energy. In Japan I was more confident to do publicly what I privately regarded as important; to take more risks if necessary. I felt more mature and less vulnerable. My family, and particularly Cynthia, were now much more

(From top) Presentation of Credentials, Imperial Palace, Tokyo, 24 March 1977.
John and Cynthia with US Ambassador, Mike Mansfield, Tokyo, 1978.
At a steel industry reception for Deputy Prime Minister, Doug Anthony, Tokyo, 1978.

(From top left) Resting with Mick Young after lunch at the beach, Shimoda, Japan, 1978.
Eric Walsh and the bonsai, Tokyo, 1978.
With Queensland Premier, Joe Bjelke-Petersen, Tokyo, 1978.
The most beautiful place in Japan, Oze Kogen, 1979. L to R: Peter, Cynthia, Libby, John, Mark Denton.

(Above) Farewell in Japan. L to R: Cynthia, Susan, John and Mayor of Katsuyamamura.
(Below) At the Opera House, Sydney, 1980 with Japanese Prime Minister Ohira and Mrs Ohira.

(Above) A cartoonist's misconception that multiculturalism was only about recent arrivals.
(Left) Presention to Mrs Pey Yung Ja, with her daughter, of her 'Graduation' letter, Immigration and Ethnic Affairs, 1980.

(Right) Investiture of Officers of the Order of Australia by Governor-General Sir Ninian Stephen, 1985.

(From top) With Minister for Trade,
Joe Dawkins, in Moscow, 1985.
On the workshop floor, Qantas,
1988.
In free fall, 1989.
Taking delivery of a Boeing 747
at Seattle with Annita Keating,
1988.

(Top left) With an old and loyal friend, Frank Hambly, Canberra, 1985.
(Top right) At the bar with Mick Young and Brian Johns, 1988.
(Left) In Canberra, 1991, with wife, Susie, and Ken Ejiri, Chairman of Mitsui, Japan.

(Right) In 1990 on Sydney Harbour with Susie and Alexander Dubeck. He was first secretary of the Communist Party of Czechoslovakia in the Prague Spring of 1968.
(Below) One of Mick Young's last parties at his home, Sydney, 1995. L to R: Eric Walsh, Mick Young, Susie, John.

(From top) Presentation of the Grand Cordon of the Order of the Sacred Treasure by Japanese Consul General, Nakamura, 1998. With Gough and Margaret Whitlam at 'Sacred Treasure' investiture, December, 1998. Also present at the Japanese Consul General's residence, 1998, the grandchildren. L to R: Miriam, Naomi, Joseph, Alice, Danny, Hannah, Ben.
With foster-daughter, Neary Eng, in Phnom Penh, 1991.

(Top) At mother Elma's 80th birthday celebration with sister Beth, Adelaide, 1986. (Centre) With the 1954 alumni of Lincoln College, (University of Adelaide) in Kuala Lumpur, 1999. L to R: Narinder Singh, 'Doc' Krishnan, Lynn Kulasingham, John, Sam Abraham. (Below) At daughter Susan's 40th birthday, Balmain, 1999, with children (L to R) Susan, Peter, Rosalie and Libby.

involved in my work and daily life. There was more integration of family and public life.

As diplomatic novices Cynthia and I both did an induction course in the Department of Foreign Affairs in Canberra. We were told about the administration of the department, how an embassy should be run, and budgets and financial delegations. There was guidance on social behaviour and etiquette. Cynthia was advised that she should 'sit in the middle of a lounge. You could be ignored sitting on the end'. We also did a short, intensive Japanese language course. I proved to be a dunce in languages again. I found it embarrassing and irritating. This was to stimulate me later to try to improve Asian language skills in Australia. Cynthia was much better with Japanese language than me.

We arrived at Haneda Airport, Tokyo, on 3 March 1977, to be met by a clutch of Commonwealth ambassadors. For new chums it was a pleasant and unexpected new world. The Embassy residence staff lined up to welcome us when we arrived in town—another quaint but enjoyable introduction to our new life. It was a long way from the country towns of South Australia.

The Japanese have a high regard for ambassadors. They give them a lifelong title 'Ambassador'. It could turn your head. We enjoyed the diplomatic status and perks while we were there, although sometimes it was over the top. The president of a major private university in Western Japan was in something of a nervous dither as he met me. In a half curtsy he welcomed me as 'Your Majesty'. I took a shine to him.

A priority in the first few days was getting the children into university and schools; Sophia University run by the Jesuits for Susan, Sacred Heart for Rosalie and Elizabeth, and St Mary's for Peter. There were very few lay teachers at these educational institutions and the fathers, sisters and brothers were very professional educators. But the students were from wealthy Japanese families or, more likely, were the children of foreign business executives or diplomats with generous expatriate living allowances. It was an unreal atmosphere, remote from the real Japan, just like diplomatic life itself.

There was no Methodist Church in Japan so we joined the American Episcopalian Church, St Albans. It was our introduction to incense in the liturgy. Peter faked a coughing fit each time.

The Embassy, about five kilometres from the centre of Tokyo, had been rented by the Australian Government in 1940, occupied by the Japanese military during the Second World War and purchased in 1952 for £135,000 from the Maquis Masaaki Hachisuka, an eccentric aristocrat and pioneer aviator with lands and a small castle in Tokushima, Shikoku. He had a reputation among the Japanese of pocketing spoons and forks from the Imperial Palace. The Japanese garden at the Embassy had a 900-year-old spring and two bonsai trees over 400 years old that were worth more than the quite incongruous castle-like and uncomfortable residence that Hachisuka had built in 1928, after the Japanese-style house was destroyed in the Great Kanto earthquake of 1923. He loved things English. The dining room had a raised platform for 'high table' in the manner of Cambridge University, where he had been briefly, and not very successfully, educated.

The residence staff were marvellous and a great help to the family, friends and visitors who went through the residence in thousands over the three and a half years that we were there. The butler, Uehara san, about 35 years old, was always obliging and helpful. The chief maid, Naoko san, rarely spoke English but understood everything. She was the corporate memory and knew where every ambassador and his wife had left a pair of shoes over the last 30 years. Shimura san was brilliant in the Japanese garden, sweeping the leaves on cue at 7.00 every morning. But he could never get the hang of Australian trees with their deep roots. The head cook, Handa san, was superb but temperamental. All food menus were presented in French. Cynthia changed that the second day. In the best tradition of Japanese lifetime employment the handyman was over 80 and couldn't change a light bulb. The other staff covered for him.

We had never had domestic staff before so it was quite a new experience. The British Ambassador told me, 'I would never employ staff that had been employed by Australians'. As employers we were too casual.

Cynthia's parents and my mother and sister, Beth, visited several times. They enjoyed the luxury of embassy life. They had never had such treatment. They had just a tinge of doubt as to whether Australian taxpayers should have been paying for all this.

My first official task was to present credentials to Emperor Hirohito. In preparation I brought gear from Australia. The second-hand morning suit was from 'Man about Town' in Sydney. The Japanese generally don't like second-hand goods but Naoko san kindly commented that a second-hand suit made me look an experienced ambassador! The shop attendant in the Strand Arcade, Sydney, who sold me a top hat, said that the last such sale he had was to Sir John Kerr!

Presenting of credentials on 24 March 1977 was a boys' only affair, with five senior officers from the Embassy accompanying me. Cynthia and the children couldn't go further than the Palace Hotel, across the road from the Imperial Palace. The hotel flew the New Zealand flag by mistake that day. It taught me about our place in the world. The Imperial Palace household staff called next day to apologise.

We went to the Palace in three horse-drawn carriages and received a briefing from the Grand Master in the Ceremonial Hall. We were told that in no circumstances should we turn our back on the Emperor without first taking three steps backwards. We might have a hidden dagger. We were then shown to a drawing room to await the Emperor.

On my own I was then ushered into the Ceremonial Hall 'into the presence of the Emperor'. I presented my formal 'Letter of Credence' from Elizabeth the Second. I also presented the Letter of Recall of my predecessor. The credentials reflect another era. It is no wonder that many Japanese scratch their heads about what it means to be an Australian.

> Elizabeth the Second
> by the Grace of God Queen of Australia
> and Her other Realms and Territories,
> Head of the Commonwealth:
> To all and singular to whom these Presents shall come,
> Greetings!
>
> Whereas it appears to Us expedient to nominate some Person
> of approved Wisdom, Loyalty, Diligence and Circumspection to
> represent Us in the character of Our Ambassador Extraordinary
> and Plenipotentiary at Tokyo
>
> with the especial object of representing the interests of
> Australia.
>
> Now Know Ye that We, reposing especial trust and confidence
> in the discretion and faithfulness of Our Trusty and Well-

beloved John Lawrence Menadue have nominated, constituted and appointed, as We do by these Presents nominate, constitute and appoint him the said John Lawrence Menadue to be Our Ambassador and Plenipotentiary at Tokyo for the purpose aforesaid. Giving and Granting to him in that character all Power and Authority to do and perform all proper acts, matters and things which may be desirable or necessary for the promotion of relations of friendship, good understanding and harmonious intercourse between Australia and Japan for the protection and furtherance of the interests confided to his care; by the diligent and discreet accomplishment of which acts, matters and things aforementioned he shall gain Our approval and show himself worthy of Our high confidence.

And We therefore request all those whom it may concern to receive and acknowledge Our said Trusty and Well-beloved John Lawrence Menadue as such Ambassador and Plenipotentiary as aforesaid and freely to communicate with him upon all matters which may appertain to the objects of the High Mission whereto he is hereby appointed.

Witness Our Right Honourable Sir John Robert Kerr, a member of Her Majesty's Most Honourable Privy Council, Knight of the Order of Australia, Knight Grand Cross of the Most Distinguished Order of Saint Michael and Saint George, Knight Grand Cross of the Royal Victorian Order, Knight of the Most Venerable Order of the Hospital of Saint John of Jerusalem, one of Her Majesty's Counsel learned in the law, Governor-General of the Commonwealth of Australia and Commander-in-Chief of the Defence Force,

this Sixth day of December in the year of Our Lord One thousand nine hundred and Seventy-Seven, and in the Twenty Sixth year of Our Reign.

By His Excellency's Command,
(Signed) Andrew Peacock, (Countersigned) John R Kerr

The Emperor handed the credentials to the Cabinet Minister in attendance and shook my hand. We then had a conversation. He expressed a lively interest in Australia and the personal attitudes of Australians towards Japan. I really think he was inquiring about attitudes to himself. He mentioned the Australian Prime Minister, Mr Fraser, but did not mention either the Queen or the Governor-General; wisely I thought.

I then introduced my colleagues to the Emperor. He said a few words of greetings and then farewell. I shook the Emperor's hand again and we all departed.

The Emperor looked precisely as I had expected, short and slight, dressed in a morning suit, bespectacled and moustached. He was shy, painfully so I thought. Seventy-six years old, he seemed worn down by the years. Perhaps he had stood taller as a young man. His voice was very high pitched and tremulous. I could not picture him as the Commander-in-Chief of the Japanese Imperial Army that I had seen as a boy in newspapers in Australia.

I sat next to the Emperor at a luncheon at the Palace almost a year later on 9 March 1978. He had regular lunches with ambassadors and I had heard from Japanese officials that the Emperor was often very forthcoming with foreign guests. It must have been a relief from the guarded, sad life he lived in the palace. On this day, he was certainly forthcoming and lively despite his 77 years. He seemed much more sprightly than some palace retainers of advanced age who stood around like crows with their beady eyes on him. He seemed a small, lonely bird in a golden cage.

In a similar manner to our discussion when I presented my credentials, the Emperor again asked very pointed questions about Australia. I recall them vividly. 'What is the Australian attitude towards Japan? We have had a difficult history but what are relations like now? Are Japanese visitors to Australia welcome? Do young people have the same attitudes as older people? What are the attitudes of veterans' organisations?' To my relief he was not interested in koalas, kangaroos, beef or coal. It was somewhat in code but I was certain that he was wanting to visit Australia to find out for himself. He felt, not surprisingly, that there had been great hostility towards him from Australians. During the Occupation, Australia was the most hardline of all the allies. Judge Webb from Queensland, President of the International War Crimes Tribunal, wanted the Emperor executed.

I believe that the Emperor wanted to come to Australia to put a line under the past and in a personal act of reconciliation underscore a new beginning in the relationship. Personal expiation was necessary. I have no doubt that that was what he was about. I was very moved by it.

With the credentials presented it was down to the work of learning to be a diplomat. In my first speech to the Australia-Japan Society in May 1977, I said, 'I am new to diplomacy but I hope that far from being a disadvantage this will enable me to bring an open mind and a fresh approach'. The Japanese co-chairman at that lunch was former Prime Minister Kishi, who had been charged with war crimes but rehabilitated by the allies to join the anti-communist side in the Cold War. Kishi's presence was an uncomfortable reminder that the grim past wasn't all that far behind us.

I knew I was being watched by the 'professional diplomats'. Foreign Affairs, Canberra, had explained to the head of the Foreign Ministry in Tokyo, Arita Keisuke, that I was not a professional diplomat, so please be understanding. A year later Arita san told me the story and, with a grin, said that I was doing better than the Canberra forecast!

I made calls on the Foreign Minister with a copy of my letter of credentials and then called on senior ministers, the heads of about ten of the main departments, the Crown Prince Akihito and Princess Michiko, Prince Hitachi and his charming wife and the Emperor's brothers—Princes Mikasa and Takamatsu. Some quick changes in the back of the car from morning suit to lounge suit didn't cause the driver or others to blink. The Japanese are very good at averting their eyes—like airline stewards who don't want to serve you.

Following normal practice I followed up with calls on the business institutions, trade unions, consumer, housewife and farmer groups. Because of my newspaper background I called on all the major television and newspaper companies. In almost all cases I arranged return lunches or dinners for the presidents of all those organisations.

I visited Daisekiji, the main Temple of Soka Gakkai, a new Buddhist religious movement. I was used to sometimes stumbling over Catholics as they genuflected in the aisle, but on this occasion we were guided by a real devotee who prostrated himself before each statue of the Buddha. Even horizontal he didn't pause in his briefing.

I was not particularly attracted to the dreary round of diplomatic dinners and parties which are so much part of the life of bored diplomats. There were a few exceptions and I worked hard at relations with United States, Canadian, New Zealand and ASEAN colleagues. I tried to attend National Days of most countries but usually went for only about 20 minutes and escaped before the speeches started.

Mike Mansfield, the United States Ambassador and former Democratic Senate Majority Leader for many years, was a great colleague and well respected. I had met him several times before with Gough Whitlam on visits to Washington. He felt that it was his duty to correct Washington's ignorance about Tokyo, to represent Tokyo to Washington rather than the other way around. Mansfield and I gave a joint briefing to a group of visiting Canadian Army officers. If I had closed my eyes I would have concluded that Mansfield was a Japanese Minister with a strange accent. The State Department became a little sceptical of reports from their 'Tokyo ranch'. Mansfield had a fairly direct view of US diplomacy: most problems could be solved with a small dash of US liberalism and a large dash of US dollars. He wasn't far off the mark.

It is also the habit of new ambassadors to call on other ambassadors. I got to about 40 calls in the first six months but then concluded that I was wasting my time. I started with the Dean of the Corps, an amiable man called Coffi, who hailed from the Ivory Coast. It is the distinctive feature of Ivory Coast foreign policy that they leave their ambassadors in a post long enough for them to become Deans of the Corps!

It became fairly obvious to me that 'Ambassadors Extraordinary and Plenipotentiary' receive an adulation and status which is not warranted by the value of the work they do. The role is often confused with results. Some ambassadors worked hard in Japan but they were the exceptions. If I didn't front to other Embassy functions for a period, I often was asked if I had been away. I hadn't; I had been working.

I think I was the first ambassador to call on the two *burakumin* organisations. They are an 'untouchable' group of over one million, but ethnically and racially indistinguishable from other Japanese. When Buddhism came to Japan in the 14th century, devout Buddhists wouldn't kill cattle so a group developed that did the dirty work, killing animals and tanning leather. They extended into nursing, laying out the dead and disposing of night soil. The Japanese Government has, by legislation and government policy, removed discrimination against *burakumin* but social discrimination is still deeply and widely entrenched. They are not discussed in polite company. The private detective industry in Japan thrives on checking connections to avoid *burakumin* marriage partners. They can be traced from certain villages and areas.

In my meetings with the *burakumin* leaders they compared their situation unfavourably with blacks in America. Blacks who succeeded in America, like Martin Luther King and Muhammad Ali, were clearly identifiable role models. In Japan, however, *burakumin* were racially indistinguishable from other Japanese and kept their identity secret. The prejudice remained that *burakumin* were dirty and criminal. Both organisations were very surprised and perhaps confused by my call.

After many previous private visits to Japan I thought I knew the ropes. I didn't. Certainly not how to undress discreetly without too much exposure. On our first official visit to Nagoya, the maids in the *ryokan* stayed in the room to take our clothes as Cynthia and I undressed. We weren't used to that. After the bath I was ushered into the banquet room in my *yukata* for dinner with the Mayor of Nagoya and distinguished guests. They were all in western dress. Cynthia wisely retreated to the tatami bedroom to finish getting dressed and comb her hair. She came to the dinner about ten minutes later and whispered, 'I have your comb and underpants in my handbag if you have any problems'.

We attended many traditional Japanese dinners. But as the senior guest I was usually looked after by the most experienced and invariably the oldest geisha. Cynthia enjoyed that. But that was about the only thing she enjoyed when geishas entertained. They are there to entertain men and wives cramp their style.

After the novelty of these dinners wore off, Cynthia usually found an excuse not to attend. The novelty wore off for me not much later. Why wouldn't it, with games which involved dripping sake into a cup until the surface tension broke or stacking matches carefully one on top of another until the whole structure collapsed. Sober and in the cold light of next day it seemed silly. But geishas were attentive, the food was marvellously prepared and presented on beautiful plates, the service was excellent; no detail was missed. The male ego was well and truly stroked. One embassy wife was apoplectic when a geisha carefully applied a hot towel to her husband who had spilled soy sauce on his crutch.

Entertainment at a bar or club was men only with the *mama san* and her band of young hostesses. But my family was on to me. After drinks at a flash Ginza bar that only my Japanese business host could have afforded, the *mama san* sent a sheath of beautiful red roses for me at the Embassy. Unfortunately, they were Cynthia's favourite flower and colour. With the cooperation of Susan, Rosalie and Elizabeth, Cynthia ostentatiously hung the roses head down in our living room. I dared not remove them and provoke the wrath of the sisterhood. Yellow roses became Cynthia's favourite.

Japan was a great experience and pleasure for the family. This was the first time, since we were married in 1957, for the whole family to do so much together. The Chancery Office was next door to the residence. Cynthia and I attended most social events together. We did a lot of family bushwalking and travelling. For the first time in her life, Cynthia had domestic help. The children were growing up. She had a freedom that she had never had before to get out and do things. In our personal and family life it was the most enjoyable time in our marriage. Cynthia enjoyed it immensely. She became well known and regarded in many parts of Japan. She went to Japan as my wife and I left as her husband. She really seized the opportunity to pursue her own interests: painting, women's groups, studying and travelling. The Japanese loved her openness and spontaneity. We climbed most of the mountains; Kitadake, Takao and, of course, Fuji, which was crowded and dirty. 'A wise person climbs Fuji once. Only a fool does it twice.'

We visited 43 prefectures, all except Okinawa. We stayed at over 100 *minshuku* where we could stay cheaply, particularly as at that time the Australian dollar was worth about 200 yen. We loved the experience of meeting Japanese in their own homes. Following the official part of our visit to a prefecture we often stayed privately at a *minshuku* on the Friday and Saturday nights. Sometimes we didn't book ahead but got a recommendation from the railway station. The family found it embarrassing when Cynthia checked for clean bed linen before we booked in. Foreigners were expected to be different and Cynthia did not disappoint. The children didn't always share our enthusiasm for *minshuku* and backpacking. After a very hot day in Kyoto and after visiting thousand-year-old temples, Peter sat in the gutter and protested wearily, 'Not another bloody one-thousand-year-old temple'.

I can't think of a time in our lives when we were better treated, pampered in fact. If we looked lost or helpless for 30 seconds someone usually stepped forward to help—even in the mountains. Being an ambassador helped, but beyond that the cocoon of politeness and courtesy shielded us from any worries, unpleasantness or shocks.

Australian friends visited us regularly. Eric Walsh came often but I could never get him outside Tokyo. Mick and Mary Young came several times. At Shimoda I told Mick to slowly immerse in the hot spring. He disregarded my advice and leapt out clutching himself and yelling something about 'orchestra stalls'. We tried jungle baths for mixed bathers. We swam like crocodiles with eyes just above the water looking for Japanese beauties. We only met male crocodiles like ourselves.

Japan left an indelible impression on the family. Cynthia later ran a *minshuku* travel business to Japan. Our eldest daughter, Susan, who first went as a Rotary Exchange Student to Japan in 1976 and then stayed on with us at the Embassy and married a Korean, now lives in Japan with her four children. Her husband runs a successful business in Tottori, in western Japan. Our youngest, Elizabeth, studied in Japan in 1985 at Keio University and home-stayed with many of Cynthia's friends. Rosalie missed Australia and returned to attend Cynthia's old schools Lameroo High School and MLC in Adelaide. Peter loved St Mary's College in Tokyo.

Working with political, business and public service people in Tokyo was in no way as interesting or as real as our experiences with country people across Japan. People are always more interesting than dollars or tonnes. But those experiences gave me background and enthusiasm for the task at hand.

The Australia–Japan relationship in 1977, as it is now, was dominated by trade and investment. By 1977, Japan had become Australia's largest trading partner, with $6 billion two-way trade per annum, running 2:1 in Australia's favour. We then supplied about 80 per cent of Japan's wool, 50 per cent of its coal and iron ore and over 60 per cent of its bauxite. Embassy staff used to lay bets that I couldn't make a speech about Australia–Japan relations or answer questions without mentioning dollars or tonnes. I always lost.

I remember Sir John Crawford, who was Secretary of the Department of Trade in 1957, telling me in Tokyo 20 years later, that in the negotiations for the Commerce Agreement in 1957 he had secret meetings with the Japanese for fear that the RSL or other groups in Australia would be protesting at the door. I recall Ambassador Nobuhiko Ushiba, a senior Japanese Foreign Ministry official who participated in those negotiations, saying that the Australian Government was so forthcoming in 1957, with Jack McEwen as the Deputy Prime Minister and Minister for Trade, that the Japanese Government thought it was a trick. They couldn't believe that the Australian Government was so generous. The trade relationship started from a very rocky patch but by the time I went to Japan, trade was developing dramatically. It continued like that for another 15 to 20 years. It was a good time to be in Japan. In 1999, it is harder, with the Japanese economy going sideways and few real signs of long-term structural change. The trading relationship between our two countries, which always lubricated the overall relationship, has now passed the high-water mark. Future relationships will probably be more difficult, certainly different.

I was always conscious in Japan in the late 1970s about the imbalance of the Australia-Japan relationship; that because of size and influence Japan was more important to us than we were to Japan, with its important relationships with the United States, the Soviet Union and China. For our part there was a feeling of unrequited love or *kataomoi*. But because of the imbalance we had to work harder at the relationship.

In the 1970s it was a pleasure to be associated with business pioneers and champions of the Australia-Japan relationship: Shigeo Nagano, the President of Nippon Steel, who told me how he slept on a camp stretcher under canvas in the Pilbara before the iron ore mines commenced production; Ken Ejiri, the President of Mitsui trading company, who lived in Australia for many years and whose son married an Australian woman; Rod Carnegie, Managing Director of CRA; Russel Madigan, Managing Director of Hammersley Iron, and Ken and Bailes Myer from the Myer family in Melbourne. Ken, with a Japanese wife, had a personal love of Japan. They were all looking to the next 20 years. I often wonder how much performance-based executive packages, linked to short-term share prices, now focuses business executives on short-term results.

It was clear to me that Japan in the late 1970s got the big decisions right and nowhere more successfully than in export and education. Government policies were linked with large corporations to make them export industries and world leaders. The same policies that were later pursued by the other industrialising countries of north Asia had been tested and proven in Japan. They all knew that economic prosperity, even survival, depended on export. That export drive was based on adapting, rather than inventing, new technology.

Cynthia and I saw at first hand 'education mammas' making enormous sacrifices to secure the best education and opportunities for their children, ferrying them back and forth to cram schools or *juku* and staying up late to supervise homework. My Embassy driver sent his son to a *juku* at the age of five. The education system was too rigorous and disciplined for our likes but it produced dramatic economic results.

Japanese learned well the lesson of Takeda Shingen, a famous Japanese general, that 'People are the castle, people are the battlements and people are the moat'. I was impressed by the care that Japanese put into people relationships. I often cringed at how poorly we reciprocated. I am still embarrassed by it; courtesies not being acknowledged let alone reciprocated, being late for appointments and showing little interest in what Japanese guests are saying.

But human relations and obligations, which are a key to Japan's social stability and cohesion, have their downside. In the 1930s and 1940s mindless cooperation with leaders and social cohesion at the expense of dissent and opposition led Japan and the region to disaster. To be different is not wrong but many Japanese thought it was. In Japanese the word *chigau* means both to be wrong and to be different. They are the same thing.

In peacetime, innocent personal obligation in gift giving became grossly exaggerated by some into large-scale corruption. In the 1970s I saw the aftermath of the Lockheed scandal in which bribes were paid by Lockheed to Prime Minister Tanaka to secure sales of aircraft to All Nippon Airways. The malaise has spread. Financial regulation is suspect when 25 per cent of the largest private banks in the country are headed by former Ministry of Finance staff and where rules are so vague that it is hard to tell whether laws are being broken.

One reason for Japan's economic strength in good times is the same as the reason for its weakness in difficult times: close and opaque relationships between politicians, bureaucrats, regulators and businessmen, particularly bankers. The key problem in 1998 was the massive bad debts of the banks and the lack of transparency. Bankers' mistakes were covered up by other members of the official family. In the end it is taxpayers who foot the bill.

In a mono-ethnic and consensus-based society like Japan there is not sufficient grit in the system to force change. The dissenter is punished. The Japanese have a phrase for it—*mura hachibu*—literally 80 per cent village, which implies that the other 20 per cent must comply or face being ostracised. So reform is hard. Every society and nation needs dissenters and Japan has fewer than most. It lacks the vigour that openness and cultural diversity have brought Australia.

Many rejoice in Asia's current setbacks, ignoring that earlier setbacks have been surmounted. They even ignore 40 years of remarkable achievements as if they never happened. It reflects both an ideological and cultural prejudice that sooner or later Asian business theory and practice will revert to the superior western norms. Undoubtedly some Asian economies were badly managed. But even one of the best managed in the world, Hong Kong, was not free of the contagion of vast speculative capital flows and the panic that ensued.

We are all inclined to try to fit awkward facts into our own terms of reference and cultural experience rather than be open to new attitudes and new ways of thinking and doing. This is most clearly the problem with the IMF and its barrackers around the world.

The long-term factors contributing to Japan's and most of Asia's development are still present: high levels of savings, a national commitment to education and export, a strong work ethic, social cohesion and mutual community obligations. Drugs, crime and family breakdown are within reasonable bounds. The principal mistake of the region has been that politicians and bureaucrats have been too close to businessmen. That is a societal problem more than an economic one. The problem is made more difficult in a way by Japan's success. Wealthy people and wealthy nations find it hard to change; they have much to lose. Japan has also one of the oldest populations in the world. Old and rich people don't make revolutions or babies.

My three years on the trade front in Japan were dominated by the sugar dispute, arguments over beef imports and the continuing besting of Australian coal and iron ore exporters by the Japanese steel mills. I learnt from the sugar dispute the value of having a single seller and from the beef disputes particularly that external pressure was necessary to get the Japanese to open up markets. It was even more obvious in the Meiji reforms in Japan after 1868 and the post-1945 reforms. They were driven from outside, and particularly by the United States. Powerful Japanese domestic vested interests made change difficult and still do.

It is true of most individuals, groups and nations, that we need an external challenge or catalyst to force change. In Australia we didn't make the necessary economic reforms in the 1980s because we woke up one morning and decided we should change. We changed because Asia was forcing us to change.

I regularly saw both the Australian and Japanese negotiators in the iron ore and coal trade. It made me uneasy. Japan saw itself as the *oyabun* or boss and Australia as the *kobun*, or client. Without blinking the chairman of Nippon Steel on a speakers panel with me referred to the 'Japanese plan for the Pilbara'. They expected to make decisions on whether the next iron ore project would be in Australia, Brazil or India. Japan effectively set the long-term market for iron ore and coal in the Asia Pacific region. The market is deliberately oversupplied. Within that framework there are annual negotiations over price and tonnage details but they are only finetuning.

In Japan I came to better understand Japanese obsession with diversity and security of supply. I learned how vulnerable the Japanese feel. Their vulnerability stems from historic concerns about earthquakes, typhoons and volcanoes and, more recently, from their lack of resources in an industrial age. So much of Japan's folk religion, Shinto, tries to explain their vulnerability in the face of nature. Despite their high income levels, the Japanese will never believe that they are rich. Japanese were nonplussed if I asserted they were. For them a country that lacks physical resources can never be rich. A country like Australia is, by definition, rich. This feeling of vulnerability leads the Japanese to pursue policies of self-sufficiency at home, particularly in food, and diversity of supply from abroad, particularly raw materials.

Because I came to understand their sense of vulnerability I admired the way the well-organised Japanese steel industry bought raw materials as a single buyer. In the case of iron ore and coal, Nippon Steel was the lead buyer in Australia for the other steel mills in Japan. In other countries it was Kobe Steel or another steel company. The Australian exporters, whether it was of coal or iron ore, were many and facing a single buyer. That put the Australian side at a distinct disadvantage. The smaller and weaker Australian exporters would offer a lower price to the Japanese in return for an increased market share. In the process they dropped the whole market price for Australian exporters.

Through my experience in Japan I gained insights about Australia. Perhaps the 12 different homes I lived in and the 12 different schools I attended in my first 15 years prepared me for looking at Australia from the outside. I never saw Japan as a model for Australia, but because it was successful and different I saw it as a valuable mirror or outside reference point that forced me to rethink about my own country. In Japan I sensed that Australia was living on borrowed time, that we had to be more open and outward looking. While the Australian standard of living wasn't falling in the late 1970s, our relative position was declining rapidly. The lucky country was under threat. Would we become the 'cheap white trash' of Asia? In a speech in 1980 I pointed out that 'Australians 20 or 30 years ago would go to Singapore or Hong Kong and regard them as poor run-down cities … We thought we were an island of affluence in a sea of poverty and it is just not true any more. Unless we face up to that, we will become the backward country'. In 1981 I pointed out that 'Asian countries are steadily drawing ahead of Australia. That is startling news'. The same sentiment was expressed many years later by Paul Keating speaking about Australia becoming a 'banana republic'.

I can't recall one person disagreeing with what I was saying in scores of speeches. But no one was getting up in the aisle and saying that we needed to change and that he would lead the charge. A crisis was not at hand to force a rethink. The lucky country didn't stir, at least not until the mid 1980s.

I seized every opportunity in Tokyo to alert Australian ministerial visitors to the economic challenge which countries like Japan and others were presenting. There was little continuing interest in Japan by ministers, except from Doug Anthony, the Deputy Prime Minister and Minister for Trade. He had a daughter in Japan as an exchange student. That informed and stimulated his interest. In the Trade Department, senior officials Doug McKay and Jim Scully were interested. Most of the senior people in the Foreign Affairs Department had experience in South-East Asia and were not well informed on the quite dramatic developments that were occurring in Japan, Korea and Taiwan.

Malcolm Fraser visited twice. He was well received and pleasant company and very encouraging in my less conventional role as Ambassador. He didn't have the enthusiasm of Doug Anthony. The Treasurer, John Howard, never came to Japan while I was there. Foreign Affairs Minister, Andrew Peacock, was more interested in the United Kingdom and the United States, where he felt more comfortable. En route from New York to Sydney, he stayed one night in Tokyo. I met him at Narita Airport. I thought it would be a good opportunity, coming in from Narita, about an hour and a half's drive, to give him a briefing on what was happening in Japan. I found it very difficult to engage him at all. I tried many angles: the state of domestic politics in Japan, the latest political or business scandal, Japan's difficult relations with Korea or the unending dispute over beef. None of it worked. Perhaps he was tired after the travel. He gave me, however, a lengthy brief about London and New York, Princess Margaret and Shirley Maclaine.

Phil Lynch, the Minister for Industry and Commerce and responsible for tourism, came once. We got a cable from his office saying that he didn't want to attend anything cultural. We arranged a dinner at his request with Yohachiro Iwasaki san, who was investing in a resort at Yeppoon near Rockhampton. Iwasaki was the pioneer of Japanese tourism to Australia, but he had it wrong. Japanese wanted multi-destination tourism to Australia, not a single visit to an out-of-the-way place like Yeppoon. Iwasaki had first made his money supplying railway sleepers to the Japanese army in Manchuria in the 1930s. The Iwasaki dinner was held in a basement restaurant and Lynch, perhaps because he was tired from his travel, fell all the way down the stairs and finished on his knees before Iwasaki.

Shadow ministers were also hard to find. Bill Hayden didn't come and neither did Paul Keating, the Shadow Minister for Minerals and Energy. Very surprising I thought. His discovery of Asia was still 13 years away. It was to prove the more dramatic because of the lateness of the conversion. Gough and Margaret Whitlam visited twice and stayed as guests at the Residence. Even though he was retired from Parliament, Japanese wanted to meet him. The dismissal had made him an international, as well as a national, figure.

I found the activities of Australian state governments in Japan wasteful and confusing. At the conclusion of my posting I sent a report to Minister Peacock:

> I have been concerned that over the last eighteen months the number of Commonwealth Ministers visiting Japan has been so few. In the same time there have been a large number of state

premiers and ministers. State government aspirations in Japan are a wasteful fact of life but we should not let the Commonwealth's ministerial role go by default.

The only two state premiers the Japanese took seriously were Sir Charles Court and Sir Joh Bjelke-Petersen. They had resources for sale, were development-minded and well-disposed to business.

When Mick Shann had been Ambassador before me, Sir Charles Court, on his calls around Tokyo, roundly criticised the Commonwealth Government and Rex Connor. Mick Shann chose not to accompany him and cramp his style. When he came when I was Ambassador, and at the request of Doug Anthony, I insisted that I went with him to try to protect the Commonwealth's interest. I hope that my presence restrained him somewhat. I found him good company. He always presented well and was highly regarded.

Joh Bjelke-Petersen was an embarrassment. He came to Japan bellowing like a bull about how he was going to tell the Japanese that they had to take more beef and coal from Queensland. Bureaucrats would politely hear him out. He was never particularly coherent. Having failed to present his case effectively, he would issue press statements saying how he had been telling the Japanese what they had to do. His statements bore little resemblance to what he had said in the meetings I attended with him.

New South Wales, Victoria, Queensland and Western Australia had offices in Tokyo. At the Embassy we held monthly discussions with their commissioners to share information and to try to promote the national interest. I told them what I was doing, the issues that were before us and who was likely to visit. I would then invite them to report what they were doing. After the first two meetings it was very clear I wasn't getting anything from them. My initial reaction was to feel that they were holding out, playing the political game that I had seen so much of in Canberra. But I came to the view that they were not doing anything significant. They had little to report except the improvement in their golf handicaps.

The Secretary of one State Premier's Department told me that most of the reports he received from their Commissioner in Tokyo were extracts from the *Japan Times*; not occasional extracts but long articles to which he attached his name. The Treasury official at the Embassy prepared a monthly report on the Japanese economy which I gave to the state commissioners. That report was invariably floated down to Australia as a report, with suitable topping and tailing, from the state office. The states were an awful waste of money and confusing to the Japanese, but they were something I had to learn to live with. In later years the quality and work ethic of the state government offices improved. It is not surprising that New Zealand, with no states and with only one Tourist Commission, has a much clearer focus and identity in Japan than Australia.

The confusion in Japan about Australians is not a new problem. When the first Australian whaling ship, *Lady Rowena*, landed in Hokkaido in 1831, the Japanese residents in the northern island confused Australians with Russians. Where else could Caucasians have come from? It has been a problem ever since. Taxi drivers take visitors to the Austrian Embassy by mistake. We are confused with New Zealanders. Quite senior Japanese recalled to me the cities they had visited in Australia: Sydney, Canberra and Auckland.

To project a clearer Australian identity I tried to interest the Department of Foreign Affairs in selling the Embassy and Chancery site in Mita and developing an Australian Centre on the fringe of the Tokyo CBD, to bring together all the major Australian activities in Tokyo: the Embassy, state governments, Qantas, commodity boards, private companies, newspapers and others. It could have been a showcase for Australia, to counter the pervasive ignorance and misconceptions about us. Reaction to my proposal was mixed. The Department of Foreign Affairs was lukewarm, believing that it would be a mistake for Embassy activities to be too closely linked to commercial activities. Good diplomats need to stand back from business to get a proper perspective for their reports! The estimated cost of an Australian Centre was about A$80 million, plus land. Nine years later, one-third of the land at the Embassy site was sold for A$775 million. The Government built a new residence, an ugly stockade-type chancery and pocketed A$640 million. Many Japanese later expressed surprise to me that, along with diplomatic immunity and being free of taxes, the Embassy was in the property business.

For many Japanese we were bronzed Britishers with little identity of our own. Shigeo Nagano, doyen of the resource trade with Australia, was awarded an AC in the Order of Australia. I called on him to congratulate him and explain the Australian Order and that it was in recognition of his contribution to Australia. He replied, 'I've always wanted to go to Buckingham Palace'. I had to let him down gradually and explain that the investiture could either be in Tokyo or in Canberra but certainly not London. He was clearly disappointed that the Queen wasn't going to tap him on the shoulder with a sword.

Not surprisingly, the Japanese also find it hard to understand how the English Queen Elizabeth could be Queen of Australia. I was reminded of it when Zelman Cowen visited Japan in October 1977. He was making a private visit before becoming Governor-General and was keen to see the Emperor. The Japanese Foreign Ministry told me that the Emperor would see him but added that they were pleased that Cowen was coming as a private citizen because the Japanese Government would have difficulty in extending an invitation to the Queen's representative when he was in Japan. 'What is the status of the Queen's Representative in Australia when he is outside Australia?' It was, nevertheless, a very pleasant private meeting with the Emperor, who had been briefed that Zelman Cowen had been an athlete at Oxford University. Somehow that was translated into him being a champion marathon runner.

Zelman Cowen briefed Australian journalists over breakfast at the Embassy about his call later that day on the Emperor. Towards the end of the breakfast, Murray Sayle, an Australian journalist living in Japan, asked, 'In the story I write can I describe you an as eminent jurist?' Zelman Cowen said, 'Yes, I suppose that would be correct'. Then Murray Sayle added, 'Well, could I be a bit more precise. Could I describe you as an eminent Queensland jurist?' Zelman Cowen modestly said, 'Well, I come from Queensland, I guess you'd be correct in that also'. Murray Sayle then commented, 'Sir Zelman, do you realise that the last eminent Queensland jurist who came to Japan tried to hang the Emperor?'

In my first public speech in Japan to the Japan-Australia Society in May 1977, I said, 'While I'm in Japan I hope to see permanently laid to rest the myth of White Australia'. In my report to Minister Peacock at the end of my posting I said, 'Through insularity the Japanese have a very limited view of the outside world. 98 per cent of them have no real knowledge of Australia. Those that do not know us well have one basic unfavourable view of us, that we are racist'.

The ghost of White Australia followed me all over Japan. I spoke to scores of chambers of commerce, Rotary clubs and business groups throughout the country. In Japan, ambassadors are always a drawcard regardless of the merits of the individual or what he or she says. It was also a pleasant opportunity to get around and see the country. I told these community groups about Australia and how relations were improving with Japan. But at question time, and invariably the second or third question, depending on whether they had had a sake or two, was 'That is all very well, Ambassador, but what about White Australia?' Coming from a country with a racist past and present, I found that red hot. I pointed out that, despite our history, Australia in the 1970s had the least discriminatory migration policies in the region. But they didn't believe me. Perhaps the intense feeling about White Australia in Japan arose because in the late 19th century Australia was closed to Japanese at the only time in their history when they were interested in migration following the Meiji Restoration in 1868 and the opening of Japan to the world.

I was irritated and challenged by the Japanese questions, and determined to do something about it, particularly when I returned to Australia. On reflection, and particularly after the reaction I have encountered following John Howard's equivocation on Pauline Hanson, I think that I got it partly wrong. Japanese were not so concerned about our discrimination against Asians and Africans. It was discrimination against Japanese that offended. Some leading Japanese businessmen told me in 1998 that we have admitted too many Chinese!

The encouraging feature through all the state-sponsored racism, both in Japan and Australia, was that people kept their doors and hearts open. People on both sides ignored their governments and the race orthodoxy of the time and treated people as they found them. Three hundred and sixty-seven Australian soldiers married Japanese women after the Second World War, despite the unscrupulous and frightened of that era promoting racial stereotypes and discouraging inter-marriage.

But the Australian army occupation of Japan also had its sad side. 'Abandoned children' of Australian servicemen in Kure invited Cynthia and me to a 'Thank You Party' to express appreciation for the 'warm assistance from the Government and the people of Australia'. Before I went to Kure, I read the Embassy files including details of Cabinet decisions ten years before. Forty thousand dollars was provided by the Gorton Government in 1968 on two conditions. The first was that the money was for all 'mixed blood' children with no acknowledgement of any Australian paternity and secondly no further claims for financial help were to be made. It was humbling to receive thank you gifts from these children who had been discouraged and had given up hope of ever finding their fathers. They were then about 25 years old. Many were 'Australian-looking' but their behaviour was very Japanese. I had a quite uneasy sense of dissonance. The irony of them thanking me has remained with me ever since. How could they say thank you for the way they were abandoned by their fathers and the Australian people? If they had pointed their fingers I think I could have better understood. As an Australian I felt unworthy of their thanks.

In my many years of involvement with Japan, it is the Working Holiday Scheme between the two countries that I recall as my most worthwhile contribution. Australia had established such reciprocal schemes with the United Kingdom, Canada, Ireland and the Netherlands. Under these schemes young people, up to the age of 25, would get a 12-month entry permit. They could then visit the other country and work six months and have six months holiday. The income earned would enable them to stay and travel around the country and so get a better understanding than they would as tourists. But no such scheme had been established between Australia and an Asian country; a legacy of White Australia.

From 1977, when I arrived in Japan, I made a number of proposals to the Australian Government that we should establish such a scheme with Japan. I also publicly pressed the case. My advocacy went on for over two years, but I made no progress. The bureaucracy in Canberra, both Foreign Affairs and Immigration, didn't say no. It is easier to do nothing; enthusiasm or passion is unseemly.

We got a breakthrough when Japanese Prime Minister Ohira, a very good man, visited Australia in January 1980. In preparation, I had a luncheon discussion at the Commonwealth Club in Canberra with Ambassador Okawara, my counterpart in Australia, to see what could be announced to mark the visit. He was very well connected and respected in Japan. I told him that I had been promoting the Working Holiday

Scheme but confessed that I was having difficulty in selling it to the Australian bureaucracy. I explained the scheme. He said, 'Leave it to me. I will see what can be done at the Tokyo end'.

At Prime Minister Ohira's press conference at the conclusion of his visit, he said that Japan would be delighted if it were possible to negotiate a working holiday agreement between Australia and Japan. He said that Australia had expertise in such schemes and that perhaps an agreement with Australia was possible. Suddenly there was renewed interest. The Japanese had helped me outflank the Canberra bureaucracy.

I returned to Australia at the end of the year, September 1980, as Secretary of the Department of Immigration and Ethnic Affairs. I was able to pick up the proposal and conclude the agreement. There was no real opposition, only caution and lethargy. There were plenty of precedents for such a scheme. All that was required was a little enthusiasm to push it along. Malcolm Fraser and Ian Macphee, the Minister, were strong supporters.

It was a real breakthrough, considering the racial history of both countries. I regard it as more important than the dramatic growth in Japanese tourism that came later when I was at Qantas. From that scheme, over 70,000 young Japanese have come to Australia on working holidays and about 20,000 young Australians have gone to Japan. It provided a real enrichment of the relationship between the people of our two countries.

The Australia-Japan Foundation was also an important arm of the Australian Government's 'people-to-people' contacts in Japan. I was sceptical of the many cultural programs which emphasised the unique and the exotic and seldom got beyond elites in both countries. We needed to encourage people to deal with each other, to introduce them so that the wider community could become participants rather than observers or window shoppers in cultural exchange. Groups and individuals were funded by the foundation. There was a two-way flow of writers, journalists, playwrights, academics, book publishers and trade unionists. The foundation was very successful in broadening the relationship and, as a result, Australia became better known to a wider cross-section of Japanese. The foundation became the model for similar arrangements with China, Korea, India and Indonesia. There was early hope that Japan would establish a counterpart Japan-Australia Foundation. The Japanese

Foreign Ministry established a 'koala group' to advise, but it recommended against a bilateral foundation, in favour of leaving it to the multilateral Japan Foundation.

While I learned a great deal about Japan, the main benefit for me was to see Australia differently. I saw Australia from an outside vantage point, relatively free of the tribalism and parochial cultural conditioning which is inevitably so much part of all our lives.

I was also thinking differently about my own personal life. In Japan, our Methodist tribal roots were uprooted. We were footloose. There was no Methodist Church in Japan and the tribal comfort I found in Methodism was absent. My Methodist autopilot was of little use. I was forced to consider many things anew. We met many Australian Marist priests in Japan and, particularly, Father Tony Glynn, whose 40-year lifetime of service in Japan left an indelible impression on our family. Together with Weary Dunlop, I believe he made a greater contribution to Australian reconciliation with Asia than any other Australian. We saw him often and stayed with him in his spartan presbytery near Nara. We liked what we saw. He lived a life of disinterested goodness.

Cynthia was very supportive of the Marists in Nara, who established accommodation for Indo-Chinese refugees who had been picked up by Japanese ships. The parish near Nara had many *burakumin* who welcomed other outcasts. Cynthia organised a monster auction in the Embassy garden in Tokyo to raise money for the refugees. It was a huge success. She didn't have much competition, as Japan didn't have many fundraising events for refugees. Foreigners in need rate very low on the compassion scale in Japan.

Our oldest daughter, Susan, was married at the Episcopalian church in Tokyo to a young Korean man, Jong Moon Chun, in 1980. We invited Father Tony Glynn as a guest. Fifteen years later I was to recall that day:

> On my first daughter's wedding day, Tony Glynn invited me to come with him while he celebrated Mass. I thought I was going as a bystander but it didn't turn out that way. I had a great sense then of the Real Presence; Christ present both spiritually and materially.

I was on the edge of a mystery. It was a deepening experience for me, an epiphany. The Eucharist took on a new meaning; the reconciling and liberating event at the centre of the universe. A quickening pace of discovery was at hand.

Japan had opened a new world for me, learning more about Australia and myself. Three years after Japan I joined the Catholic Church—but more about that later.

Seventeen years later, in 1997, I was awarded the Grand Cordon of the Order of the Sacred Treasure, by the Emperor of Japan, in recognition of my 'distinguished contribution towards the furtherance of friendship, cultural exchange and mutual understanding between Japan and Australia'. As I posed with Gough for a photo at the investiture at the Japanese Consul-General's residence in Sydney, Gough Whitlam announced, 'a sacred Treasure and a secular Treasure'! It was a very simple and friendly occasion with family and friends. I knew how family an affair it was to see Joseph Chun, my youngest grandson from Japan, standing in the front row picking his nose. It was the signal to wind up my speech.

The most satisfying job of my life

Immigration and Ethnic Affairs

'For those who've come across the sea
We've boundless plains to share;
With courage let us all combine
To Advance Australia Fair'

W̲e all loved Japan, but there was a longing to go home. As a result of my Japanese contacts with the minerals trade, Jim McNeill, the Chairman of BHP, asked me to join the board of BHP after I left Japan. But I decided against it. At 45, life as a professional board director looked premature.

When Malcolm Fraser was in Japan in mid-1980, he asked me about my plans. I told him that I would like to go back to Australia to head the Department of Immigration and Ethnic Affairs and do my bit to end White Australia forever. That sentiment appealed to him. He took it up with Ian Macphee, who was the Minister. I knew Macphee by reputation but I didn't know him well.

Malcolm Fraser gave full support to Macphee and me to eliminate racism and discrimination in immigration. The three of us were of a common view. I was not on a frolic of my own. Not once did Fraser tell Macphee to change course. And neither of them told me to do anything differently. The *Sydney Morning Herald* of 3 December 1980 commented that, 'the combination of the Immigration Minister, Mr Macphee, a small "l" liberal, and Mr Menadue, who once contested the Federal seat of

Hume for the ALP, has activated radical changes in Australia's immigration aims'. When my appointment was announced, the *National Times* carried the story under the heading 'Man from Tokyo returns to bury White Australia'. I thought that summarised my mission pretty well.

The job as Head of the Department for three years was the most satisfying I have ever had. It was thrilling to be part of nation building and to see and feel the vitality which new and diverse people brought to their adopted country.

By 1980 a large number of Indo-Chinese refugees were coming to Australia. On a per capita basis Australia took more Indo-Chinese refugees than the US. Changes were under way. However, I found the department in its administration, attitude and personnel still very much shaped by the past. There was a resistance to change, particularly among the older members of the department who had cut their teeth on immigration programs from the UK. They were decent men but with very different mind-sets. There were only a few women. The resources of the department for processing migrants and visitors were still overwhelmingly in Europe, particularly the UK. The posts in Asia were few and under-resourced. I set about changing that.

In my first week in the department in September 1980, there was a major immigration advertising campaign in Manchester. I got reports from delighted staff about how 11,000 people queued up to inquire about immigrating to Australia. I didn't feel the same delight. I told the staff that if we put a similar advertising campaign into Manila or into Singapore we would have had even more in the queue. I sent a senior officer from Canberra immediately to tell the UK Regional Office that things had to change. Special advertising in the UK only was cancelled on the spot. We had to advertise on a non-discriminatory basis and where the most skilled applicants could be found. For the first time we commenced advertising the business migration scheme in the *Far Eastern Economic Review* in Hong Kong.

Amongst the younger staff who had worked in the Indo-China refugee programs, the changes I commenced were welcomed. There were also a lot of younger women in the department and I found them much more open. They were a great help.

As an illustration of past practices, I was shown files on applicants in Sri Lanka. There were obviously some fancy photographers in Colombo—the negative was underexposed or overexposed so the desired complexion could be produced in the photograph on the application form. Applicants feared that if they looked too black they wouldn't be admitted.

I made quite a number of public speeches which got me into hot water with editorial writers and cartoonists. I said that with a non-discriminatory policy I didn't care if a thousand migrants to Australia came from the United Kingdom or from Malaysia, provided they were qualified and met the criteria. The *West Australian* on 25 November 1980 reported:

> Menadue said that he had no preconceived ideas of Australia's racial mix or its racial mix of immigrants. One year there might be 10% British and 90% Asian and the next year it could be reversed. We want the best people. Menadue made it clear that he was determined to smash the image of Australia's White Australia policy.

Some elements of the RSL called on Macphee to get rid of me. Graffiti appeared on the walls of the department: 'Menadue = mongrelisation'. I was criticised that as Secretary of the Department I seemed to be determining policy. The *Australian* on 31 December 1980 said in its leader, 'Immigration policy is a matter for Cabinet. Now clearly Mr Menadue has his own policy line on immigration. It is not one we believe the Government or the great bulk of the Australian public would, or should, support.'

There was a lot of media interest generated in what I was saying. I had had the privilege of working in Asia and seeing Australia from the outside and I was determined that a non-discriminatory policy should be genuinely implemented. People whose judgment I valued urged me not to back off in the face of the attacks.

Macphee came under criticism from some of his parliamentary colleagues, not so much on the issue of non-discrimination in immigration but that, as Head of the Department, I was so public on immigration issues. But Macphee understood what I was trying to do and was very supportive. I knew he had a problem with some of his colleagues so I pulled my head in for a couple of months. Fraser did not complain at all.

We took advantage of government policy to cut expenditure by proposing cuts in programs that reflected the earlier preferential and discriminatory days of 'Bring out a Briton'. Since 1945, over two million migrants had received assisted passages at a cost of over $500 million. More than 50 per cent of the money went to UK immigrants. We proposed to end all assisted passages immediately. Macphee told me that in Cabinet Deputy Prime Minister Anthony and Treasurer Lynch said that there would be an outcry from the Government's pro-British supporters if we did so. Fraser supported Macphee and in April 1981 the Government removed the favoured treatment that UK immigrants were receiving. There was no outcry. Part of the annual savings was used to fund expanded English learning for non-English-speaking migrants.

Immigrants still had privileged access to hostels when they came to Australia. Most were from the UK and they lingered a long time. To cut expenditure further the Government agreed to Macphee's recommendation that migrant hostels would be available only for refugees and special humanitarian cases.

We explained the changes overseas as well as in Australia. In the *Financial Review*, on 2 July 1981, Greg Heywood reported from London,

> In an eight day trip throughout Britain, Australia's Immigration Minister, Ian Macphee, and his Permanent Head, John Menadue, have trodden on a few sensitive toes. They have stated outright that Australia does not want British migrants unless they are skilled tradesmen or businessmen. Those offended are British Government officials and those who see migration to Australia as an alternative for the underprivileged ... hopeful that Australia might draw off some of their army of unemployed. The British are getting no joy from the visit.

At a dinner at Lancaster House on the visit, Jock Pagan, the anglophile NSW Agent-General, leaned across the table and told Lord Carrington, the Defence Minister and former British High Commissioner in Canberra, that he disagreed with what Macphee had been saying. Carrington reacted that just as the UK saw its future in Europe, so Australia might see its home in its own region. Pagan said that he felt at home getting into his Bentley in London. Carrington, the European, said that he felt at home in London getting into his Mercedes Benz.

But it wasn't just British migrants who had been getting preference. Under the Netherlands Emigration Scheme, Dutch tradesmen were selected by Dutch authorities—not Australian officials—and without proper regard to Australian requirements. The scheme was terminated. Preferential treatment of New Zealanders, who didn't require any documents to enter Australia, was more problematic. Malcolm Fraser determined that it should be changed. But the reform, insisting that all New Zealanders entering Australia must at least carry passports, and vice versa, wasn't easy going.

In preparation for the Commonwealth Heads of Government meeting in Melbourne in October 1981, we were concerned about lax procedures for people entering New Zealand, who could then come on to Australia without adequate checks. On grounds of non-discrimination, I favoured visas for New Zealanders and still do, but knew that it would be politically hard for any Australian Government to make that stick. Fraser agreed with the sentiment but insistence on a passport was as far as he was prepared to go. Many of his Cabinet colleagues didn't want any change.

At a negotiating meeting between Ian Macphee and 'Ossie' Malcolm, his Australian-born New Zealand counterpart, the Australian High Commissioner in New Zealand, ex-Senator Jim Webster, set us back by saying he agreed with the New Zealand position of opposing passports. We thought the Australian High Commissioner was paid to be on the Australian side. But we made the change and from July 1981, all travellers entering Australia from New Zealand had to carry a passport. Unfortunately the announcement was made on the eve of Anzac Day.

In November 1981, after agreement with the states, the Commonwealth Electoral Act was amended to prevent future 'British subjects' in Australia voting in Australian elections if they were not Australian citizens. 'British subjects' included not only UK citizens but citizens of 41 other countries from former British colonies like the Bahamas, Bangladesh, Zambia and Zimbabwe. Our purpose was to remove discrimination against immigrants who were not British subjects. By removing the preference to British subjects we were also keen to encourage British subjects to take Australian citizenship. In 1981 there were 1.2 million people in Australia who were residentially qualified to be Australian citizens but had chosen not to become Australian citizens. Approximately 70 per cent of them were British subjects.

Macphee and I were particularly concerned about racial violence in Western Australia against Asian immigrants which, we were advised, was provoked by some immigrants from Southern Rhodesia. Macphee agreed that we should attempt at immigration interviews to assess whether applicants were sympathetic to the non-discriminatory policies of Australia and would settle happily in Australia, or try to carry on their racism in their new country. It was important in terms of suitability for settlement in Australia. It is very difficult to administer such criteria. Racists are usually smart enough to hold their tongue in interviews. But we made an attempt.

Steadily discrimination was being dismantled. We relocated staff out of Europe into Asia and the Pacific. As a result we were able to get a better balance of immigration inflow. We had a wider range of choice. By the mid-1980s Europe was relatively affluent and the best and most enterprising migrants had probably left. We were seeing in Asia the development of education and the growth of a middle class. As a result of a non-discriminatory policy coupled with non-discriminatory administration, we were able to get more adaptable migrants from around the globe. In 1976/77, before I joined the department, 15 per cent of the settler intake was from Asia. In 1980/81, the first year of the Indo-China refugees, Asians made up 24 per cent of our total intake. In 1983/84, the year after I left the department, 38 per cent were from Asia.

One issue that did worry me was that treatment of the 50,000 'illegal immigrants' in Australia was not evenhanded. Illegals were people staying in Australia without proper papers. Australians had an erroneous view, and probably still do, that illegals are here because they jumped ship or arrived on refugee boats. That number is miniscule. The largest number of illegals in Australia were British tourists who came legally and then stayed illegally after their entry permit expired. Those who were reported as 'illegals' by neighbours, contacts or just busybodies, were invariably non-white and non-English-speaking. The assumption was that if you were white you were probably legal. If you were Asian or from the South Pacific the chances were you might be in Australia illegally. So the reports we received about possible 'illegals', which we had to act on, gave us a very heavy skew against non-whites. I don't think we successfully overcame discriminatory treatment.

The bias in our procedures was clear on the issue of visas for visitors. In 1982, 27 per cent of overstayed visitors were from UK but only 0.2

per cent of applications by UK visitors were rejected on the grounds of being likely to overstay or engage in employment. This low rejection rate was despite the large departmental representation we had in the UK. The 1985 Report of the Human Rights Commission on the Migration Act of 1958 not surprisingly commented, '… it may be construed (from the above figures) that assessments for granting or rejecting visitors visas are made in a racially discriminatory manner'.

Despite my concern over the bias in our procedures, I was determined that we should have a strong enforcement policy. That attracted unfavourable publicity. In October 1981, 146 bogus refugees arrived in Darwin. They had come from Taiwan and Hong Kong via a boat from Thailand for the last leg to Australia. It was an organised racket. They were all detained and quickly deported on Macphee's direction. Strong enforcement was also shown to a group of Liberal Party supporters in Melbourne who persuaded a Romanian soccer player to seek asylum, big noting themselves that they would get Macphee to fix it. He refused.

We both strongly believed that an important reason why Australians supported immigration was confidence that the Australian Government controlled the program. If the Australian community, then or now, believed that there was no real control at our borders, that people entered and stayed illegally, there would be a serious loss of confidence in the program. There is a harshness about a strong enforcement policy, but I felt that a liberal policy had to be firmly enforced.

In the department we were under pressure to develop a population policy for Australia. What was an optimum population? After discussion with Macphee we resisted, for several reasons that I still find compelling. The primary reason was that 'population policy' was really code for 'stop immigration'. It was coming from the green anti-development groups. It is ironic that almost 20 years later the Greens have been joined by Pauline Hanson to resist immigration. We also believed that, in contrast to a heavily populated Asia, Australia has space, resources and opportunity. With a small population we have a moral obligation and it is also in our self-interest to increase our population. We were also certain that immigration had brought great vitality and development to Australia, so why should we turn our back on new, enterprising people in the future? Since my days in Japan I have always favoured a significantly higher population for Australia: nearer 50 rather than 18 million.

Fortunately, we had with Fraser and later Hawke and Keating, prime ministers who were optimistic about Australia and confident of new people and their contribution to nation building. In my years as head of the department, 1980–83, the annual immigration intake was about 100,000 persons. We rejected what we saw as the timidity of the 'population policy' advocates in the early 1980s.

After I had been one year into the job, Cynthia, at 46, was to begin her struggle with cancer. In a routine check in Canberra she found a lump in her breast. Further checks confirmed the possibility of malignancy. We came to Sydney where Dr John Morris, a family friend and Head of Nuclear Medicine at the Royal Prince Alfred Hospital, arranged further tests. They confirmed our fears and Cynthia underwent a mastectomy in December 1981. She recovered quickly and got back to her *minshuku* tours and book writing.

While Cynthia was often in Japan four or five times a year with her tours, we nevertheless, spent a lot of time together in Sydney. At balls, dinners and community gatherings we enjoyed meeting the ethnic communities and seeing first hand how they were transforming and invigorating Australian life. How unlike Japan it was. At the Australian Institute of Mining and Metallurgy Conference in August 1982, I spoke of what I was witnessing:

> Thanks to our post-war immigration program, Australians are now more understanding and knowledgable of other nations and cultures. There is a growing awareness, both here and abroad, of Australia as an independent but integral part of the international community. Immigrants, more and more, are expanding this awareness. Through them, and together with them, Australia is being constantly stimulated in a whole range of areas. An immigration program is the only tool readily at hand to challenge complacency and parochialism. The contribution of innovative immigration to the development of the United States comes to mind as an example of people who ran risks, but greatly prospered through a steady infusion of people determined to make a better life for themselves and their children.

Almost two decades later, I still see immigration as the best means at hand to raise the levels of enterprise and initiative in the Australian community. Historically Australia has always been myopic and inward-looking. Immigration is the catalyst to change that, more than anything else. The richness and diversity of Australia that we have developed over the last 20 years, indeed over the last 200 years, is our greatest national achievement.

Every year students from non-Anglo-Celtic backgrounds—Korean, Vietnamese, Chinese, Polish and Russian—dominate university entry. The children of non-English-speaking migrants are twice as likely to go to university as English-speaking school leavers. The crime rate amongst migrant communities has been consistently lower than amongst Australian-born. Being younger, migrants are usually healthier. All the research that I have seen also shows that migrants boost jobs. Environmental problems in our cities are due to bad policies and bad planning rather than immigration.

I have always had a soft spot for refugees. Perhaps it comes from my boyhood and the stories of the holy family fleeing to Egypt to escape Herod. Refugees, almost by definition, are risk-taking people and have been a very important part of our developing maturity. Since the Second World War, Australia has provided a home for about half a million refugees and displaced persons. They abandon the past for a better future. Most recently, in the case of Vietnam and to a lesser extent Cambodia, those who had to flee were associated with the old regime. They were vulnerable and exposed. They are grateful for the freedom and opportunities that we older Australians take for granted. Their energy is invigorating. I find their enthusiasm and commitment to Australia quite infectious.

In June 1981, Macphee and I visited the refugee camps in Malaysia and Thailand. It was a moving experience to see tens of thousands of people waiting expectantly to leave. Would our visit, like so many other visits, help them get a ticket out? In the closed refugee camps scores of them secretly gave me letters that they hoped I could pass on to their families. Young refugee officials were a joy to see, patiently assisting in processing and responding to medical and social problems. Some aid workers, however, were very insensitive, like some fundamentalist Christians from the US raising the hopes of the mountain people from Laos that they might settle in the US with large five-bedroom houses, two cars and hi-fi.

On Malaysia's east coast we learned of the hostility of the locals to the boat people. The Malaysian Prime Minister, Dr Mahathir, had been reported as saying to the locals, 'Shoot them'. His Foreign Minister, Ghazali bin Shafie, however, told us with a wink that Mahathir had really said 'Shoo them'. Macphee asked to discuss refugee matters with Mahathir but he was too busy. Mahathir did find time, however, to see a junior North Korean minister while Macphee was in Kuala Lumpur. Mahathir's dislike of Australia is long-standing.

Refugees do present risks, which we acknowledged in the department. When there are people moving quickly in large numbers, processing is under pressure. Undesirables join the flow; mistakes are made in selection. We also faced problems in refugee camps in the region with unattached Vietnamese minors, young boys of 15 or 16, who had been separated from their families. We were asked by the United Nations High Commissioner for Refugees (UNHCR) whether we would take some of them. After careful consideration we decided to take several hundred. I don't know how they settled into Australia but it was a decision that we made knowing it was risky. Do you leave young, single males in a refugee camp or do you take a chance and give them an opportunity for a new life?

In the course of my work, Cynthia and I met many very committed English language migrant education teachers. It was through these associations that Cynthia learnt of a young Cambodian woman, Neary Eng, at the Cabramatta Hostel. The teachers were impressed with Neary as a very able young woman who needed some additional support and opportunity. Cynthia and I fostered Neary in our own home for over five years. With hard work she obtained her School Certificate and became a qualified nursing sister. Cynthia and Peter particularly helped her to learn English and become familiar with the Australian community. She became an Australian citizen at the earliest opportunity and a very good citizen she is. We have kept close contact with her. It was a great pleasure for me some years later when I was a director of the Overseas Telecommunications Commission, to take her back with me to Phnom Penh. It was very moving to meet her father, who acknowledged that he was no longer able to look after her and thanked me for the way we had fostered her. Neary has had a kidney transplant. She married and has a baby. Her siblings and their families all now live in Sydney. We set out to help Neary but, as in so many matters of the heart, she contributed much more to our family. Through Cynthia's sickness, she was an enormous strength and point of equilibrium in our family.

In my job I came to see at first hand that refugees and people fleeing persecution do it tough and often experience precious little of the milk of human kindness when dealing with officials in secure jobs. In 1982 many Poles fled their country after the imposition of martial law. Many were in camps in Austria. The Australian Embassy in Brussels reported that NATO officials were urging countries like Australia not to accept these Poles as refugees. They should stay in Europe and return to Poland to carry on the fight against communism. We disregarded the NATO advice.

We had representations from Coptic and other Christian leaders in the Middle East urging us not to deplete their small Christian communities by accepting their fellow Christians as settlers in Australia, even though they were facing various degrees of discrimination. We decided to ignore the representations and treat each application on its merits.

In 1982, we introduced a global Special Humanitarian Program (SHP) for people who were not 'refugees' under the strict UNHCR definition, but who were suffering gross discrimination. We gave priority to those with close links to Australia. Applicants could apply 'in country'; they would not have to flee their country in order to apply. Prior to that, all of Australia's humanitarian resettlement entrants were classed as 'refugees' only if they had left the country in which they had experienced persecution. By 1998 over 70,000 people had settled in Australia under the SHP.

The program was largely a reaction to the installation of US-backed military governments in El Salvador and Chile. Under the program Australia could react humanely to those suffering discrimination within their homeland but unable to leave to seek refugee status elsewhere. It was quite an achievement to implement the SHP without antagonising bilateral relations. Perhaps, in part, we were successful because the military governments concerned wanted to get rid of their critics. It was also because we studiously avoided the word 'refugee'.

Establishment of the SHP was also influenced by President Reagan's policies towards Latin America. The US was a very generous funder of refugee programs generally, but as a result of US pressure, the UNHCR would not declare many displaced people in Latin America to be 'refugees'. The US Administration could not bring itself to acknowledge that people might want to flee right-wing governments, particularly those they had installed or supported.

Macphee was straightforward in agreeing to help these people in need, regardless of whether they were under pressure from dictatorships of the left or the right. Fraser was very supportive.

Despite our success in aligning non-discriminatory procedures with a non-discriminatory policy, the British link was never far away. I was approached by the UK High Commissioner in Canberra to agree to the migration of a number of 'supergrass'. These were, in most cases, British citizens who had informed on the IRA. They were to be extricated from the United Kingdom with cover and aliases. I consulted Macphee who said, 'No'. Whilst the Irish had enriched Australia, Macphee was determined that Australia must keep out of the violence that had bedevilled Northern Ireland. They would not be allowed to bring their contagion to Australia. The High Commissioner then spoke to Fraser but Fraser trusted Macphee's judgment. As a Scot, Fraser probably didn't feel inclined to help the English anyway. Macphee was adamant that he wouldn't change. He thought carefully and stuck to his decision. Australia had ceased being a British penal colony. Why should we start again?

By coincidence Mick Young was the Shadow Minister for Immigration and Ethnic Affairs. He had a high regard for Macphee, which was reciprocated. Together with Eric Walsh, we often had dinner together at a Canberra restaurant, usually the Charcoal. Ian Macphee sang 'On the Road to Mandalay', Mick Young 'Danny Boy' and Eric Walsh 'Kevin Barry'. I tried to sing 'Joe Hill'. But the Macphee-Young-Menadue connection raised queries. A journalist was under ASIO telephone surveillance and from this ASIO picked up speculation, in a conversation with another journalist, that because of the relationship between the three of us there must be an immigration racket running. The matter was referred to the Prime Minister The journalist gossip was rejected.

There was genuine political bipartisanship and personal cooperation on immigration. Macphee and I both separately briefed the ALP Caucus Committee. The Minister didn't think it necessary to send along one of his political staffers to check on what I said. Things have now changed in Canberra. Trust is not the same.

We organised public meetings around Australia to discuss

immigration. Mick Young shared the platform with us. There was some predictable opposition, mainly from new English immigrants who were disappointed to find that they weren't coming to the White Australia that they had expected.

In looking back now I think the debate should have been more rigorous. We were cautious about public debate, given our history of racism which was not far below the national surface. I believed then and still believe that in a referendum on the question, 'Should we have more Asian immigrants?', the response would be 'no'. I believed, however, that Australians were pragmatic and generous. To a question: 'How do you get on with your Chinese neighbours?', I was confident that the answer would be 'They seem OK'. Asian immigration does require strong and committed leadership and a view about our future rather than a nostalgic look backwards.

With each generation of new settlers, Northern Europeans, Southern Europeans and Asian, there are inevitably problems; 'they don't speak English', 'they are taking our jobs', 'they are into crime', 'they live in ghettos', 'they bring disease', 'they are ruining the neighbourhood'. Interestingly, it is often the second last wave of immigrants who are most sceptical of the last wave. I recall the opposition to Indo-Chinese refugees in Cabramatta in the 1980s. A young blonde woman in a bar was asked on television what she had against the Indo-Chinese. She replied in a very heavy East European accent, 'We was here first'.

Over time, the new arrivals settle in, become integrated, shift out of ethnic concentrations as they become more prosperous and confident and succeed in mainstream education, business and sport. But immigrants face problems in every society. In times of change and difficulty we all have a tendency to project our personal anxieties onto others and blame the person or group that looks different or foreign. Scapegoating is as old as human society. It is worse when we have high unemployment and when differences are politically exploited.

By mid-1982, almost two years into the job, I was looking at a move back to Sydney. Talbot Duckmanton was finishing his term as General Manager of the ABC. The Chair of the ABC was Professor Leonie Kramer. My media interest had survived my seven years with Rupert Murdoch. But my other interest in Sydney and the ABC was personal. Cynthia had recovered well from her mastectomy and she ran her *minshuku* tours to Japan out of Sydney. We wanted to be close to her. All the family loved Sydney. I also felt that the ABC didn't adequately reflect multicultural Australia. It had little sense of life in the new and outer suburbs. If it had, the SBS would never have been established. The ABC was still North Atlantic oriented, with heavy dependence on traditional news services, particularly the BBC, but it neglected Asia even though it was still streets ahead of its commercial competitors in this regard.

I applied for the position of General Manager of the ABC, made the short list, but was defeated by Keith Jennings, who resigned from the job within 12 months on the grounds of ill health. He had previously been a senior executive at the University of Sydney with Professor Leonie Kramer. My referees, Sir Roderick Carnegie, Chairman of CRA, Ian Macphee, Minister for Immigration and Ethnic Affairs, Mick Young, Shadow Minister for Immigration and Ethnic Affairs, and Sir Geoffrey Yeend, Secretary of the Department of Prime Minister and Cabinet, all supported me but a decision was made before their referee reports were received. Not surprisingly, they were extremely annoyed and told Professor Kramer in very strong terms about the lack of due process and waste of their time. I learnt that being a front runner is risky; the media had unhelpfully promoted me as the person for the job.

So back to work with John Hodges, the new Minister for Immigration and Ethnic Affairs, in midwinter in Canberra 1982. Macphee was promoted to Industrial Relations. He was a big loss to the department and the immigration cause.

Hodges was the Liberal Member for Petrie, in Brisbane. It was to prove a difficult working relationship. He had on his staff people from Joh Bjelke-Petersen's private office. They had a sceptical view about me and my background, and I was similarly sceptical about them.

I had a particular problem with Hodges over the Big Brother Movement (BBM). Cavan Hogue, on secondment from the Department of Foreign Affairs, had come to see me a year earlier and told me in his laconic style, 'Mate, I have found another spider under the colonial rock'. Hogue had unearthed the BBM, a special deal going back to 1921.

BBM provided opportunities for white boys from the UK to migrate to Australia. Over 10,000 had come. There was a special annual quota of 300. The BBM 'lads' were not screened by immigration officers for compliance with government policy and procedures. Special equipment and establishment allowances were paid by Australian taxpayers. BBM paid a peppercorn rental on office space in Canberra House in London. Sir John Pagan, President of the NSW Liberal Party, was also President of BBM. The organisation was very well connected politically, with dukes and knights by the cartload. They staged a fighting retreat for 18 months.

Back in May 1981, Macphee had directed that any preferential treatment of BBM had to end. In July 1981 in London, at a meeting of the Cooke Society, Pagan privately complained to Macphee and me about the department being uncooperative with BBM. Macphee politely and firmly explained that BBM did not conform with a non-discriminatory global policy.

Later in the year, Pagan was back in Canberra and again pressed the BBM case with Macphee, this time with more threat. Pagan was staying at the Lodge with Fraser and inferred to Macphee that he had one last chance to be helpful or the matter would be raised with Fraser. True to form, Fraser never urged Macphee to back off.

Coincidentally, Mother Theresa asked Macphee in Melbourne at the same time to take special action to admit waifs from Calcutta. Macphee's response was the same as to Pagan. They can only be admitted if they came within a non-discriminatory global policy.

With the loss of government funds for passage assistance, BBM said they could become self-sufficient but required three things: continuation of the free accommodation in Canberra House, continued immigration processing of their own and retention of their special quota.

When Hodges replaced Macphee as Minister in May 1982, BBM put on an intense lobbying campaign directed at Hodges. He gave them encouragement. I explained to Hodges that we didn't have similar schemes for 300 boys each year from Indonesia or Malaysia who were in need, perhaps even in greater need than English boys. In a memo to him I recommended that all special financial assistance be abolished, that no free accommodation be provided, that all BBM nominees meet normal entry criteria and that departmental officers process all applications.

There was a long, drawn-out disagreement. I decided to force the pace and directed our office in London that BBM should not receive free accommodation. A copy of my directive went to Hodges. However, the 'landlord' in London was the Department of Foreign Affairs and their senior officer in London, the Deputy High Commissioner, rejected my direction as being 'too hard' on BBM. The dukes and knights obviously still had influence. I lost that one.

Friction continued in the department with respect to BBM until the Fraser Government lost office and John Hodges lost his seat. The new Government terminated all preferences for BBM within weeks.

Social stability in Australia has been built on a strong core culture of English language, shared values, freedom of speech and religion, tolerance, and our parliamentary and legal systems. An immigrant superstructure of diversity has been built on that strong, unifying substructure. Our success has also been because the core culture has never felt threatened because the process of new people coming to Australia has been slow and orderly.

We held public forums in late 1982 to discuss a paper on 'multiculturalism for all Australians; our developing nationhood'. The paper prepared by Professor Zubrzycki, outlined four pillars for building a 'viable multicultural Australia': social cohesion, cultural identity, equality of opportunity and participation in society. The public forums were well received, with predictable protests from those who in later years rallied to Pauline Hanson.

A key to the success of settlement and the multiculturalism that went with it were the programs to promote equality of opportunity and to demonstrate to new settlers that they were valued. New settlers knew that they didn't have to shun or disown their own culture, language and traditions. They sensed that what they brought to Australia was valued. It is hard to appreciate and learn from another culture and join the mainstream unless you are grounded and confident in your own. New settlers who are forced to abandon their own culture and identity through assimilation are not much value to Australia or themselves. Government policies made it clear that people with differences were valued. Esteem went to them despite differences.

In the department we didn't welcome diversity for its own sake. There were some aspects of diversity, the treatment of women and children in some ethnic groups, that were clearly unacceptable in the community. But we recognised that changes and moderation would occur over generations.

Government programs in English language, education, welfare and health have avoided the development of a migrant underclass. We had, through the Galbally Report and succeeding programs, quite successful means to create equality of opportunity for new settlers. Multiculturalism was more than new cuisine and interesting folk dancing. There have been difficulties and there is obviously a sacrifice which first generations make for the success of their children. It is the second generation that we see topping classes in university and high school examinations.

My days in the department persuaded me of the importance of compulsory voting in promoting social cohesion. Australians should not be allowed to opt out of the democratic process. I think in Australia's interests there is an overriding greater good in compulsory voting, that people who come to this country as well as those who are born here are expected to participate. With voluntary voting, the alienated and disadvantaged would drop even more out of the system. Compulsory voting keeps them in. Their vote is important and politicians can't ignore them. Alienation would be worse if we did not have compulsory voting.

In the department we were also active in promoting citizenship but in retrospect it deserved a lot more attention than we gave it. It is the glue that unites us. There should, in my view, be more encouragement for citizenship; perhaps access after a certain period to government benefits should be available only to citizens. I hope we don't go the way of the jingoism in the United States but we should promote citizenship more positively and effectively to bind Australians together. Importantly, we need always to underline that it is loyalty to Australia which binds us together, not blood or ethnicity.

In Australia in the 1980s there was overwhelming support from politicians and all parties for the migration program. There were niggles around the edges from right-wing and anti-development groups but there was strong support. That has been a great feature of migration and multiculturalism in Australia. It has been supported by all the major opinion leaders, whether they were in politics, business, unions or the media. The only significant exception over many years has been John Howard. He first broke bipartisanship in immigration in 1988 when he was Leader of the Opposition and again as Prime Minister in 1996.

To live and succeed in this part of the world we have to have a migrant program that reflects our geography. Change will happen slowly and at an acceptable pace but I would expect that by the middle of the next century the Australian population will be very different from what it is today. I think it is an exciting prospect. Four of my grandchildren are Australian-Korean. I think this will be increasingly common in Australia in the future. A republic is part of the process of defining ourselves, as is a new flag.

The other important issue we worked on in the department was foreign language learning. We set the pace in the early 1980s, with not many supporters. I felt quite lonely. My experience in Japan gave me the energy to try and do something about it. What I saw and felt in Japan was my own language inadequacy. I had some social Japanese but not much more. On too many occasions I found it painfully embarrassing not to be able to communicate, even when I was playing golf with Prime Minister Ohira.

During return visits to Australia from Japan, on leave and consultation, I made many speeches about foreign language learning in Australia, pointing to the dramatic shifts away from foreign languages in universities and schools. Between 1955 and 1980 in the NSW Higher School Certificate, there was a drop from 60 per cent to 18 per cent in students studying a foreign language. To the teachers of Japanese in 1981, I pointed out '20 years ago, 40 per cent of Australian matriculation students took a foreign language. The figure is now about ten per cent. Last year less than three per cent of students sitting for matriculation studied an Asian language.'

We took this issue up in the department because of my interest and because the only major groups in Australia who were interested in second languages and language development were the European ethnic communities. One of their gifts to Australia was love of their own language. They wanted language maintenance in Australia for their children. So I tried to build a national language policy coalition based on the European ethnic communities in Australia. In 1980, there were over 1.3 million first-generation migrants of non-English-speaking origin. The 'top four' foreign languages were Italian, Greek, 'Yugoslav' and German — almost 50 per cent of the total. The only Asian language of significant size was Chinese. I didn't believe that we could succeed in Asian language development without the support of the European-based ethnic communities. They were pointing the way out of monolingualism.

The ethnic communities responded enthusiastically and we developed a campaign across Australia to develop a national language policy for schools and universities. In 1981, Ian Macphee and I persuaded Wal Fife, the Minister for Education, to make a joint Cabinet Submission on the development of a national language policy. With Fraser's support Cabinet agreed that it should be further pursued through the Senate Committee on Education and the Arts, chaired by Senator Baden Teague. That Committee agreed on 25 March 1982 to examine all aspects of language learning and use in Australia.

I tried through Charlie Perkins, who was Head of the Aboriginal Affairs Department, to find common ground for preservation of Aboriginal languages. I put to him that one reason why there was increasing support for the preservation of Aboriginal languages and dialects was that there was now a significant continental European community in Australia which was interested in preservation of their own languages. By extension one could make a strong case that languages should be preserved for all Australians, whether Aborigine, Greek or Chinese.

It was hard building links between Aborigines and ethnic communities. Many Aborigines resented that Asians seemed to have preferential treatment and felt Aborigines were not being asked whether they wanted new migrants coming to Australia. I appreciated that there were problems but I believed that conceptually there was something that we could build on. I think that the retention, inadequate though it is, of Aboriginal languages in Australia owes something to multiculturalism, a policy which Aborigines never embraced.

In a speech on multiculturalism I used a poem by Kath Walker to describe what we were trying to achieve:

> Pour your pitcher of wine into the wide river
> And where is your wine? There is only the river …
> … Do not ask of us
> To be deserters, to disown our mother,
> To change the unchangeable.
> The gum cannot be changed into the oak.
> Something is gone: something is surrendered, still
> We will go forward and learn.
> Not swamped and lost, watered away, but keeping
> Our own identity, our pride of race.
> Pour your pitcher of wine into the wide river
> And where is your wine? There is only the river.

I made dozens of speeches to business, ethnic and educational groups through 1980 and into 1982, about the need for a national language policy. I proposed that foreign language study should be compulsory at all education levels and a prerequisite for university entrance. There were very encouraging responses in newspaper editorials, almost all of them drawing attention to the continuing advocacy on languages that I had commenced in Japan.

The first National Language Conference was organised by the Department of Immigration and Ethnic Affairs and the Federation of Ethnic Community Councils, in Canberra in October 1982, to bring all of our work together and to provide a platform for the future. It turned out to be a disaster, as one's best laid plans often are. Minister Hodges was really not on board as far as Asia, multiculturalism and language were concerned. I didn't speak at the conference launch as the Minister was the obvious keynote speaker. We prepared some speech notes for him but he didn't use them. The thrust of his speech was 'What's all this about a national language policy? The world is all learning English. We don't need to change'. My friends in the ethnic communities groaned.

Despite the ministerial setback we had created momentum. Public debate was under way; other organisations were picking up the issue. More and more emphasis came on to the need for Asian languages.

A major breakthrough came when the Senate Committee on Education and the Arts reported in February 1985. I had left the department by then. The committee made two major recommendations. The first was that language policies in Australia should be developed on four guiding principles: competence in English; maintenance and development of languages other than English; provision of services in languages other than English; and opportunities for learning second languages. The second major finding was that language policies should be coordinated at the national level. The development of a national language policy was under way after five years of speech-making and lobbying.

In 1987, the Australian Government adopted a national policy on languages and in 1994, the Council of Australian Governments, comprising the federal, state and territory governments, adopted a report on funding of Asian languages in Australian schools and universities which I felt was the culmination of the work we had commenced 14 years

230

earlier. There is now funding through commonwealth and state programs for Asian priority languages, Japanese, Chinese, Korean and Indonesian. In his 1999 Budget, Peter Costello announced $30 million funding for these priority languages over the next three years.

A new concern, however, is that while young Australians are now learning Asian languages as never before many Australian employers are reluctant to employ them. Many boards and CEOs don't appreciate the value of Asian language skills. Our Asian linguists are now returning to Asia or turning to multinational companies in Australia to use their language skills. Hardly a week goes by that I don't get a telephone call from a young Australian who has become proficient in an Asian language, asking me, 'After the encouragement I had to learn an Asian language, why are Australian companies so uninterested?' I don't have an adequate answer, without dumping on Australian business.

In the early 1980s, apart from the ethnic communities, there weren't many who were talking about foreign languages, just a few academics and a few businessmen. Professor Stephen FitzGerald, formerly Australian Ambassador in China, was one. We were probably the two principal advocates of Asian languages. He was an expert in the Chinese language and I wasn't an expert at all. In retrospect, perhaps I had one advantage. Because of my own inadequacy I felt personally and keenly how important language skills were. Later when I went to Qantas it was a major priority, developing Asian language skills for cabin crew and customer contact staff.

The three years as Head of the Department of Immigration and Ethnic Affairs were the most personally satisfying of my public life. In such a line department I was very conscious of being part of nation building. This was much more so than as the Head of a coordinating department like Prime Minister and Cabinet where we didn't have direct responsibility for programs.

When I left the department in March 1983, I wrote to senior officers about what we had achieved and some of the problems ahead:

> I doubt whether officers in any other department derive such satisfaction from seeing and being able to measure the results of

their work. Immigration is changing the face of Australia for the better and will continue to do so ...

More than any other factor, immigration has changed our national outlook and character. From the narrowly focused, distinctly parochial and predominantly Anglo-Celtic society of the immediate post-war years, Australia has progressed to today's more diverse, more tolerant, more mature, less insular and more confident and internationally respected nation.

How can we reconcile our historic links to Europe and the old world with the geographical imperatives and opportunities of the Pacific? The Department of Immigration and Ethnic Affairs has a more critical part than others in shaping our future relations with the region,

I regard the acceptance in Australia of over 70,000 Indo-China refugees as a decisive turning point in our history and a turning very much to our advantage both in our relations with our region and the contribution which these refugees, and indeed other refugees, are making in Australia. Refugees 'select' themselves better than a migration officer can select a migrant. Refugees are highly motivated, risk-taking, and know that they cannot go back, unlike some other new arrivals who complain from the day they arrive.

I do not underestimate the problems which a large Indo-Chinese refugee program presents, particularly in times of high unemployment. But so far the response by the Australian community has been excellent, and, if we are careful, I believe it will continue.

The bi-centenary on 26 January 1988 will celebrate two things. For one part of our community it recalls the successful settlement and development of this country by immigrants from other lands. To others it recalls the beginning of the dispossession in their own country. How can we, the post-1788 migrants, establish our legitimacy in this country without coming to terms with the legitimate aspirations of the historic owners of this country?

An important issue of principle ... is whether assistance for new settlers should be delivered through 'mainstream services' or through special and separate programs. I see no difficulty in principle with the latter. But special programs have clear limitations and do engender some hostility. I would hope that as far as possible all institutions, programs and organisations reflect and are responsive to the changing nature and needs of a diverse Australian community. The need for special programs is very often a commentary on the entrenched Anglo-Celtic bias of so many of our institutions.

Immigration was not a divisive issue at the last election and hopefully we can keep it that way.

John Howard was the first Prime Minister for half a century to turn it into a divisive issue.

A non-discriminatory immigration policy is the only ethical course for Australia. It is also in our best interests. The successful integration of new arrivals still depends on the four pillars we spoke of in 1982. The diversity and vigour that immigrants contribute must be underpinned by programs to promote social cohesion, equal opportunity and participation of all in an evolving and dynamic society. I am optimistic provided we don't lose heart and confidence. Immigration is the greatest success story in our history and I was pleased to be part of it.

— 1983 —

Marking Time with Mick Young

'Life is a long lesson in humility' (Sir James Barrie)

Mick Young had been very confident that Bob Hawke would win the 1983 election, but was doubtful whether he would show the necessary discipline and application in government. The doubt proved groundless.

The Whitlam Government had transformed Australian political life. But there were obviously political lessons to be learnt, and I hoped that my experience in 1974–76 as Head of the Department of Prime Minister and Cabinet would be valuable for the Hawke Government. I also thought that I could do things better the second time around.

I was aware that my role on and after 11 November 1975 still rankled with some in the Labor Party. Obviously working for Fraser, first as Head of the Department of Prime Minister and Cabinet and then as Ambassador in Japan and Head of the Department of Immigration and Ethnic Affairs, didn't endear me to some Labor people. Alan Ramsey, in the *National Times* (22 July 1983) drew on some of that sentiment:

> Despite two changes of government, Menadue has survived the subsequent nine years and still remains one of the elite in the bureaucratic first division. This factor alone speaks volumes for his fast foot work as well as his political connections and his management ability. He is a superb survivor with sharp instincts to seize the main chance.

234

Ramsey is given to some personal hyperbole, but I think that he captured at least something of the way I had operated. It hurt.

I talked to Mick Young who spoke to Bob Hawke about my future. Hawke was not at all forthcoming. Our relations were courteous but never close. I think the main reason is that I was identified with Whitlam, and Whitlam and Hawke were invariably competing with each other in the Labor movement. The events of 11 November 1975 were probably a factor as well.

There was a suggestion that Bill Hayden might go as High Commissioner to London but he stayed as Foreign Minister. He was not impressed with the idea that I might be appointed head of his department. I accepted that I would continue to pay a price for November 1975 but I was looking for a change and a chance to head a reasonably senior department. I thought most of my objectives had been achieved in the Immigration Department. But it wasn't to be. I became Head of the Special Ministry of State (SMOS), with Mick Young as the Minister. It turned out to be something of a marking time for both of us.

Mick had two principal areas of responsibility. The first was electoral reform. There was a lot to be done in the electoral system, particularly with the funding of elections, the disparity between the value of votes in rural and urban electorates and complicated voting procedures. Mick Young brought in Hugh Hudson, who had been Education Minister in South Australia. He looked after electoral issues with Mick and did a superb job. I was only marginally involved.

The other main responsibility Young had was the Australian Federal Police (AFP). He did a very good job, despite the interruptions. He had a very clear vision of the AFP becoming the best police force in the country. He ensured that it was well funded. The AFP had a reputation for honesty, in contrast with the state police forces, but Mick Young was very conscious how it was denigrated by state police as educated show ponies who didn't know much about real police work. The AFP were delighted to have a senior Cabinet minister; most AFP ministers, before and since, have been quite junior.

It did seem an unlikely combination: the Irish union organiser in charge of police. The poacher turned gamekeeper! The AFP were a little worried as to what it would mean for them. But Mick Young quickly established quite remarkable personal relationships with the senior people in the police as he did with every one. The Commissioner was General

Ron Gray, from the Army, whose social background couldn't have been more different, but they developed a great respect for each other. I knew that some senior departmental officers were concerned about Gray's direct access to Young and not via the department. Mick made it very clear that the department was not to be informed each time he saw or spoke to Gray.

Mick learned quickly what appealed to military types. He always ensured that Gray had a spare seat alongside him where he could place his hat with its braid and stars. Mick liked that. He was tutored in the ways of the military by Greg Dodds, who was with the Army when I recruited him as my personal assistant and interpreter in Tokyo. He became Mick's senior adviser in Canberra.

Mick Young won hearts, even that of the Police Commissioner. Gray knew that Young was genuine. To Mick, mateship was not a suit of clothes; as Robert Haupt put it, 'It was him'.

The quality of the AFP was improving rapidly, in part because of the large number of well-qualified women recruits. That did, however, present a problem. Male egos were dented as women were invariably the prize winners in graduation classes. The problem was 'solved' by raising the minimum height requirement for all recruits, excluding many women. Mick and I missed this subterfuge.

It was quite a treat going with him to a formal AFP 'dining in' night. In the department we prepared some speech notes. He wisely ignored them and, aside from some unprintable stories, won police hearts by telling them what he personally expected of them in protecting the community and how they had to understand young people more. He would be loyal to them and they had better be loyal to him. He had them eating out of his hand.

The police also knew that Mick Young was tough. He was very much formed by his experiences as a shearer. In the Australian Workers' Union split of 1956 there were political, industrial as well as physical brawls across inland Australia and particularly western New South Wales. Large union meetings were held in Broken Hill, appropriately in the boxing stadium. Mick Young literally began his public life in the boxing ring, which was the platform for the meetings. Jack Wright, an old union friend of Mick's and later Deputy Premier of South Australia, told me of those days. He said that if all else failed, Mick was good with his fists. The nuggety shearer with strong arms and hands didn't take a backward step, industrially or physically. The federal police did not trifle with Mick Young. He was a funny but also a very tough and serious person.

I remember his first ministerial duty. Prince Charles and Princess Diana had been invited by Fraser and were arriving at Alice Springs within a few weeks of the election. Hawke couldn't go so he decided to send Mick and Mary Young. I remember him saying, 'This is a wonderful way of telling the Queen that Australian politics has really changed—an Irish ex-shearer to meet Prince Charles'.

Mick encountered early problems over the 'Ivanov-Combe affair'. Ivanov was a KGB agent at the Soviet Embassy and David Combe was the Federal Secretary of the Labor Party. A Foreign Affairs and Security Committee of Cabinet met to consider a report from ASIO about David Combe's association with Ivanov. It was an unwise association but nothing more. Young, as Minister in charge of the AFP, was a member of that Cabinet Committee and briefed on the matter. Unwisely he told Eric Walsh. They had shared a lot of confidences over the years but in this case it went awry. Eric Walsh mentioned it to a Melbourne businessman who was an agent of the Australian Security and Intelligence Service (ASIS). The agent reported back to ASIS; the circle was complete. Prime Minister Hawke was confronted with a problem. A security matter had been discussed in Cabinet and information had been passed by Mick Young to Eric Walsh and from him to an intelligence agent and back to ASIS. It was a very sad occasion for both of them. Fortunately, their relationship was later fully restored but it was a difficult period.

Young had to stand down as Minister and Kim Beazley became acting Minister. He was very supportive of Mick and through that period a close personal bond developed. Kim Beazley went to great lengths to ensure that there was no suggestion whatsoever that Mick would not be coming back to his portfolio. Mick Young was the epitome of loyalty and Kim Beazley reciprocated in full measure. Mick was upset that one or two of his junior colleagues were over-keen to get his job, urging Bob Hawke to fill the ministerial vacancy. A Royal Commission headed by Justice Hope subsequently exonerated Mick from having been guilty of anything more than an indiscretion. He returned to the Ministry. But it had been a period of turmoil for Mick and for us in the department.

Mick Young was a remarkably well-balanced public and private person. His political home was on the left but knew that ideals without power in public life were of little value. Some on the left preferred to be in opposition; they could keep their ideals pristine by never having to exercise power. Election defeats were confirmation of the stupidity of the electorate and their own ideological purity. Some of the 'realists' on the right were so hungry for power that they would sell their grandmothers. Political realism meant power for its own sake and favours you could do for your tribe. Of all the public figures I knew I always felt that I could trust Mick Young's judgment better than anyone else's. He got the balance right between idealism and realism.

As Secretary of SMOS, I was a member of the Council of the Order of Australia for about twelve months, in 1983/84. The chairman of the council was Sir Harry Gibbs, the Chief Justice. I proposed that Lionel Murphy receive an AC, the senior award in the Order of Australia. Gibbs asked that the matter be deferred as he would like to consider it further. At the next meeting Gibbs said that he had spoken to Murphy and Murphy was not interested in such an award. I was very surprised. My proposal lapsed.

Mick Young's difficulties with the Royal Commission over the Ivanov-Combe affair made life difficult. But at a more personal level our family's increasing focus was Cynthia's health. Her *minshuku* tours to Japan were going extremely well. She was taking groups of 15 or 20 Australians and showing them the pleasures that she had experienced in visiting out-of-the-way villages and country people. In February 1983, her book, *Taishi Fujin–Minshuku no Tabi* or *Ambassador's Wife, Minshuku Travel*, was published in Japanese by Simul Press. By mid-1983, in great pain, she had to leave one of her tours in Kyushu. Friends in Japan got her on a plane back to Sydney. Dr John Morris, at the Royal Prince Alfred Hospital in Sydney, diagnosed a secondary cancer in the liver. Cynthia underwent intensive chemotherapy treatment with painful side effects. She was very courageous but the pain was obvious.

Several factors influenced Cynthia's and my decision to join the Catholic Church. A sense of vulnerability, particularly for Cynthia, forced a rethink in our lives. What is important? I remember that six months later, at

Christmas 1983 at Glenelg, South Australia, Cynthia and I were sitting on the esplanade after a vigil mass on a Saturday evening. We had by then both joined the Catholic Church. Recalling the proclamation of the priest at mass—'I am not worthy to receive You, but only say the word and I shall be healed'—Cynthia said, 'I may never be healed in my body but I know I have been healed in my spirit'. I knew she had. She had come to terms with life and what it might hold for her. In her search, through pain, she was finding answers. It is the way answers often come.

The institutional journey to the Catholic Church was not as important as the spiritual journey that we made together. But the two journeys were linked. Cynthia was always a few steps ahead of me in both.

We never regarded ourselves as 'converts' and I am hurt when I am called a 'convert'. It is a Catholic tribal word for outsiders. I am sceptical of those who jettison and repudiate their past. It all needs to be integrated. I find it hard to take seriously ex-communists who take a wild lurch to the political right or non-Catholics who then become more Catholic than the pope.

Joining the Catholic Church for Cynthia and me was a very simple occasion. Our 'Methodist' baptism was recognised by the Catholic Church. Eucharist was celebrated by Father John Glynn at the Marist Chapel at Hunters Hill. He was the elder brother of Father Tony Glynn whose goodness and simplicity had impressed us so much in Japan. The Eucharist was the one reason above all else why I joined the Catholic Church and remains as the central factor in my continuing life in the church. 'This is the Lamb of God who takes away the sin of the world' is a remarkable claim. I believe it.

Many other factors influenced me. I was attracted by the universality, diversity and apostolic nature of the Catholic Church. In Japan the Methodist Church seemed a very small tributary in a large universal church. The Catholic Church was the big league.

I also came to appreciate the importance of tradition within the Catholic Church whereby truth continues to be revealed through the church's teaching. That appreciation is despite the fact I know that Catholic teaching on many important issues will change in the future, as it has in the past on such issues as anti-Semitism, usury, slavery and the sun revolving around the earth. I was also attracted to a sense of stability and order within the Catholic Church. One of the difficulties with many churches is that they get blown off course by passing fashions. I hope that the 'barque of Peter' will be more open and reforming, but I was attracted by the fact that the Catholic Church seemed stable in the way it proceeded in the world.

At a personal level I felt great affection for Pope John XXIII. He still remains for me an extraordinarily attractive and trusting person, together with Martin Luther, another great reformer. Without John XXIII, and the Vatican Council reforms he initiated in 1962, I don't think I would ever have joined the Catholic Church. To me the Second Vatican Council was really a substantial vindication of the reformation. Joining the Catholic Church was, I think, also a sign of my growing maturity. I joined a church of my own choosing, one that was not my parents' church. By the time I joined the Catholic Church my father had died. I think he would have found it hard to accept. My mother didn't really understand my change but she expressed confidence in me and my decisions.

With the worsening in Cynthia's health, I was more than ever keen to get back to Sydney with her and three of the children. Susan was married with a family in Japan. Cynthia's medical treatment was at the Royal Prince Alfred. She was in and out of hospital as either an in-patient or out-patient month after month. In July 1983, I threw my hat in the ring again for the Managing Director position of the ABC. A new ABC Board headed by Mr Ken Myer had been appointed by the Hawke Government. Competitors this time around included Bruce Gyngell, Peter Westerway and Ranald MacDonald.

A close friend within the ABC gave me a written report on the ABC and its prospects. He concluded, 'With your diplomatic experience you should walk it in so long as you are aware of Ken Myer's idiosyncrasies'. I wasn't and I missed out again. I know that Ken Myer thought I would be hard to manage. I wasn't as deferential in discussion and interview as perhaps he would have hoped. The position went to Geoffrey Whitehead from New Zealand.

It was a real family letdown. Cynthia was very upset. A pall of disappointment descended when the headhunting firm rang me in Balmain to say that I had missed out again. So it was back to Canberra and commuting regularly by car to Sydney. I determined I would be with Cynthia each time she went to hospital for a check-up or treatment. She was an inspiration to us all. She visited Dr Ainslie Mears, in Melbourne, to help her in meditation. It gave her peace and strength.

I was also finding work hard going. Mick Young had prepared himself almost all his life to be a minister in a Labor government and quickly found himself sidelined through a Royal Commission. Professionally, I also found that I didn't have much enthusiasm for electoral and police matters.

A rocky personal period
Department of Trade with Lionel Bowen and John Dawkins

'Dead, my old fine hopes
And dry my dreaming
But still
Iris, blue each spring'
(Shushiki)

When Jim Scully retired as
Secretary of the Department of Trade, Mick Young was again helpful.
He discussed with Lionel Bowen, the Minister for Trade, and Bob Hawke,
the possibility of my becoming Secretary of the Department. Hawke
was not keen on the idea. Ian Macphee, who had a good relationship
with Labor ministers, also spoke to Hawke on my behalf. Hawke and
Macphee had been rival employee and employer advocates and were
close acquaintances. I was not accepted with acclamation by senior
ministers but Bowen was anxious for change within the department. In
December 1983 he appointed me Head of the Department of Trade.

The period ahead was the most difficult of my life. Bowen was
very generous and pleasant but relations with his private staff were often
difficult. The major continuing difficulty for me, however, was the
worsening in Cynthia's health right through 1984.

I was of the view that in the Department of Trade we had to promote a
much more outward-oriented economy. We had an urban business culture
that was addicted to protection. It had its back to the outside world and

looked internally to the Australian market. The Department of Trade was spending a lot of its resources on the promotion and development of export markets for minerals and farm products when there also needed to be an industry restructure and the development and export of manufactured goods and services areas where there was growth in world trade and potential jobs for Australians.

There needed to be closer links between industry and trade policy. But that was anathema to Treasury, which invariably captured its minister in the name of economic orthodoxy. 'Leave it to the market.' The same argument about industry and trade policy is unresolved 15 years later. We need to export more manufactured goods and services to provide jobs for Australians.

My view was then and still is that Australia had to be as open to the world as possible—in capital, trade, people and ideas; this offers better opportunities for long-term growth in jobs. Nationalism and isolationism, with attendant racism, have been the great scourges of this century. At the same time I am sceptical of unfettered international markets, and believe that governments should intervene to promote openness and then correct and alleviate social problems flowing from openness.

Conservatives do acknowledge that markets fail from time to time and that a social safety net is necessary, but then they dissemble when reminded that an adequate safety net requires higher taxation. Government intervention and higher taxation is, in my view, necessary for openness and economic reform to be socially acceptable. The alternative is Pauline Hanson and a return to fortress Australia.

In my first public address on 1 February 1984, after becoming Head of the Department, I outlined the agenda that I would be focusing on. It was very much influenced by my experience in Japan and seeing Australia from outside.

> It is commonplace to refer to the economic success stories of our region, Japan, Korea, Taiwan, Singapore. Clearly there are many features of their societies and economies which are not translatable. For success we don't have to eat with chopsticks or sleep on tatami. But I believe that there are a few areas which are critical to their success, where we can learn and benefit … Their economic policies and programs were export oriented and all their people understand that jobs and income depend on export.

This nexus between exports and jobs had been highlighted by research undertaken by the Department of Trade which showed that every $100 million of export income generated 5000 jobs.

It was also clear that we needed a greater commitment to export to pay the growing foreign debt servicing burden. I pointed out in many speeches in 1984 that, 'Foreign borrowings have increased sharply over the past three years and by the end of 1982/83 the stock of foreign borrowings had reached $33.6 billion compared to $13 billion in 1979/80'.

Over the ten years before I joined Trade, Australia's export performance had been at the lower end of the OECD league ladder. A contributing factor to our poor export performance was that we had become the victims of our own propaganda. The resources boom of the 1970s and 1980s showed our cargo cult mentality. It fed a complacency already widespread in the 'she'll be right' country. It created excessive expectations and inflated the dollar, so making exporting harder. The resources boom disguised many of the structural problems in the closed Australian economy. Results of the European Management Forum's survey for 1983 showed that Australia had dropped five places on the 'competitive scoreboard', from seventh to twelfth during the year. We had done particularly poorly in the key area of outward orientation, the area in which our neighbours were streaking ahead of us.

The result of this lack of outward orientation was that manufacturing industry in Australia had not created one new job in the period 1965–82. Whilst total employment in Australia increased by 1.5 million over this period, employment in our manufacturing sector had fallen by around 100,000.

At every opportunity I could find, I also advocated much more attention to services such as education and tourism to revitalise our export performance. On 11 February 1984 I said:

> Trade in services currently accounts for around a quarter of total world trade and is growing faster than the trade in goods. International comparisons indicate that the relative size our services sector, which accounts for around 70% of total employment and output, is broadly comparable with that of countries with similar per capita incomes. On the other hand, our exports of services, comprising about 16% of our total Current Account earnings, are relatively low.

We needed a program of export development with export incentives which was linked to industry policy. One couldn't be divorced from the other. We had to develop an industry structure that was internationally competitive and could export and in the process provide jobs. It was much more than getting the 'fundamentals right' as Treasury kept saying. We could never compete in manufacturing and services on cost alone. We had to develop firms and industries that could compete on innovation, quality and service. Research and development and the lifetime training of Australians were essential.

The Hawke and Keating governments made some quite courageous decisions to open the Australian economy to the world: the float of the Australian dollar in December 1983 and major reductions in industry protection. The Reserve Bank was more influential than Treasury in promoting this openness. We are still seeing the benefits of those steps. What was lacking was an industry policy and adequate social programs to support the opening of Australia to the world.

I was not able to achieve much in industry policy. In Canberra in 1985 Treasury dominated economic thinking and had well and truly captured Paul Keating. Treasury wanted both a dismantling of protection and less government support of industry. It was called 'industry welfare'. My view was that openness had to be supported by a positive policy to promote industry. John Button made attempts to develop an industry policy to promote exports and jobs but he was out-gunned. The economic reform policies of the Hawke-Keating years were necessary but they neglected the industry and social downside and the politics of managing change.

Columnists like Brian Toohey were right that Treasury espoused one fad after another. In the 1970s it was 'monetarism', fixing inflation by controlling the money supply. In the early 1980s it was 'twin deficits'; by cutting the budget deficit there would be a cut in the current account deficit. Then Treasury promoted the free flow of capital. Having lost the argument time after time, Treasury is now into another fad: cut the wages of the poor to reduce unemployment.

In the department in 1984, we commenced a study on the export of educational services. After we had completed the study, I spoke at a dinner with 19 vice-chancellors of the major Australian universities in the Scarf Room at the ANU about our thinking and plans for the export of educational services. I outlined ways in which I thought we could promote education services offshore and encourage more Asian students to come to Australia. The Americans and British had been doing it very successfully. We were not serious competitors. With the universities under financial pressure, this was a commercial opportunity for them. It would also transform university campuses and, hopefully, student attitudes towards Asia.

The dinner turned out to be a frost. The vice-chancellors were not impressed with my commercialism. My main critic was Professor Peter Karmel, Vice-Chancellor of the ANU. He had been my mentor from Adelaide University days. We held similar views on most public issues but we didn't agree on this one. He was upset at commercially exploiting educational services on such a scale. After the dinner, Karmel buttonholed me on my proposal. His concerns also came back to me through an old friend, Frank Hambly, Secretary of the Vice-Chancellors' Committee: 'What is Menadue up to in advocating selling overseas educational services in this way?', he had asked his colleagues.

You always remember the speeches that don't go well but in retrospect it helped quicken reform. In the mid-1980s education exports were minimal. They now have grown to $3 billion annually with almost 150,000 foreign students in Australia each year, mainly from Asia. The Australian International Education Foundation estimates that educational exports will be worth $5 billion in 2001.

While I was spending a lot of time on work plans, Cynthia was making plans for the children and their future without her. At her initiative we sold the family home in Birchgrove and moved to a smaller house in East Balmain. We distributed half of the money to the children on the condition that it was used on deposits for their own houses in Balmain. The result is that all the children have houses within walking distance of me. Cynthia's foresight proved to be good for the family as well as a wise property move.

With chemotherapy, Cynthia had periods of intense pain followed by some remission of the cancer. But by mid-1984 it became clear that her future with us was in months rather than years. I had hoped that she could accompany me on a business trip to Europe. Her doctor prepared a report that could be shown to a doctor or hospital overseas in the event of a relapse or crisis. The report brought me up sharply. I had been told it all before but here the prognosis was spelled out in chilling and clinical detail. We didn't make the trip.

The morning hours of 27 October 1984 are the most sacred hours of my life. Cynthia called me at about five o'clock in the morning from the Royal Prince Alfred. She had been in and out of hospital. This time she had been in hospital for a week. She knew that the end was near. When I arrived at the hospital she reminded me again that she had been healed in spirit. In that important respect she was healthier than she had ever been. But she didn't think her body would last much longer. We held hands and together prayed the Lord's Prayer; it was for the last time. As her breath came in gasps, I knew what the 'breath of life' meant. I called the three children in Sydney, Rosalie, Peter and Elizabeth. We were all together with Cynthia for the last hours. The oldest, Susan, was in Japan, making arrangements to fly to Sydney with her eldest child Naomi and her new baby Miriam.

A priest anointed Cynthia and administered the last rites of the church. God came and quietly took her just after midday. I had never been so close to dying before; I was also never more conscious of life. There is a cycle of living and dying for all people and all things. I saw the face of God that day.

Aged 49, we had known each other for 32 years and been married for 27. We had grown together in the most formative years of our lives.

The requiem mass in St Augustine's, Balmain, was a great celebration of Cynthia's life. Mick Young gave the eulogy. The co-celebrants were John and Paul Glynn and Ed Campion. Protestants and Buddhists, believers and non-believers, took communion. How pointless differences seemed. Cynthia's mother, Nel, and my mother, Elma, attended. Cynthia's father, Max, had died a few months earlier. When he learned that Cynthia had cancer, I think he lost the will to outlive her.

Exactly a month later Rosalie's son, Ben, was born. Cynthia had referred to the coming child as her 'grip on immortality'. Ben was a wonderful testament for me and the children to ongoing life. The Japanese Haiku poet, Issa, put it beautifully,

A yearly sweep for our parental tomb:
The youngest child comes carrying the broom.

For months after Cynthia's death I had vivid dreams of talking to her on the telephone. We spoke about everyday family matters, children, birthdays, meals, shopping and schools. Time and time again we agreed to meet, at a restaurant, at a theatre or at the shops. She never came. There was a lot I now had to do to tend the family. It was good therapy for grief, although in retrospect the children were probably more concerned about me. However much we had tried to prepare for the loss, the experience was something different. The ache was there every day.

Amongst family and friends we quite deliberately spoke of Cynthia's life and death, knowing that healing wouldn't come from hiding the loss. And there was plenty of ebullience and humour in Cynthia's life to recall with joy. In Western cultures we seem to flee mortality rather than come to terms with it and speak about it. We privatise grief when we need to acknowledge it as a normal part of life. I later came to notice when friends lost a loved one how even their friends were awkward and reluctant to talk about the loss or even mention the name of the deceased. It probably said something about their own fragility.

Elizabeth had one year to go to complete her HSC at Ascham. She lived with Neary, our Cambodian foster daughter, at the house at East Balmain. Rosalie was very supportive. I commuted back and forth to Canberra again. It was very tiring, a full week in Canberra with interstate travel thrown in and a drive back to Sydney on Friday night. Through it all, family and friends and particularly John and Nitaya Morris, friends in Balmain, were a great help. The Good Samaritan Sisters were wonderful pastors. I wish the nuns ran the church, or at least their spirit did.

Slowly we got things together but the pain of loneliness was always there. All that I had publicly constructed was of little help in the face of grief. The controlling public person was privately lost.

Back to work in Canberra after a couple of weeks, I found the staff in the department were very helpful and tolerant. It was nice to be 'mothered' by so many of them. On free nights, Mick and Eric took me under their wing for dinner like old times, before I retreated to the quiet of my apartment with its powerful memories.

Within a few weeks of my return Lionel Bowen retired and was replaced by John Dawkins in December 1984. It proved to be a difficult working relationship. His views were often conveyed indirectly to me through staff. Through one of them he put the suggestion that I might like a diplomatic appointment in Geneva. He was not at all empathic.

Dawkins was very interested in administrative changes. He had shown that particularly as Minister in charge of the Public Service Board. In the Department of Trade he decided to hive off the Australian Trade Commission into a separate statutory organisation, Austrade, to make it more commercially oriented and skilled. We went through a major organisational change. I thought it would be appropriate to shift Austrade out of Canberra, closer to the business community. It would also provide a chance to shake out public servants who were not very interested in business. But the Minister decided that he wanted to keep the head office in Canberra so that he could keep an eye on it. I am not sure to this day whether the new Austrade has been a significant help in our trade efforts.

I had difficulty with Dawkins over my speeches on foreign debt. As I had pointed out in my first public address as Head of the Department, I was concerned about Australia's ballooning debt. It had more than tripled over five years, from $13 billion in 1979 to $41 billion in 1984 and was approaching the levels of financially endangered Third World countries. In one speech I commented: 'These figures are unprecedented in recent Australian economic history. It is therefore not surprising for some questions to be raised about the prudence of much of our overseas borrowing. They argue ominously that Argentina, Brazil and Mexico have debt commitments that are not much greater than ours'. The 'banana republic' comments of Paul Keating were still a few years off. I made many speeches along these lines, which were well received by a number of businessmen, although they were fairly cautious what they said publicly. Newspaper editorials picked up the subject. The Minister put a note around the department about public servants being careful about public statements. He didn't raise the matter directly with me. It was the only time in my public career that a minister rebuked me for public comments.

But he had reason to be disappointed with me. Following Cynthia's death and the difficulties thereafter, I didn't perform well. It was my time in the wilderness. At work I was able, with considerable difficulty, to keep things together throughout 1985, but with commuting back and forth to Sydney to care for the children, the pressure became too much.

Just a year after Cynthia's death, I entered a period of depression. The demands of my situation were greater than my spiritual and psychological resources could cope with. It was like being in a black hole with no escape. I required medical attention and went on sick leave for several weeks. I was becalmed for a couple of months. I reduced my work load. Apart from family, a few close friends and doctors, I never disclosed to anyone the nature of my difficulties. Although commonplace, depression is not something we like to admit to. Medication helped me regain some equilibrium but the cure had to come from within. I gradually got going again. I was carried on eagle's wings.

Eleven years later in a speech to a church group, I spoke about my experiences and how, after Cynthia's death, grief, depression and recovery, things were never the same again. The function was organised by 'Catalyst for Renewal' which I helped co-found with a group of Catholics. I took as my text for that speech Jacob's battle with God, which Thomas Merton describes as the prototype of all spiritual struggles. Sons of Methodist preachers need a text for such occasions.

> Jacob stayed behind alone. Then a man came and wrestled with him until just before day break. When the man saw that he was not winning the struggle, he hit Jacob on the hip and it was thrown out of joint. The man said, 'Let me go, daylight is coming'. 'I won't unless you bless me,' Jacob answered ... Then he blessed Jacob. Jacob said, 'I have seen God face to face and I am still alive'.

Several things in that text resonated with my own experience, struggling with grief and then depression. The first was that the struggle was exquisitely personal. Secondly, my experience was that the struggle was not over quickly; it continues. Thirdly, I learned that blessings come after the struggle and not before. I was humbled first; all that I had publicly constructed, some success, esteem and security, were unavailing. They turned to ashes in my mouth. And lastly, I found that spiritual discovery is grounded in human experience and is not something apart. So often when we plumb our own humanness we touch the divine. My experience was intense and very personal, but it is just part of being human. In one way or another it happens to each of us.

In those experiences I had insights that went to the core of my being. At last I really listened to my inner voice, a voice that had never given up on me. I stopped running from myself.

The ground had been tilled on and off for years, but the spiritual plant took on new life. Little intellectually had changed; it was an experience of the heart. Thomas à Kempis described this experience: 'It is good for us to encounter troubles and adversities from time to time, for trouble often compels a man to search his own heart. It reminds him that he is an exile here' (*Counsels on the Spiritual Life*).

I confess that in difficulties before, I had had a formula like Boxer in *Animal Farm*, 'The revolution is failing, I will work harder'. But this time the formula didn't work.

In my experience, happiness is not the goal of life, although it is essential for an integrated life. The goal is to find meaning. Happiness is the by-product of finding meaning. I always come back to St Augustine to help me articulate that search for meaning: 'You have made us for Yourself and we are restless until we find rest in You'. Religious literature is littered with this 'restlessness for rest', this spiritual thirst, longing, homesickness. It is found in rock drawings, carvings and oral stories. They reflect the yearning of us all for answers to the questions, 'Who am I and what am I here for?'; 'How can the created connect with the Creator and other created beings?'; 'What makes sense in this world?'; and 'What matters in the end?'

I spent a large part of my life trying to put these questions aside, not in riotous living, but in earnest work and good causes, as important as they were. I discovered that the spiritual struggle was about trying to find my true self, not giving myself to others by seeking their esteem or doing what they want or satisfying others, as seductive as that was. It was learning to be content with myself, that I could accept the good with the bad; in short, coming to terms with my being human and forgiving myself. It was being prepared to let go, to accept that participation in life, rather than mastery of life, is sufficient.

But I have moved well ahead, trying to describe what unfolded for me over many years following Cynthia's death and the change it triggered. Back in Canberra in late 1985, I slowly put depression behind me and my enthusiasm for life and work returned. I felt more confident and mature. Many years before, I had met Susie Bryant, when she worked for Dr Stephen FitzGerald, whom I knew well. He ran a successful consultancy for Australians doing business in China; Susie was the business manager and ran it very well. She had also been personally helpful in assisting Cynthia and me move our belongings in Reid as we changed apartments. Out of the blue, she had turned up from a nearby apartment and offered to help. I thought at the time how attractive she was.

We met again in mid-1985. She had moved into an apartment above mine in Reid. I complained that her sink water was coming through the fan into my kitchen. Then she disappeared. I found later that she had moved to a house nearby in Reid, where she lived with her two teenage children, James and Emma. Perhaps taking pity on me as a lonely widower, she invited me over for coffee.

It being winter, she went to some trouble to make me feel welcome by lighting a fire. Unfortunately, the fireplace hadn't been used much and the lounge filled with smoke from burning green pine cones. Picked up in the street, they were free firewood. I was to learn that it was very much out of character for Susie not to do things well. We commenced seeing each other and going out together. It became a warm and loving relationship. Life started taking on meaning again.

Susie had a strong association with the army. Her father and first husband were in the regular army. Her son James is now a major in the army. This was a world I knew little about, as I quickly learned. I attended a graduation parade at the Australian Defence Force Academy (ADFA) in Canberra for James. An old Canberra associate, Sir Edward Woodward, was on the Council of ADFA. He kept peering at me trying to place my face in an unfamiliar environment. He finally came to within almost a foot of my face before exclaiming, 'You're John Menadue, aren't you! What are you doing here?' Menadue and the military did not fit together.

My children were welcoming of Susie. She was very helpful and supportive as a friend who gave good advice. The children also thought that I would be happier. It worked out very well.

I was made an Officer in the Order of Australia in 1985 for 'public service'. Those words meant a lot to me; my father would have particularly enjoyed them. For three years I felt awkward wearing the lapel badge. After the bicentennial in 1988 I wore it regularly.

A rocky personal period

Unexpectedly, in February 1986, Jim Leslie, the chairman of Qantas, inquired about my interest in joining Qantas. For me there was the bonus of living in Sydney as well. Leslie spoke to the Qantas Board at its next meeting and processes were put in motion for my appointment.

It was an appointment by the Qantas Board but the Minister for Transport, Peter Morris, and other ministers wanted to know what major government business enterprises were doing in the appointment of chief executives. I had known Peter for many years, a good friend, and I knew his brother, Dr John Morris in Balmain, even better. Peter Morris was very supportive. Bob Hawke again was not very helpful, but with the chairman of Qantas and the Minister for Transport in my corner that was sufficient.

I was appointed as the chief executive. There was a lot of unfinished work in the Department of Trade but I was pleased to go to Qantas in Sydney.

Susie came to Sydney at about the same time and we were married a few months later in June 1986. She sacrificed a lot in coming to Sydney, leaving James and Emma, a house that she had bought and lovingly renovated, as well as her job as a business manager. I was blessed with a second happy marriage. Not many have such good fortune. But marriage at 51 is different to marriage at 22. I became more aware of how set in my ways I was and that marriage, like all good relationships, must acknowledge the individuality of the other. One, but separate. In my first marriage the relationship evolved more naturally with less apparent effort or thought on my part. It was two unformed people growing together. In my second marriage I was more aware that I needed to consciously take action to adjust and change, to be less self-centred. I was able to stand back and see more clearly the influences at work in my life — some helping and some hindering relationships.

A new marriage and Qantas were big changes for me. My energy came back. I was able to put behind me the melancholy of the last 18 months. Grief, depression and recovery taught me a lot about myself.

Understanding what boards are about

CEO of Qantas

'The Qantas Board is what a Government needs when it hasn't got a House of Lords' (Senator Gareth Evans)

I should have paid more attention to that quip of Senator Gareth Evans who, as Minister for Transport and Communications, became the Minister in charge of Qantas. He understood better than I did how valued a Qantas board seat was.

I joined Qantas in April 1986 as chief executive officer but not as a board member. The Government wanted to keep as many board places as possible for its political friends. I became a member of the board in September 1987.

I was the first CEO to come from outside the airline. I put my efforts into Asia and customer and staff relations, and paid too little attention to the board. In the end I confronted the board and paid the price. I didn't pay it gladly but I felt I was truer to myself.

Some of what I tried to do at Qantas was rather flatteringly described by Dexter Dunphy and Doug Stace in *Under New Management* in 1990:

> Few Australian managers have inspired more commitment from their subordinates than John Menadue. Personally he is a quiet, unassuming person, not given to flamboyant behaviour.

Nevertheless he found powerful ways to dramatise the change program already underway when he joined Qantas. Faced with widespread employee cynicism about the commitment of Qantas senior management to constructive suggestions from employees, Menadue instituted grass roots discussions. He ensured that problems raised were promptly dealt with and effective action taken. Similarly, shortly after his appointment, Menadue planned a trip overseas and had himself booked economy class. Qantas executives always travelled first class. The word spread that Menadue was placing a new emphasis on customer service and was personally testing the quality of service. He provided a high profile to give focus to the renewed service ethic of the airline.

In my first year at Qantas, 2.5 million passengers were carried on 29 Boeing aircraft in its worldwide network. There were over 12,000 staff. There was no domestic network, a major handicap; Qantas acquired Australian Airlines six years later in 1992.

I found Qantas an organisation that had enormous technical and operational depth, a feature of most government enterprises. The safety culture amongst pilots and engineers was a joy to see. It was best described to me by a ground engineer in talking about his work: 'This is no job for a cowboy'. Qantas was highly regarded as a brand name around the world. It was a great aviation pioneer; a very family-oriented company with strong employee loyalty. But as the Australian international flag carrier, it was complacent, particularly in customer service, marketing and costs. It was overstaffed, particularly compared to airlines such as Singapore Airlines and Cathay Pacific, whose labour costs were about 40 per cent lower than Qantas's.

Under industrial agreements, Qantas pilots when repositioning flew first class, at the expense of commercial passengers. To try to embarrass them to change I booked economy for my own travel. Pilots were hard to embarrass. It kept me modest, or almost so, to know that over 30 senior pilots in Qantas received substantially higher salaries than the CEO. Crew baggage was unloaded before customer baggage. The work culture needed to change.

The Qantas of the late 1980s doesn't exist any more. In some respects that was inevitable, but there have been some downsides: preoccupation with short-term share price, excessive executive salaries and a loss of employee loyalty.

The first important thing I attempted at Qantas was to seize the opportunities in the growing markets of Asia. QF1 and QF2 up and back to London each day were regarded as the premier routes, even though they were struggling financially against strong competition, particularly from the Asian airlines. Profits were seldom made on the continental European routes either. The Pacific routes were all in the red as a result, in part, of large US carriers cross-subsidising from other routes.

The most obvious market I was concerned about and had knowledge of was Japan. Everything told me it had great untapped potential. My first overseas visit as CEO, in June 1986, was to Japan. It was also our honeymoon and Susie's introduction to Japan, as well as an opportunity to meet our oldest daughter, Susan, in Tottori. At a press conference in Tokyo I was asked, 'As Ambassador and since, for eight years, you have made dozens of speeches about exorbitant airfares on the route. Do you still hold that view?' I said I did. The Japan Airlines (JAL) reaction was swift. Its public relations officer, a long-time British expatriate in Japan, gave me the rudest public tongue-lashing I have ever had in my life. I had dared to break rank on airfares.

But the public outburst created the crisis which made a breakthrough possible. On return to Australia I sent Peter Stainlay, General Manager Marketing, to Tokyo to meet JAL. He put a deal to them: 'Menadue would shut up on airfares if JAL would agree to immediately double capacity on the route.' It worked liked a charm.

As a result, there was a dramatic increase in the number of Qantas flights. From four flights a week, we increased to 23 per week within three years. The number of flights continued to grow and reached about a hundred per week for all carriers on the route. That dramatic increase in the number of flights from 1986 laid the basis for the remarkable increase in tourism from Japan. In 1985, the year before I joined Qantas, there were 107,590 Japanese tourists to Australia. In three years it increased to 352,315. Japanese tourism put Queensland, and particularly Cairns, on the tourist map.

This expansion was not achieved by television advertising but by increasing airline capacity. I kept Qantas as far as possible from the Australian Tourist Commission and Paul Hogan 'ocker' type commercials which I felt were nationally demeaning and not good for long-term business.

As a result of the increases of traffic on the Japan route, the profitability of Qantas soared. In my second and third years at Qantas close to 60 per cent of profits were coming from that route. In the year ending June 1989, the Japan route made a profit of $101 million out of a total operating profit of $177 million. Over ten years, the profits on the Japan route, which I estimated at around $750 million, substantially underwrote Qantas's financial position. In 1991/92 the Japan route made a profit of $79 million (147 per cent) out of a total international profit of $54 million. The highest Japan route profit was $134 million in 1993/94, which was 84 per cent of the total international profit of $142 million.

We established very good relationships with JAL and Japanese travel wholesalers, particularly Japan Travel Bureau (JTB), through staff exchanges. I appointed a Japan Advisory Committee in Japan, which included the President of Mitsui, a former Japanese ambassador to Australia, a director of the Industrial Bank of Japan, a former head of the Japanese Department of Transport and a leading Japanese academic.

While the profits on the Japan route far exceeded my wildest hopes, I was concerned about our dependence in the Japanese market on major travel wholesalers like JTB, Kinki Tours and Kintetsu. The five top wholesalers controlled over 60 per cent of Japan's outbound travel and had the ability to turn business on and off to particular destinations depending on airfares, ground costs and exchange rates. They could reward or punish Qantas as they chose. In my last year at Qantas in 1989, we attempted to combat their dominance and undertook a major study to build alternative sales partners who would focus on selling Qantas airlines seats and tour packages. We needed to establish control of our own destiny and not rely on Japanese intermediaries. With large profits on the route it was tempting to think it would never end. I left before we could implement a new strategy.

There was a general build-up of other Qantas capacity into Asia, particularly to Hong Kong and Singapore. But I was cautious about Cathay Pacific and Singapore Airlines, which strongly pressed for more flights out of Australia to carry Australian passengers to Europe but were reluctant to give Qantas flights to carry passengers from Hong Kong and Singapore to other parts of Asia. Negotiations on air services into and out of Australia were formally in the hands of the Commonwealth

Government, but the real negotiations were between the airlines. We had the knowledge and expertise. We also had a lot of self-interest to protect. Governments invariably rubber-stamped what the airlines agreed. Qantas is still protected, but less so.

We did develop Bangkok as an alternative hub to Singapore and expanded services through Bangkok to London and Frankfurt. We also began a triangular route, Hong Kong–Singapore–Bangkok, as we slowly negotiated rights in those countries. My view was that in the long term Qantas had to be an intra-Asian operator where there was enormous growth and high fares. The alternative was to purchase a significant stake in an Asian carrier such as Thai International. Asian carriers were competitive in services on long-haul routes but on regional routes in Asia fares were high. We wanted to be a regional carrier on Asian routes.

There was delay in the start of services to Taiwan because of objections from Beijing, which held the view that as Taiwan was a province of China, a foreign carrier could not operate there without Beijing's approval. There were quite a number of precedents, however, of overseas carriers establishing a separate company to operate to Taiwan. We established Asia-Australian Airlines, with a slightly different livery. It was all cosmetic. But the arrangements between Canberra, Beijing and Taipei took about two years to complete. I appointed an old Canberra friend, Sir Geoffrey Yeend, with good connections in Taipei, to be our negotiator with Taiwan. In the end the main opposition came not from Beijing but from the Australian Department of Foreign Affairs, which was nervous about upsetting China. The Australian Ambassador in China and a former senior advisor to Bob Hawke, Ross Garnaut, suggested that Ansett would be a more appropriate Australian carrier to operate to Taiwan.

I was cautious about Korean Airlines' campaign to operate to Sydney. At that time there were severe restrictions on passports, travel permits and taking currency out of Korea. I was also certain that the interest of Korean Airlines was to get access to the Japan–Australia traffic by bringing it via Seoul to Australia and return. That would not be of much benefit to Qantas or Australia. I did make an oral agreement with the President of Korean Airlines during the visit of the President of Korea, Rho Tae-Woo, to Australia in November 1988. We would initially operate joint services between Sydney and Seoul. In this way we would ensure that the services focused on Korea–Australia traffic. I told the Australian

Government that I had shaken hands on a deal with Korean Airlines. But Korean Airlines would not later confirm the arrangement in writing.

Some Asian carriers expected too much of Qantas; particularly, that we should continue as a 'donor' to the region. A case in point was Malaysian Airlines System (MAS), which had been effectively grounded after its break with Singapore Airlines in the 1960s. With Keith Hamilton as the CEO, Qantas sent engineers and managers to Kuala Lumpur to help put MAS back in the air. Qantas made a large contribution over many years. Twenty years later, having established a very competitive airline, MAS executives were disappointed that I was resistant to their frequent requests for more flights to carry passengers, not between Australia and Malaysia but between Australia and Europe via Kuala Lumpur. I felt that with the new economic tigers in Asia, Qantas was no longer in the foreign aid business; we had strong regional competitors.

Like most Australian companies, Qantas did not have the Asia-skilled people we needed and could not recruit them. We had to introduce our own programs for the skilling of Qantas staff. The 1987/1988 *Qantas Annual Report* described the program: 'Qantas introduced a series of initiatives to support the Government's plans to realign Australia's education priorities towards Asia. Costing $6 million over three years, the program will help Australians gain the language skills and knowledge of Asia considered vital for commercial success in the region'. The program was cut back after I left.

Our Asian priority did have some setbacks. In 1988, John Howard, Leader of the Opposition, attacked Australia's immigration program. It was a subliminal call to revert to the discrimination and anti-Asian immigration of the past. He spoke in code of the need to slow down migration and alter the migration mix to preserve social cohesion. His shadow Minister for Immigration, Phillip Ruddock, resigned in protest and Ian Macphee, the former Immigration Minister under Malcolm Fraser, crossed the floor to vote against him.

In response to Howard's attacks, I organised a 36-member group called 'Our Australia' to raise money and screen television commercials to 'promote a continuing non-discriminatory migration program in Australia … to promote in Australians a sense of pride and confidence in the elements that unite us'. The founding group included Sir Peter Abeles, Rabbi Raymond Apple, Jimmy Barnes, Archbishop Clancy, Sir Roden Cutler, Janet Holmes a Court, Kevan Gosper, Tom Hughes, Sir

William Keyes, Sir Gustav Nossal, Sir Nicholas Shehadie, Tim Besley, Simon Crean, John David, Mark Ella, Professor Stephen FitzGerald, Sir Gordon Jackson, Dame Roma Mitchell and Saul Same. We raised over $180,000 in donations. MOJO/MDA produced the commercials almost at no charge and Channel 9 donated over $1 million of free television time. Later the ABC supported the campaign. We went to air in early January 1989. This was a private venture of mine but Jim Leslie was happy for me to do it. I hope it helped to blunt Howard's nostalgic look backwards. Eight years later he was at it again.

On family matters, Susie and I sold the house that Cynthia and I had lived in and bought a modern terrace house in Balmain. Elizabeth, who was studying law, and Emma, Susie's daughter, who was studying fashion design, lived with us for a time. Neary Eng went off nursing, very confident about her future. She had acquired a broad Australian accent. Susie later enrolled as a full-time psychology student at Macquarie University and completed an honours and a masters degree.

My mother, Elma, died from a heart attack in 1987, aged 81. My sister Beth, in Adelaide, was a great support for Elma, particularly in her later years of ill health and, I think frustration, in a church old folk's home. Elma liked independence. I am indebted to her for teaching me determination and resilience.

Qantas in the 1970s and 1980s was a relatively small operator in world terms—particularly when large operators like American, United and Delta went offshore as a result of airline deregulation under President Carter. The international aviation market was changing dramatically. At Qantas we had to respond, make alliances with the new international carriers, grow in size, compete against them head to head, or go out of business.

With the help particularly of Peter Stainlay, we identified our key markets and the partners we wanted to develop strategic alliances with around the world. The north Asian market was the key to a strategic partnership with Japan Airlines. In South-East Asia we set out to court Thai International, which unlike Singapore Airlines had its own large domestic market and did not rely on transit traffic. In Europe we identified

Lufthansa as the carrier in the centre of Europe that could provide synergy and long-term growth. We needed to get to a daily service to Frankfurt. We always saw British Airways (BA) as a major competitor, with the UK a fairly stagnant and relatively small market. We did not trust British Airways. It was more than dislike of the Poms. We found it unreliable in negotiations on routes and traffic. It was the 'by the way' airline, invariably introducing a new demand when we thought negotiations had been concluded. In the US, American Airlines was a big and growing carrier with a high quality computer reservation system, Sabre, which was critical in generating business. The trans-Pacific route was always a heavy loss-maker for Qantas. We needed a strong ally, like American Airlines, to help us tap the US market.

We set out ways to develop these strategic alliances. It took time and required a lot of personal contact at senior level. It continued after I left and was achieved 12 years later in a somewhat different form with a 'western' alliance between Qantas, British Airways, American Airlines, Cathay Pacific and Canadian Airlines in 'One World'. Alliance building was probably the most exhausting part of my time at Qantas, in that it entailed travelling around the world to develop personal and, hopefully later, business relations with these strategic partners. We had some early success when in 1988, the New Zealand Government announced that it would be privatising Air New Zealand. American Airlines and Japan Airlines joined our syndicate with 7.5 per cent each. With a New Zealand Government limitation of 35 per cent on overseas shareholdings Qantas took 19.9 per cent. Brierley Investments was the major New Zealand shareholder. The main reason Qantas put a syndicate together to purchase Air New Zealand was to keep BA out of our part of the world. Qantas sold the shareholding in 1996/97 for a capital profit of A$99 million.

I was confident that in any privatisation of Qantas it would have been possible to bring American Airlines and Japan Airlines on board as minority shareholders, with the possible addition of Lufthansa. With these strategic alliances, Australian ownership and control could be assured.

By later selling 25 per cent of Qantas to British Airways in 1993, Paul Keating effectively put Qantas in their hands. For a country with increasing ties to Asia and aspirations to be a republic, it was disappointing that while fulminating about the British capitulation in Singapore in 1942 Paul Keating was inviting Colin Marshall, the Chairman of BA, to take over Qantas. Paul Keating was no match for the politically tough

BA which had honed its skills in its wars with Laker Airways, British Caledonian and Virgin Atlantic.

Customer service took a lot of my time. Public enterprises like Qantas had great records in engineering and technology but customers were a bit of a nuisance. We introduced a range of training and customer awareness programs and gave greater delegation to front-line managers. They were told that if they bent the rules in service provision they would get my support.

As Australians we often felt that providing and receiving service was a little demeaning—it was something that other nationalities were good at, perhaps the Italians, but not us. We looked customers in the eye and if they didn't like it, well bad luck. But things were changing, forced in part by the economic recession of the late 1980s. We were also influenced by changes around the world. Organisations from Walt Disney through to traditional ones like ourselves acknowledged that customers wanted improved services. It was not just a matter of safety with a smile.

Air travellers required a seamless service; there wasn't any point in just providing good airport-to-airport service. Passengers were concerned about the whole travel chain: buying their tickets, standing in queues, delays in delivery of baggage, treatment by ground staff and the availability of ground transport. There was a revolution coming in customer service. Airlines were somewhat behind improvements in other industries, but it was a major push that we made in Qantas. There was still a long way to go when I left.

My other main focus was staff attitudes and loyalties. There were many examples of unacceptable attitudes. Susie and I were on a Qantas aircraft that was forced to make a stop in Darwin because of a minor technical problem. Under provisions of their award, cabin crew could insist on an overnight rest break in Darwin or fly some additional hours and take the plane to Sydney that night. The pilots decided to fly on to Sydney and arrive before curfew. But the cabin crew said they were too tired and voted to stay in Darwin. So all the passengers were off-loaded for a night in a Darwin hotel. Over sandwiches and coffee at the hotel I heard the cabin crew at the next table planning their evening at the casino. I pointed out their selfish behaviour and the damage they were doing to Qantas and in the long term to their own jobs. They complained to their union about my abruptness and wanted an apology. I refused. There was clearly a long way to go.

When I was travelling, I would usually go and have a chat to cabin crew in the flight kitchen and ask, 'What are the loads like lately on the flights you have been on?' It soon became clear that to them a high passenger load was a horror trip with more work. As an absentee workforce many cabin crew staff were out of touch with others in the company and, indeed, Australian working conditions generally. The life of cabin crew was very seductive.

Amongst cabin crew there was no overt opposition to the language training programs we were introducing. The main problem was that there was a system of seniority whereby the most senior cabin crew bid for and flew the choice routes. Over a period, the least attractive routes became the long-haul ones to London and the most attractive were the short-haul routes into Asia. So the most senior cabin crew were flying the Asian routes, but they were usually the ones that didn't have Asian languages. Younger staff with Asian language skills were flying to London. Some compromises were made but a lot of the rigidities and inefficiencies in Qantas held the company back.

I also worked hard on communications with staff, whether it was one-on-one, on board the aircraft or at mass meetings in the Mascot hangars. I tried to explain to them the problems we faced, how we needed to change and be more efficient so we could compete with Singapore Airlines and Cathay Pacific. It wasn't all straightforward. After a 'CEO presentation' to the multicultural staff in the catering centre, I was asked by a woman from a non-English-speaking background, 'Who are you and what do you do?'

We did make a lot of advances in staff relations. I like to think it helped give a sense of direction and confidence to people within the organisation. Subsequently, when I had my difficulties with the board, there was overwhelming support from staff. It wasn't always easy but it was rewarding to build relationships. Some Qantas board members with union connections expressed anxiety about my growing identification with the staff. Was it my plan to cut the unions out? I said 'no', amazed by their concern.

We knew we had to reduce our dependence on travel agents with their generous margins. They had no particular loyalty to Qantas. We expanded our direct sales offices and took a substantial shareholding in Thomas Cook.

In January 1987, we introduced the Qantas Frequent Flyer marketing program to reward with prizes the loyalty of customers. We deliberately avoided a mileage scheme because of the contingent liabilities it would build up for the future. Membership grew rapidly and now exceeds two million and it has given Qantas an enormous competitive advantage. I never dared to hope it could be so successful. Frequent flyers were invited to special events where Qantas was often a major sponsor. I took Susie and the children to one such event at the Sydney Entertainment Centre. In the VIP room I asked who the red-haired guest was in the long, coloured glomesh gown. All the family groaned, whispering to me that it was Elton John.

We were able to make large and growing profits. The 1988/89 *Annual Report* described the results: 'in recent years the group's profit performance has been unprecedented'. This was assisted by a strong world economy, the 1988 bicentennial, the devaluation of the Australian dollar and particularly our expansion into Asia, especially Japan. Our business and profit growth also drove a dramatic upsurge in Australian inbound tourism. In 1987 the year before the bicentennial, the OECD placed Australia at the top of the growth tables with a 27 per cent increase in arrivals, about five times the OECD average.

In the three years while I was at Qantas, revenue from passengers and cargo increased 60 per cent from $2 billion to $3.3 billion and operating profit after tax increased by 660 per cent from $23 million to $177 million. The net profit before tax was $226 million. The results were deliberately understated by special provisions and write-offs to ensure that in future years Qantas could show a steady and rising trend in profits in preparation for privatisation.

Profit as a percentage of revenue increased from 0.2 per cent to 5.4 per cent. The Boeing fleet of B746s and B767s increased from 23 to 36. The Commonwealth Government shareholder also had reason to be pleased with the results. We were driving the enormous expansion of tourism—arrivals increased from 1.4 million in 1986 to 2.2 million in 1989. Shareholder equity increased from $484 million to $916 million and company reserves from $280 million to $760 million. Dividends paid over the three years were $85 million. But on reflection we were growing too fast, given the constraints we operated under as a government authority. In the end these constraints forced privatisation and brought me into conflict with the Government and the board.

One of the handicaps under which Qantas laboured was that the Government imposed wage guidelines on government business enterprises (GBEs). We had no flexibility to trade wage increases for increased productivity. As a consequence we lost skilled staff dramatically, some with over 20 years experience. We couldn't match the wage rates paid in the private sector.

I discussed the problem with the chairman, Jim Leslie. Referring to his private sector experience with Mobil he said, 'You'll just have to match the rates in the private sector'. I decided after a lot of thought that that was what I would do. I approved over-award payments in the middle of 1988, breaching government GBE guidelines on wages. I moved to match the market with wage increases. I didn't get approval of the Government. I was prepared to live by the sword. We needed flexibility to avoid the enormous loss of skilled staff. It was seen by the 'Industrial Relations Club' as adventurism.

The responsibility for authorising these increases was mine and I accepted that I was accountable. I did recall, however, that Jim Leslie had told me during an earlier conversation that the chairman should protect his CEO. In his view it was better for an organisation to lose the chairman, rather than have the CEO sacked! The reverse happened.

It was, of course, difficult for the Government, with its Prices and Incomes Accord. The Government and the ACTU through Bill Kelty were determined to avoid any breakout by the public sector in wages which could then spill into the private sector, even though the private sector was going for its life, particularly the smaller firms who were increasing pay and taking Qantas's skilled staff. Kelty saw himself as the policeman to limit wage gains to assist the Government in achieving other social gains. Union members would later come to resent what he did. In Kelty's view the Accord had to be held. But I also had a real problem to deal with.

I was called before the Industrial Relations Commission, in August 1988, to swear a statutory declaration that I would abide by the terms of the Accord and the GBE guidelines. I duly signed. It was getting pretty willing by then. We quarantined the wage increases I had approved.

This episode obviously created problems in my relationship with the Government, which wanted us to be as flexible as possible in the market but didn't want to give us freedom to negotiate wage increases in return for productivity gains. We were stuck. In the end the problem rebounded on me.

The other problem I had with the Government was over a profit share plan. I found it hard to give money away. In my first year with Qantas, we had made an operating profit before tax of $104 million, up from $44 million the previous year. We gave some additional travel entitlements to staff as a bonus. In 1987/1988, when our operating profit was $153 million, the board unanimously agreed with my recommendation that we put in place a long-term profit share plan for the staff. The board was of the view that if or when Qantas was privatised there would be a staff share issue, but not being privatised at that stage, we could at least proceed with profit sharing. It was designed to say thank you to staff, improve staff relations and align staff and company objectives. It was part of my plan to change the 'them and us' culture. The staff were delighted but some union officials didn't like my initiative. Improvements like this should come through the unions!

Jim Leslie and I saw Minister Gareth Evans in Canberra and explained the profit share plan to him. We left with him a document outlining the plan. He was delighted that Qantas was making such large profits. The plan was also something which was philosophically attractive to the Government. I remember him rubbing and clapping his hands and saying, 'It's terrific comrade; it's terrific'. I am not sure that Jim Leslie enjoyed being called 'comrade', but Evans's support was clear.

We proceeded to pay out the profit share, a week's extra pay for all staff. I then got a telephone call from Evans: 'You've got to stop that profit share'. I told him that I couldn't as the cheques were in the mail to the staff. It was true. Evans said that the scheme had not been approved. It would be true that I didn't have a document saying 'approved' or signed off by the Minister but the indication I had had was that he was extremely pleased with what we were doing. In my view, he had approved the scheme in every sense except signing a piece of paper. So it was another strike against me with the Government. The profit share payments were not withdrawn but we were not to do it again without formal Government approval. What we had done had been interpreted by the Government as an over-award payment. It was nothing of the sort.

Understanding what boards are about

I decided in the middle of 1988 that we needed help in presenting our case in Canberra. I was busy on other things and not keeping the Government happy. Not that I wasn't looking after Canberra in all respects. I was always being bombarded by requests for upgrades for political friends. On my recommendation the board unanimously agreed to appoint Mick Young as a consultant. He had retired from Parliament. He was an ideal person for the job. Few in Australia could do it better but I had not anticipated the hostile media response. It was another job for Labor mates, easy copy for journalists preoccupied with personalities, drama and colour to the exclusion of serious reportage and analysis.

With our rapid expansion we needed an injection of share capital. Jim Leslie and I told the Government on numerous occasions that we needed an equity injection of about $600 million to maintain a proper debt to equity ratio. But there was a major political reason why the Government was not prepared to accede to our requests. Paul Keating, the Treasurer, wanted to keep the pressure on for privatisation. We were to be starved of share capital to force privatisation.

My own view was that Qantas would have to be privatised. It was not something that philosophically I was attracted to but I was swayed over a period to the view that the Government, whether Labor or Liberal, was a bad shareholder. It wouldn't provide Qantas with equity injections and it wouldn't provide us with the flexibility to conduct the business. Down the track that is still my view, particularly for a business like air transport. My view was then, and still is, that a competitive market is more important than who owns the enterprise. The public, however, remains rightly concerned to have government enterprises in essential industries that will pursue public objectives; that the rights of citizens expressed through their elected representatives are as important as the rights of consumers expressed in the market. We have passed the high-water mark in the tide of privatisation.

In Qantas we were never impressed with Ansett Airline's business performance after years of living comfortably in a highly regulated domestic airline regime, but we took our hats off to the political clout that Sir Peter Abeles and Rupert Murdoch, major shareholders, had with the Hawke Government. Hawke and Abeles also had a remarkably close personal relationship. We saw major benefits in merging Qantas and

Australian Airlines. Linking international and domestic services would provide an improved service to customers. It would enhance our marketing, spread our costs and lead to a substantial improvement in the utilisation of aircraft, particularly as most Australian Airline aircraft were idle at night. Profits could be lifted substantially. But the merger was always stymied by the Government's support for Ansett, which saw a merged Qantas-Australian Airlines as a strong competitor. At Qantas we facetiously called Ansett the 'government's airline'. We were the public airline.

One episode particularly alarmed me about the influence which Ansett had on the Government's aviation policy. I made extensive notes at the time, which I quote from below.

In March 1988, we put to Minister Gareth Evans a proposal for a merger of Qantas, Australian Airlines and Air New Zealand in what became known as the 'tricycle'. We knew that the New Zealand Government was interested in privatisation of Air New Zealand. Both governments were also committed to closer economic relations and a single aviation market covering both Australia and New Zealand was inevitable and desirable. Further, a carrier with the combined capacity of Qantas, Australian and Air New Zealand would be a stronger competitor against the mega carriers on the Pacific, United and American Airlines. The tricycle was also, we believed, a way of getting the Australian Government off the privatisation hook. Our proposal envisaged that there could be a public float of the new merged entity, hopefully in the first quarter of 1989. Under our proposal, Ansett would operate on the Tasman and so link its services in Australia and New Zealand.

Evans was very enthusiastic about the tricycle, but he found it hard going. In all important matters involving aviation, the views of Sir Peter Abeles and Rupert Murdoch were influential with the Government. We didn't speak directly to Abeles or to Murdoch. The Government was the shareholder. Government policy was involved and that was not for us to negotiate. But Evans kept us briefed on discussions. I sensed his growing frustration about intervention by his ministerial seniors, Hawke and Keating.

The only legal and commercial leverage Ansett had was the domestic two-airline agreement which did not expire for another two years, in October 1990. In our view, that could be managed without real difficulty.

At the first round of discussions Evans had with Ansett, Abeles expressed major reservations about the tricycle proposal. He was particularly concerned about competition on the Tasman. Having worked comfortably in a regulated domestic system, he wanted similar arrangements on the Tasman, shared capacity. Qantas would have to withdraw capacity on the Tasman so that Ansett would have less competition. During the debriefing Evans gave us we pointed out that it would be bad public policy to extend the regulated domestic capacity controls to the Tasman. Regulated domestic aviation was coming to an end, so why extend it to the Tasman? But Evans was adamant that that was what he wanted: 'It is as solid as the Rock of Gibraltar.' We were told to produce a formula to make regulation work on the Tasman. We told him that we could do that but reiterated that it seemed bad public policy. I said that we would be 'responsible duopolists'. My attempted humour was not well received.

Evans told us that Bill Kelty was briefed on the tricycle. He wasn't opposed to it but had said that there 'wasn't sufficient in the proposal for Peter Abeles'. Paul Keating also got involved. At one meeting with Evans in Sydney, we had to leave the room so that he could take a phone call from Keating on the tricycle. On our return, Evans described the situation: 'Paul Keating said that there had to be enough in the arrangement to get the support of Murdoch and Abeles'. It was very clear from Evans that it was Murdoch, not Abeles on the Ansett side, who was now the prime negotiator.

The next concession made to Ansett was that the tricycle would not be allowed to operate its B747s on domestic routes in Australia. That would be too competitive for Ansett. The final crunch was that the tricycle could not operate its B767s either, despite the fact that Ansett had B767s on domestic routes itself.

After the B767 rebuff we said to Evans that, as far as we were concerned, the tricycle was off; too many concessions had to be made to Ansett. Leslie queried with Evans after one round of concessions why he made the concessions 'without talking to us about it'. Evans said, 'Rupert was only in town for two days, so I had to make a deal'.

There would have been problems getting the agreement of the New Zealand Government and Air New Zealand to the tricycle, but it was necessary to clarify the Australian position before approaching the New Zealanders. It was disturbing to see a very attractive proposition being derailed to protect Ansett. I made my views very clear to Evans. He warned me not to go public.

I had kept Dr Peter Wilenski, Head of the Department of Transport and Communications, informed of what was happening. At the end I recall him saying, 'at least we have established one thing; a point beyond which the Government will not go to oblige Murdoch and Abeles'. It was, he said, 'a dismal example of political power ahead of public interest'.

Together with Leslie I reported to the Qantas Board at a special meeting within a day or two of what had happened on the tricycle. I was conscious of what Gareth Evans had said to me about not saying anything publicly but I thought it was necessary to outline to the board my concerns. After the meeting and within an hour, Evans rang me. He had obviously been briefed by a board member about what I had said and reiterated to me not to go public and that I should be careful about what I said on the subject.

In my final note on the subject on 15 April 1988, I noted 'the demands of Abeles/Murdoch and the Government's willingness to concede was the reason for the collapse of the three-way merger. Senator Evans acknowledged that this was the case.'

On the same day I had a discussion with Ted Harris, chairman of Australian Airlines. My note for file summarised our discussion.

> I outlined to Ted Harris the events that had led to the scrapping of the three-way merger. Although he did not know all the details he said that my outline was quite consistent with his knowledge of events. He said that cronyism and deals, regardless of the public interest, was the driving factor in public life in Australia. There was no point in being too idealistic.

Three months later I had a lunch with Graham Richardson at the Imperial Peking at The Rocks, to discuss what might be done by Qantas to counter the Ansett influence with the Government. His advice as always was to the point, 'There will have to be enough for Peter [Abeles] in any proposal to get Hawkie on-side'.

With the Ansett veto on the tricycle, Evans suggested that we should consider a two-way merger of Qantas and Air New Zealand without Australian Airlines. We opened discussions with Air New Zealand at a luncheon in Sydney in April, with the New Zealand Minister for Transport, Prebble, and Air New Zealand senior executives. Jim Leslie and Gareth Evans were present and myself.

There were two outcomes. The first was that it was pretty clear that the merger wasn't going to go very far. There were traditional rivalries between the two airlines and between the two countries. Minister Prebble said that winning support within the New Zealand Cabinet for the merger would be like 'pushing shit uphill'. Subsequently the New Zealand Government decided that it would go ahead with privatisation of Air New Zealand.

The other outcome was that Gareth Evans told me after lunch in very colourful language that he would not deal in future with Jim Leslie. I was left to manage the problem as best I could. That luncheon obviously triggered a lot of earlier antipathy. They were both from Melbourne but came from different sides of the political tracks. Every CEO needs a chairman as a buffer. I lost my buffer.

There were also increasing problems I was having in my relationship with Jim Leslie and Evans's veto on him made things even more difficult. A feature in the *Sydney Morning Herald* on 22 July 1989 put it this way: '[Jim Leslie's hands-on role] was fine while John Menadue was learning the ropes at Qantas but as Menadue's authority grew and his grasp surer, there were signs of trouble in store'. I was probably impatient, not spending sufficient time with him. He was very sensitive about his status. I recall that at the opening of the new Qantas cargo terminal at Mascot, Peter Morris, the Minister at the time, had asked me to travel in his car to have a chat. Leslie was very upset about being left out. If there is any advice that I would give to a chief executive, it is always make sure that you have got the chairman on-side, whatever your personal feelings. That is, if you want to survive! Another piece of advice would be, never surprise the chairman.

The chairman appeared to be particularly concerned about his own reappointment. He probably felt that I was not a friend at court. But I wasn't lobbying for or against him or anyone else for that matter. I wasn't even lobbying for myself. I remember him saying to me, 'You'd be surprised, the supporters I've got'. I hadn't been cultivating my Canberra contacts as much as I should have been. With the growth path we were on and the work pressures we had, I hadn't bothered, although I knew there was criticism in Canberra for the way I had breached the GBE wage guidelines and a backlash over the profit share plan.

So I was running out of supporters in quite a few places that mattered, or, as the *Sydney Morning Herald* on 24 September 1989 put it, 'It is ironic that such a skilled former ambassador should in the end have been brought undone by lack of diplomacy'. But I was strongly supported among the executives and staff of Qantas. That is where I had given my time and attention. The company was very profitable and doing very well even though there was some overheating and costs were rising.

The trigger for final confrontation with the board was concern about the low level of salaries for executives in GBEs compared to the private sector. The government view was that if GBE executive salaries were to be increased to stem the loss of executives to the private sector, executive positions should be spilled. Executives would then apply for those positions at the higher salary. There had to be open competition. In public policy terms I could understand why that needed to be done. It turned out that it created enormous instability within GBEs generally. One example was in Australian Airlines where James Strong decided that he wasn't going to face that situation and resigned.

Jim Leslie's initial reaction was not to spill executive positions because of the instability it would cause. He told the new Minister Willis that and in a public statement Willis said, 'the new arrangements [for spilling positions in GBEs] will be introduced only when the present incumbent agrees to vacate the position, or when the position otherwise becomes vacant'. Then I learned that Leslie was conducting a CEO search with a headhunting firm. I knew nothing about it. A very close friend of mine in London rang me to say that he had been approached about the Qantas CEO job. That floored me. I thought the dice were being loaded against me.

It had been my intention to agree to the spill and then reapply even though an increase in my salary would have made no difference to the way I worked. But I was progressively disappointed by the Government's policy towards GBEs, the attitude to share equity, wages, profit sharing and its behaviour over the tricycle. I was tired. I was disappointed by the board's performance. Then I felt that the chairman was not dealing openly with me. That was the clincher. I decided I wouldn't accept the spill. Leslie said, 'Well, the board has decided that it will pay out the unexpired two years of your contract if necessary'. I said that if I was spilled I wouldn't reapply.

I spoke to John Ducker. The deal he offered was that he would support me as chief executive if I would support him as the next chairman.

I said I wouldn't be in that, though it wasn't the smartest offer to refuse. I mentioned it later to Brian Johns and he almost had a fit: 'Menadue, you need a minder'.

Jim Leslie was off on sick leave for a period and Jack Davenport and Tris Antico had carriage of the matter on behalf of the board. I agreed I would take a couple of weeks leave while things were sorted out. They would appoint an acting chief executive. I never said that I was going to resign. My contract was being terminated by the board. They couldn't understand why I was not prepared to accept the face-saving route of resignation rather than termination. In the board *Annual Report* after I left, my departure was described as a resignation. It was not; it was a termination. Ten years later it still remains surreal for me as to why so many people couldn't understand why I would not take the path of resignation and accept some weasel words about what a good chap I was.

Within two days of going on leave there was a well-sourced press leak that I was resigning and that there had been a major confrontation with the board. The story was very hostile to me. I decided that I wasn't going to stay home on holidays and cop that. I was still chief executive, so I went back to work and circulated a memo to senior staff and others who were not fully briefed on what was happening. Almost every fax on the Qantas network throughout the world was popping up with my memo about the dispute with the board and that I wasn't resigning.

Negotiations continued about the termination of my contract. I think I could have fought it legally as a breach of contract. But I wasn't inclined to have a long, drawn-out dispute. The last thing I wanted to give was the impression that there were arguments about money. I was exhausted. A settlement was made, but on the clear understanding that my contract was being terminated.

Because I was still technically a public servant on leave without pay, I was entitled to a job back in the Commonwealth Public Service and could therefore mitigate financial loss. As a result the two unpaid years on my unexpired contract were reduced by 85 per cent. I had no intention of going back to Canberra and, having left Qantas, I resigned from the Public Service within a couple of months. I was not eligible for retired staff travel.

On the night I left, two directors—Jack Davenport and Tris Antico—and a solicitor from Freehills went through the normal separation

273

processes and insisted that I hand back credit cards, keys and all company property. I suggested they might like to do a body search in case I was taking away a Qantas biro. At the time Qantas was making 'unprecedented profits' as the *Annual Report* described it.

In the end I realised that I didn't fit in with board directors' agendas and I was prepared to pay the price. I had contributed to my problems without any doubt. I gave the Qantas Board too many two-finger gestures for my own good. I was careless about the ways of the political and business world. But I felt I could hold up my head. The children's education and the house mortgage were no longer at risk. I could be more independent and less ambitious and calculating. It was, I think, also part of my own maturing, with the public self now more integrated with my private self. The two worlds and the two journeys were merging. I had become more self-aware. I knew that life was more complex than I had supposed.

To make a difference, to produce change and get things done requires strong will and risk taking. In Qantas I knowingly broke the rules on at least one occasion. I pushed hard and upset too many people. On earlier occasions I had taken similar, but smaller, risks and survived, even prospered. But not this time.

In that last fortnight the support of staff was overwhelming. A petition was signed by 7000 Qantas staff worldwide criticising the board, the Government, and asking me to stay. In my whole career I have never had so much support. But decisions in Qantas were not made by popular vote of the staff. They are made by board members. I got overwhelming support from my 'juniors' but I didn't attend to my 'seniors'. After years of doing the bidding of Murdoch, Whitlam and Fraser in pursuit of their goals, it was quite a change.

The *Sydney Morning Herald* feature, on 24 July, commented on my departure:

> … Menadue's supporters are legion within Qantas ranks … and increased greatly in number over the past 18 months. His boosters say he has streamlined and transformed management, greatly improved internal communication and brought management and workers together.

I would have added that he produced 'unprecedented profits'.

In a farewell speech to staff a couple of days later, I said:

In situations like this, one's trust in others inevitably receives a temporary setback. But as I have said many times in workshops, trust has its rewards. The trust I hope I have shown you has been rewarded to me thousands of times and in thousands of signatures. Nothing can change that. Anger may be one of the sinews of the soul, but it subsides. Trust and personal relations are the important things that last for ever. What I like most about Qantas is the Qantas family. That is what I will miss most. I will always feel a de facto member of the family.

It is still a great pleasure, ten years later to be greeted by Qantas staff.

I decided not to ever work for a minister or a board again on a full-time basis. Not that I would get many offers! I was getting a reputation for not playing the corporate game. I would pay a price.

A year later a Qantas captain invited me up to the flight deck to watch the landing at Narita. In thanking me for my time at Qantas, he said, 'You lived by the sword and died by the sword'. I took it mainly as a compliment.

Late in the day I had come to understand better the comment of Gareth Evans that a government needs a Qantas board if it hasn't got a House of Lords. But it makes it hard for the CEO.

Separating the job and the person

'We grow neither better or worse as we get old,
but more like ourselves' (May Lamberton Becker)

Τ he telephone taught me what life would be like after Qantas. Asked, 'Who's calling?', I would reply, 'John Menadue'. Then I would be asked, 'What company are you from, sir?' I was confronted by that. It seemed that unless I belonged to a company or a group, I was a non-person. John Menadue and the job were not the same thing, or were they? A Brown Josephite sister advised me, 'Just tell them you are from good company'.

The job defines so many of us. Identity is indistinguishable from work. I learned from painful experience that they must be separated. At Qantas people revolved around me; then it stopped. The status, recognition and supporting structure I got as CEO, things that had been part of my life for so long, were gone overnight. I had spent a large part of my life constructing those props. Now I felt bereft without them, thrown back on my own resources. Adjustment was painful but self awareness often comes from personal setback. Perhaps because I was more mature I learned more from this experience: to be less controlling and less a perfectionist. Most importantly, I learned that John Menadue is not the same thing as the esteem that goes with the job John Menadue does. Slowly life began to make more sense, but not without a few months of melancholy.

Peter Abeles offered me a job with TNT, but I wasn't interested in a full-time executive position. Over several months I was able to put together a good portfolio of consultancies, mainly to assist Australian firms in their business in Asia and help Japanese firms understand Australian commercial and political life. Susie was very active in our new business. Her skill and experience in running a small consultancy was a great help. She was at ease with computers and new technology. In business decisions she was invariably wiser than I was. Initially I felt a little challenged by her advice but she was usually right.

An office in the city with a large law firm in early 1990 was a very valuable part of my readjustment. The daily routine of going to the office and administrative support were important. Later, structure became less important and I worked from home with Susie. It was very pleasant and efficient, with separate offices, modern communications and little wasteful travel time. She continued studying psychology at Macquarie University and got excellent results. She was establishing a new life and career for herself. She is a great companion; my best friend.

Working out relationships in a blended family has had its difficulties but has been rewarding and, I believe, quite successful due mainly to Susie's nurturing and good sense. Birthdays and anniversaries have been the occasions to get the family to rub along. Susie put a lot of her homemaking skills and energy into drawing everyone together. A woman, like a snail, carries her home on her back much more easily and naturally. A close confidante to her own children, Susie became a confidante to her wider family. She took particular care of my Australian-Korean grandchildren, Naomi and Miriam, who had come from Japan to Sydney as college boarders, staying with us over many weekends. Susie was very patient in supporting them in their early anxieties—how to cope with a new school, a new country and a new language and culture.

It was wonderful sharing so much together with Susie. I would advise anyone who has had a happy marriage that has ended for whatever reason, not to hesitate to remarry. It is one of the great joys of life, as Cardinal Hume put it, 'to realise that we have a privileged place in someone else's heart and life'.

My most satisfying work after Qantas was with the St Vincent de Paul Society, chairing a fundraising committee to raise $4 million for the

Matthew Talbot Hostel for homeless men in Woolloomooloo. Matthew Talbot was a recovered Irish alcoholic. He inspired the establishment of hostels to help the men of the streets. I met many gentle men at the hostel who had been broken by life through alcohol, other drugs, family distress and loss of job. Many had been forced out of psychiatric institutions. Their lives had been stripped bare but their dignity shone through it all. 'There, but for the grace of God ...'

One thing I did learn from my experience at the Talbot is how we try and shield ourselves, at least in our own minds, from possible misfortune: 'I couldn't end up homeless on the streets because I am different to the men at the Talbot'. One senior business man I approached for a donation asked if the men at the Talbot were criminals. I think it was his way of erecting a mental barrier and persuading himself that such misfortune could not befall him because he was so different to those men. But we are all broken and vulnerable in some way.

Although money raising is often a thankless and frustrating task, I found it satisfying. I learnt that if you have a good case, a good prospect list and present your argument well, you can raise money—something that I had never done before. I did get knockbacks from corporations and people that I thought could help. Widows with their mites were very generous. The liquor industry was particularly disappointing, perhaps unwilling to admit that it had profited very substantially from the problem. But I found it liberating to accept that all that I could really do was present the case for a donation as best I was able. The response was not up to me. I tried to raise some money in Japan but I knew that my story had become screwed up somehow when Japanese tourists tried booking in at the Talbot. I keep my personal links to the Talbot with some hands-on work, serving at lunch once a week. The staff and volunteers at the Talbot are the salt of the earth.

I did have one real surprise in my Talbot fundraising work. I had approached a developer neighbour of the Talbot in Woolloomooloo, for support. He promised $250,000 for the hostel if his project went ahead. I lobbied two members of the Central Sydney Planning Committee, the Mayors of Sydney and South Sydney, pointing out that it was common practice for developers to assist their case by supporting local community projects such as children's playgrounds and parks. In this case $250,000 would be provided for renovations at the Talbot. I was reported to the Independent Commission Against Corruption. After a three-month preliminary investigation, the ICAC decided against any further action. Like many others, I came to wonder about the purpose of the ICAC.

When I left Qantas after disagreement with the board, I knew I wouldn't get many board offers. But in December 1994, I got a telephone call from Canberra about a possible appointment to the Telstra Board. I was asked about my relations with Rupert Murdoch. I assumed that the caller was trying to establish whether I might have any conflict of interest, a standard query before such appointments. I said I was not aware of any conflict because, whilst I had worked for Murdoch in the past, my links were then quite tenuous. It became clear to me, however, that I had misinterpreted the question. The caller was wanting to establish whether I would be a supporter of Murdoch on the Telstra Board. I kept my counsel, and was appointed to the board. I learned very quickly the significance of the Murdoch query when I found myself on my own a few months later opposing the Foxtel joint venture between Telstra and News Limited.

The circumstances and reason for my opposition were set out in a letter I sent to the chairman of Telstra, David Hoare, on 9 March 1995. I have decided to put this on the public record because I think board behaviour should be more transparent.

> At the Board meeting on 2 March 1995, I said that I had not been persuaded about the proposed arrangements with News Limited and Australis (which would supply movie content) ... In the Board paper of November 3 [when I was not a Board member] the first criteria for pay television partner selection was 'strength in content creation, content distribution and packaging'. The paper added that News Limited's strength was that as the '... world's third largest producer, distributor and owner of films and television programming (Fox) *could guarantee content availability'*.
>
> On the basis of our belief that News Limited could supply content, I assume, the Heads of Agreement on 11 November (1994) was signed. My basic problem is understanding how such an agreement could be signed without being satisfied that News Limited could 'guarantee content availability'. Didn't we check whether News could and would deliver? Were we too

trusting? [All movie film content, except Twentieth Century Fox, had been signed up by Optus or Australis.]

It seems to me that most of our problems have flowed from this flaw in the Heads of Agreement: News Limited's failure to provide content on acceptable terms. Content is the primary issue, the rest is secondary. News Limited has clearly not delivered content and on 25 December at 3 am!, News Limited 'signed a Heads of Agreement with Australis without knowledge of Telstra, which secured the Australis programming (for the joint venture) on an exclusive basis for cable distribution'. This Heads of Agreement was for 50 years!—since amended to 25 years.

As a result of News Limited's failure to deliver on content as expected by Telstra, we are faced with a punitive arrangement with Australis which will deliver content '… significantly more expensive than planned'. Further the agreement is for 25 years. One result of News Limited's failure to deliver content is that Australis will reap a financial windfall, at the expense of the Foxtel joint venture. The increase in programming costs has clearly affected the business case which I find unconvincing. It was not discussed at our last meeting …

There was also a generous marketing incentive payable to Foxtel by Telstra for each pay television connection. The logic of this was that Telstra's telephone business would benefit from each pay television connection.

A bad deal, however, was only part of the problem as I saw it. The other was the political pressure that was being applied. The board was told by the managing director that 'the Government wants us to do the deal with News Limited', as I set out in that same letter to the chairman. I also pointed out that, 'We were told that Ministers and Commonwealth Government officials were "better briefed" [than Telstra Directors on the pay television deal.] …The legal responsibility, however, is ours'.

Before a board decision was made, the chairman, David Hoare, said that on such a critical issue there must be unanimous board support before the Foxtel joint venture would go ahead. When it came to the final decision, I said no, I wasn't persuaded as a director that I could support the business case and I objected to what I regarded as political influence being brought to bear.

It is tempting for governments to try to bend government business enterprises to their party-political advantage. I learnt that it is one of the responsibilities of boards to try to stop that happening.

When I dissented, the chairman said that my opposition had vetoed the project. Perhaps he hoped to force me to change my mind. I said that I couldn't. In further discussion some directors said that they thought it was unreasonable to require a unanimous decision. The Foxtel proposal was then agreed but there would be no suggestion in the board minutes that it was unanimously agreed. I sent the letter which I have referred to on 9 March 1995 to the chairman for the records of the company to explain my opposition. One director hugged me after the vote. He never explained why. Perhaps earlier in my career I would have kept my head down.

To clean up the books for the partial float, Telstra wrote off $818 million in its loss-making Broadband Network and Foxtel pay television business in 1996/97 after a loss of $155 million in 1995/96. A loss of $166 million followed in 1997/98.

David Potts, in the *Sun Herald* on 27 July 1997, commented, 'Telstra has been taken for a ride by Rupert Murdoch and taxpayers will foot the bill for what may add up to be the most scandalous deal ever embarked on by a government authority ... For the Keating Government to have allowed and maybe encouraged, for all we know, a taxpayer owned authority to do [this] secret deal ... was straight out of a banana republic'. Chanticleer in the *Financial Review* of 23 July 1997 described the Foxtel episode as 'the largest strategic and financial disaster this country has ever seen'. In April 1998 the *Financial Review* columnist wrote: 'Foxtel could end up paying as much as $3.7b more than it ought for movies over the next two decades'. Telstra was fortunately partly saved from itself when Australis went bankrupt and breached its 25-year deal with Foxtel.

I was also concerned about people management. In correspondence with the chairman, I described the Telstra management of staff as being like the 'Grand Old Duke of York who marched his men to the top of the hill and marched them down again'. Telstra staff numbers went down from 93,000 in 1991 to 68,000 in 1994. Then they went up again to 78,000 in 1996 and are planned to fall 25,000 to 53,000 by 2000. Telstra provided $1.5 billion in 1995/96 and 1996/97 in its accounts for redundancies.

Business circumstances do change but the management of staff numbers was erratic. In my two years on the Telstra Board, the full-time equivalent staff numbers in 1994/95 and 1995/96 exceeded the budget by almost 10,000 and 9000 respectively. At an average cost per staff member of $40,000 per annum, that was a cost overrun of about $800 million over two years. On 1 May 1996, I wrote to the chairman:

> I have been expressing concern for nine months about the blow-out in staff numbers in Telstra and the need to reduce our product unit costs. To the extent that the response has been delayed, both the Board and senior executives cannot avoid responsibility for the stronger action that will now be required.

And strong action was taken: 25,000 staff were to be retrenched.

At the Telstra Board I referred to my experience at Qantas, where revenue growth was easier than cost control. The same was happening at Telstra.

At our April 1996 meeting, the board was told that executives had been checking telephone lines to establish patterns of calls by Telstra and former Telstra executives to journalists, particularly on the *Financial Review* and to opposition politicians. I was amazed both by the act itself and the way that it was blurted out. I spoke and wrote again to the chairman but don't know what action was taken.

As a member of the Appointments and Compensation Committee at Telstra, I also attempted to initiate a discussion on and establish guidelines for the appropriate relationship between the remuneration of the lowest paid and the highest paid full-time employee of Telstra. I believed it was necessary to maintain confidence and trust among staff. Was the acceptable multiple 5, 10, 50 or even 100 times? I asked twice for a paper on the subject as the basis for discussion. Nothing was produced.

When the Howard Government was elected in 1996, I was asked by the new minister to resign from the Telstra Board, along with several others, although I had three years of my term to run. I refused; he then terminated my appointment. I sent him copies of my correspondence with the chairman. He thanked me for my services on the board. The board secretary fixed some administrative matters but I heard nothing from the chairman or the managing director either then or since. I don't think any of the other members of the board who resigned at the time heard anything either. Through the Department of Prime Minister and Cabinet I learned that a Telstra senior executive, in discussing Telstra Board names with the new government, commented that 'Menadue is not a good team member'. You pay a price for telling the emperor that he is naked.

I was later offered directorships with a casino and a slot machine company. I could hear Laurie Menadue calling from his grave!

I rejoined the Australia-Japan Foundation (AJF) as deputy Chairman and later Chairman. AJF work was made more personal and pleasurable by having a daughter and four grandchildren in Japan.

The first field in which the AJF concentrated was the training of Japanese language teachers in Australia. The tourist industry was developing rapidly but there were not many Japanese speakers available. We committed $500,000 over three years for intensive courses. This was very successful and in the process we created a momentum within the state education departments, particularly in Queensland. There was a dramatic breakthrough in the number of Australians fluent in Japanese.

The next major foundation project was a 'Discover Australia' teachers kit, including a video, distributed to over 12,000 junior high schools in Japan. We spent over $1 million on the project over three years. The origin of the kit was the experiences of many of us who had been haunted in our time in Japan by how the Japanese had been offended by the notion of White Australia. We really had to get into the school system and explain how Australia had changed. The Second World War and White Australia are frankly discussed in the kit.

A critical breakthrough was the cooperation of the conservative Japanese Education Ministry that gave us their *sentei* or approval for the kit—a first for them and us. Our associates in the Japanese Education Ministry and many Japanese teachers of goodwill have been extremely supportive. Not surprisingly they have been confused by John Howard's cautious response to Pauline Hanson. Perhaps we haven't changed as much as we said in the kit.

The other main project has been a Japanese-language Australian website in Japan. It is the most elaborate site in an Australian Embassy in the world and the most advanced national site in Japan. It allows wide dissemination of a broad range of information about Australia. It also allows the AJF to link its other projects in Japan: library, schools kit and an English-language learning project.

With only about $1 million annually for projects, the AJF has been a pacesetter with some very strategic projects. The hopes that we had for it 20 years ago have been realised. When I left the AJF at the end of 1998 the Minister of Foreign Affairs & Trade, Alexander Downer, said in a letter to me, 'the Foundation has over the years shown a very innovative approach to promoting the bilateral relationship and an ability to gear attitudes to reflect its growing maturity. Your guiding contribution to the Foundation for so many years has placed it in good stead for the future'.

My concern about Australia's relations with Asia has been the consistent thread in my public life. So I didn't need much persuading in late 1995 to take the position of Director of the Research Institute for Asia and the Pacific (RIAP), a foundation of the University of Sydney. At my insistence the work and salary were only to be part-time. But it quickly became clear that it was a full-time job. I was working about 60 hours a week, partly because of the lack of resources to do the job properly and partly because of my own enthusiasm for Asia. The university didn't know how to use me. I had had a similar experience at Macquarie University a few years earlier as a visiting lecturer.

I was foolish to think that I could do the RIAP job part-time. One reassuring feature, however, was to see that there were many organisations, similar to RIAP, established in association with Australian universities. When I was first interested in Japan and Asia, over 30 years before, there was scarcely a single organisation like RIAP in the country.

RIAP was poorly funded. I should have known what was in store for me when I learned that my predecessor used to come in at weekends to paint the office in his own time. In my first week on the job I got windburn keeping my window open trying to keep cool in a stuffy terrace office in Darlinghurst. The support I unwisely anticipated did not happen. To meet the budget and pay my own part-time salary, I had to get out on the road fundraising again. After over 12 months I woke up one morning after several days of helter-skelter activity and asked myself, 'At the age of 61 I don't have the same energy; what am I doing this for?' I decided to resign and became Principal Adviser, pulling back from my heavy workload.

One of our quiet successes at RIAP was to bring Kim Dae Jung to lecture in Sydney in September 1996 and receive an honorary doctorate from the University of Sydney. Two years later he became President of the Republic of Korea (ROK).

With Dr Rikki Kersten, who succeeded me as Director of RIAP, I went twice to Seoul to try and persuade Kim Dae Jung to visit Australia. I had admired him from a distance for his dissent and refusal over 40 years, as a democrat, to buckle under military dictatorships, even in the face of death. Living in Japan we had come to know more about Kim Dae Jung than Nelson Mandela.

Apart from personal admiration of Kim Dae Jung, we hoped at RIAP to hear from him an alternative view of 'Asian democracy'. Lee Kuan Yew of Singapore had clothed Asian democracy in Asian values which seemed a means by which some Asian leaders cloaked their autocratic behaviour.

At a private dinner party which Kim Dae Jung hosted for RIAP at the end of his visit, I had a memorable discussion sitting next to him at the table. His opening comment was to indicate that we were both Catholics—almost like a Mason's handshake! He added that his wife was a Methodist. That was also reassuring. With such intimate opening comments I asked him what it was like to face death.

In the calmest, most matter-of-fact way and with little sign of anger or emotion he described his experiences as if they were yesterday. He was gentle and modest. He said that he had faced death once after being captured by the North Korean Army; twice at the hands of the Korean Central Intelligence Agency (KCIA) and also at the hands of President Chun Doo Hwan, after being convicted of sedition following his support of the students at Kwangju. He had spent fourteen years either under house arrest, forced exile or in prison.

He said that he was very scared facing death the first time as a young soldier. After that he felt he was living on borrowed time and could face the prospect of death quite calmly. His reaction to events and his whole demeanour then and since marked him as a man well and truly tested; enriched rather than embittered by the experiences. Suffering so often produces authentic leaders. His life was transformed by the experience—and for him the miracle—of being saved by the intervention of the US CIA. He had been weighed down with cement blocks in preparation for being thrown overboard on a boat trip back to Korea after being kidnapped by the Korean CIA in the Palace Hotel, Tokyo. To be told of a miracle at the hands of the CIA was a new experience for me.

Kim Dae Jung's first act as the new President of the Republic of Korea was to pardon the two former presidents responsible for the Kwangju massacre and the subsequent sedition charges against him. His running 'mate' as Prime Minister in 1997 was Kim Jong Pil, the man who had established and headed the Korean CIA, which had hounded and tried to kill him.

After his Sydney visit and two years before his election as President, I wrote to him, 'Good wins in the end, but not always quickly or easily'. It was worth being Director of RIAP just to meet Kim Dae Jung.

Alienation and relationships

'Always and everywhere human beings have felt the radical inadequacy of their personal existence' (Aldous Huxley)

M̲ick Young's death, in April 1996, influenced me to slow down. It helped persuade me to resign as director of RIAP.

Mick struggled valiantly against leukemia for months. We were all touched by his life. Whenever I met Mick he brightened my day, even during his final illness. There were words of encouragement and a marvellous telling of the latest joke he had heard. His personality always transcended his situation. He was a wonderful friend. Father Ed Campion rang me to say that Mick had died and that in his last hours he had blessed himself with the sign of the cross. I remember that phone call as if it was yesterday, feeling both loss and joy that the shearer had come home.

When he had left Harbord at 16 to be a wool classer, his mother had told him three things: join the union, bank Commonwealth and go to mass. He skipped mass for many years but was given a rousing send-off by the Catholic tribe in a requiem mass at St Mary's Cathedral. Mick always called St Mary's 'headquarters'. There we sang 'Faith of our fathers'. At the grave side Eric Walsh led off with 'Kevin Barry' and 'Joe Hill'.

Mick was most warm when I joined the Catholic Church, even though his own ticket had lapsed. He renewed it at the end.

After I joined the Catholic Church in 1983, I was often asked by friends, 'Do you regard yourself as an institutional Catholic?' I think they were disappointed when I said that I did: that religion is more than individual, it is communal as well. We need institutions, whether family or church, to anchor us.

I described my attitude to the institutional church in an address entitled 'Men in the Church', in May 1997.

The spiritual journey without the community of believers and their support would be impossible for me and I could not conceive of spiritual growth without the Church. The branch withers apart from the vine. I need Scripture and tradition for counsel. I need fellow travellers on the journey to share experiences. I need stability and continuity so that I am not blown off course by every passing whim. Most importantly, I need the Eucharist, the double grace of God's Incarnation and Sacrifice.

That central event, the Eucharist, is not only individual, it is communal, bringing with it a search for justice and peace in the world as well as a search for the true self. One of the joys of the Eucharist, is to be linked with others in our common journey, passing the peace and standing in line to receive the sacraments — in community.

Yet my experience within that community is a mixed one. The word that jumps out at me is 'power'. It often seems that the Pope with his Roman Curia is as much a successor of the Emperor Constantine as Peter, the humble fisherman. He speaks persuasively about justice and freedom in the world but not in the Catholic Church. Trust seems lacking. At the parish level, 'Father knows best'. Bishops are not chosen locally, as they were for much of the first eighteen centuries, but are rather selected in a secret process by a few in Rome acting on advice from a closed inner-circle in the country of appointment. In so many ways the formal hierarchal church is no longer plausible.

My experience of power in the Catholic Church is not unlike the way I saw power exercised in the ALP in the 1960s, when I worked for Gough Whitlam for those seven lean years. The ALP was run by a few officials who were not chosen directly by party members and were only remotely answerable to them. Debate was suppressed, the party was static and frozen; problems were denied. Party members and voters were deserting year after year. The party controllers saw that as vindication of their ideological purity and orthodoxy. They dismissed dissenters as malcontents who should leave the party if they didn't like it—as if the party was their private property. In this top-down system, the hijacking of power from the rank and file was second nature. The rank and file knew that the party was out of touch but felt powerless to do anything about it.

As individuals we are in daily need of reform. The same is also true of the church as much as of a political party. We try to fit God into our own mould.

But change is invariably painful and I do feel concern for those who are part of a clerical culture who would like change, but are hemmed in. In times of personal crisis, we each have a fear of letting go. The same is true of institutions like the church. As the crisis deepens it hangs on more doggedly and with ever more recourse to rules and authority.

The best sign of coming reform is the gathering crisis. Parts of the institutional church will need to die before there is new life. It is true of all institutions. But there are signs of hope. It is only a zephyr at present, but the wind of change is gathering. The lay faithful in many continents, particularly women, are expressing themselves clearly in favour of reform.

For all that, I have found the Catholic Church wonderfully nurturing in critical periods of my life. I have found thousands of Catholics who share my concerns and hopes for renewal. It is a broad church. So I will stay. I will hang on. Where else could I go?

The problems within the Catholic Church are only part of a wider crisis in the community. We are all tied to institutions and systems that are disconnected. We are increasingly aware of our powerlessness, that most frustrating of all human emotions. The journey of the individual conscience within many institutions is a hard one: do I stay and compromise or get out and be ineffective?

At the age of 64, I see the use and abuse of power within institutions as the central issue in public life in Australia. All self-centred power structures ultimately break down, destroyed by their own arrogance and worldliness. We need to democratise the power exercised in Australia by political parties, business, media and the church. And power needs to be exercised at the lowest possible level in every institution—what in Catholic social teaching is called 'subsidiarity'.

In the West, secularism and the pseudo scientific approach to business has led us to where we are now, aghast at money worship and consumerism and unwilling to be constrained by the moral strictures of family, church and state. We live in a post-Christian society where the golden calf we worship is 'the market'. The sudden and cosmetic interest in business codes of ethics and its colonisation by lawyers with their rules, is one practical outcome of an ethically footloose business world. When the chairman of AMP said, 'It is not for the AMP to make moral judgements with its investments', it didn't even cause a ripple. Whatever became of right and wrong? More than anything else the explosion in executive salaries accompanied by the downsizing of staff has eroded trust and public confidence in business. As Samuel Johnson put it, 'The insolence of wealth will creep out'.

The public is also disillusioned with Parliament and parliamentarians, although I think many parliamentarians are as much disillusioned as voters. They would like reform but are locked in by the system. Our political candidates are chosen by a handful of party members. Party supporters and voters have no say in the development of policy or the selection of candidates or leaders. The political number-crunchers, with their focus groups, hold sway. Not surprisingly, supporters of a republic want to directly elect the President. They don't want to leave the choice to politicians. As a young man I thought the major problem for the ALP was a constitutional one. The problem now is institutional—its own institution.

Confidence in institutions has been eroded by globalisation and the growth of powerful multinational companies. Some of that is inevitable and desirable but increasingly governments will need to negotiate international arrangements to protect their constituents in the face of the globalisation of money, information, ideas and people. In its very essence globalisation is anti-democratic. In the 1930s we learned that national financial markets had to be regulated. In the 1990s we are learning the same about international financial markets.

Even more importantly, we need to break out of the mind-set that with globalisation there is nothing that national governments can do. A solution is made more difficult with the advocates of global free markets entrenched in national treasuries, central banks and international financial institutions like the IMF. Because of their free market ideology, ironically in an age of retreating ideology, those to whom we need to look for a solution are a major part of the problem. This self-selected oligarchy have their boosters in the media and financial houses that we see each night on the TV news. They pretend that there are no moral issues and social consequences in increasing food and fuel prices for the poor in Indonesia.

The media in Australia is dominated by two people and the values and lifestyles they project. What a wasteland the Australian media would be without the ABC and SBS. New technology like pay television offered opportunities for new players and greater diversity but, with the help of government, was hijacked by established players.

The response to this institutional decay and alienation of citizens is apathy and withdrawal. In some cases the response is political or religious fundamentalism. One Nation and the burgeoning fundamentalist churches offer misleading 'solutions' to difficult problems in uncertain times.

I am certain that the answer is in the democratic ethos. Aristotle knew what was at stake: 'Oligarchy is to the advantage of the rich, democracy to the advantage of the poor'. People have good sense. Power must be diffused and distributed whether it be in politics, business, media or the church. Only in that way will we engage the energy and win the trust of Australians. Our institutions need to catch up with our democratic aspirations.

Because of our powerlessness and lack of confidence in institutions, we develop unreasonable expectations of leaders. 'It will be better with a new President, Prime Minister or Pope!' We hope too much for the charismatic and visionary leader who will solve our problems. It doesn't happen and when leaders fail or stay too long, as they invariably do, our sense of frustration is even greater.

Despite the institutional failure and alienation, Australia is a better, more open and tolerant society than it was in my youth. Since White Australia ended only 30 years ago the progress has been remarkable. Aboriginal reconciliation is on the agenda for the first time in our European history. I am pleasantly surprised about the progress we have made in our growing openness to Asia in the last 15 years. Progress has been made in rights for women. We are much more respectful of people who are different. Conservation of our physical environment has become a mainstream issue.

I am optimistic but not certain about our future. Our economic prosperity has been built on the dispossession of our indigenous people. No wonder there is a 'whispering in our hearts'. Our small population in a large, dry, land mass is situated in a populous region so different to our own. We have to come to terms with our own region. Resolving those two strategic challenges, relations with our indigenous people and our own region, will determine whether our hold is secure or tenuous. There is no future for us in being a proxy for the British or Americans.

In this journey of mine over 64 years, there have been long periods of sameness, even boredom. There have been experiences that have been wrenching and painful. Many were joyful. There were successes and failures. I think I understand better now that the job is not important, it is what you do with the job that matters and that the job and the person are not the same. Who is the person standing there alone when all else is stripped away?

There were times when things changed forever for me, when all my conditioning, habits, attitudes and beliefs were challenged and I was forced to address life in a different way. Differences challenged my assumptions. Change didn't mean becoming like someone else, it meant being truer to myself. Over the years, I believe I have been better able to integrate my public and private selves, to be truer publicly to my private convictions. I believe I have done that better in my last ten years than I did in my first 50.

It meant acknowledging that in some times in my life I lacked the resources to deal with the problem at hand. In a talk given to a meeting organised by 'Spirituality in the Pub' in Sydney in 1996, I spoke about this.

> I have not found my identity in success, I have not found it in power. Self-knowledge, in my experience, has not been found in success but in adversity, not in strength but in weakness. In my journey I believe I have been closest to the Truth when I have felt the weakest — when I have been humbled. 'Blessed are the poor in spirit'. I know from my own experience that that is real. When I have been weak and vulnerable I have been most open.

I learnt that to be outside the group is not comfortable, but it is liberating.

I had many opportunities, perhaps good luck, that was aided by my determination and focus. Determination, however, has its down-side. I was driven and single-minded in long periods of my life, often at the expense of relationships with family and others. I am inclined to be hard on myself and others.

I no longer see the point of playing the game and being a recipient of the benefits bestowed by people in power: promotion, preferment and position. It took me a long time to work that out.

Within a few months of Mick Young's death I had a heart attack. Fortunately, there was no permanent damage. I found the 'trial run' reassuring. I often wonder whether the main event will be the same. I had an angioplasty, in which a balloon is inserted in the arteries and air pressure is applied to force the blocked arteries open. When I recounted the event to Gough Whitlam he inquired: 'Comrade, is the balloon a Catholic condom?'

I now feel in better health than for many years, with improved diet, loss of weight and more exercise. Once again my experience was that it usually requires some external event or crisis to trigger change. I had promised myself for years that I would exercise more and lose weight, but never did.

After the heart attack I attended a rehabilitation course. The course included exercise, stress tests, advice on diet and lifestyle. Almost all the members of the group were men who differed from each other in respect to the jobs they did, where they lived, their marital status, sexual orientation, ethnicity and religion. We discussed what was happening to us and our feelings and even fears for the future. All of us, having faced the possibility of death and feeling vulnerable, were very open and trusting with each other. More than ever before we were all living with the end in view.

We had never met each other before and we are probably unlikely to meet again. But the one thing we had in common was concern about relationships. There was no exception. No one spoke about job or house, rank or earnings. All the concerns were about relationships with a wife, partner, estranged sister, neglected mother, a son in need of special care. Poor relationships, loneliness and separation were worse prospects than death. The search for integration, wholeness and harmony is at the heart of the human story. I had never before had the opportunity in such a diverse group to listen and hear what really mattered. It was not about markets. It was a longing for relationships and community; without them we are incomplete. We are drawn to each other as if in a magnetic field. The most powerful urge within each of us is seeking out for another or the Other and in that way to be complete. I learned about that first in a Methodist manse.

> We shall not cease from exploration
> And the end of all our exploring
> Will be to arrive where we started
> And know the place for the first time.
>
> (T. S. Eliot)

Index

Index

Index